# AFRICAN ETHNOGRAPHIC STUDIES OF THE 20TH CENTURY

Volume 20

# VALENGE WOMEN

# VALENGE WOMEN
The Social and Economic Life of the Valenge
Women of Portuguese East Africa

E. DORA EARTHY

LONDON AND NEW YORK

First published in 1933 by Oxford University Press for the International African Institute.

This edition first published in 2018
by Routledge
2 Park Square, Milton Park, Abingdon, Oxon OX14 4RN

and by Routledge
711 Third Avenue, New York, NY 10017

*Routledge is an imprint of the Taylor & Francis Group, an informa business*

© 1933 International African Institute

All rights reserved. No part of this book may be reprinted or reproduced or utilised in any form or by any electronic, mechanical, or other means, now known or hereafter invented, including photocopying and recording, or in any information storage or retrieval system, without permission in writing from the publishers.

*Trademark notice*: Product or corporate names may be trademarks or registered trademarks, and are used only for identification and explanation without intent to infringe.

*British Library Cataloguing in Publication Data*
A catalogue record for this book is available from the British Library

ISBN: 978-0-8153-8713-8 (Set)
ISBN: 978-0-429-48813-9 (Set) (ebk)
ISBN: 978-1-138-59497-5 (Volume 20) (hbk)
ISBN: 978-0-429-48834-4 (Volume 20) (ebk)

**Publisher's Note**
The publisher has gone to great lengths to ensure the quality of this reprint but points out that some imperfections in the original copies may be apparent.

**Disclaimer**
The publisher has made every effort to trace copyright holders and would welcome correspondence from those they have been unable to trace.

# VALENGE WOMEN

The Social and Economic Life of the Valenge Women
of Portuguese East Africa

AN ETHNOGRAPHIC STUDY

BY

# E. DORA EARTHY

*With an introduction by*
Dr. A. C. HADDON

FRANK CASS & CO. LTD.
1968

First published by Oxford University Press for the
International African Institute

Published by
FRANK CASS AND COMPANY LIMITED
67 Great Russell Street, London WC1
by arrangement

First edition     1933
New impression    1968

*Printed in Great Britain by*
*Thomas Nelson (Printers) Ltd., London and Edinburgh*

# INTRODUCTION

IT is many years since I first made the acquaintance of Miss E. Dora Earthy, as it was in 1921 that, in answer to her letter asking for advice, I wrote to encourage her to maintain the interest she had shown in the social life of the Leŋge women. I recognized that with her knowledge of the language, her sympathetic character, and the close contact which her professional duties implied, she was in a peculiarly favourable position to undertake such investigations, and I urged her to obtain all the information she could of the woman's point of view in that interesting corner of Portuguese East Africa.

Studies of this kind can be accomplished only by women. And though there are many women with equal opportunities, there are very few who have sufficient enthusiasm, training, and catholicity to undertake them. Readers of the monograph will recognize the extraordinarily conscientious care with which the observations are recorded, and cannot but feel that they can fully rely on their accuracy. Miss Earthy also collected a large number of native texts, rituals, and formulae, which confirm her conclusions and have converted oral tradition into material available for students.

We should therefore feel very grateful for the great amount of time and trouble that Miss Earthy has taken in collecting this valuable ethnological material. Doubtless, as has happened to others, her motives were sometimes misunderstood by those who may have looked with suspicion upon these delvings into pagan practice and belief, but they have been fully justified. Overcoming all difficulties, some of which only those who have attempted similar work in a similar climate can appreciate, Miss Earthy stuck to her self-imposed task, and students at home will now reap the benefit of her self-denial. Her sole reward will be the thanks and appreciation of students and the satisfaction of knowing that her time and energy have been well spent.

A. C. HADDON.

CAMBRIDGE,
*July*, 1933.

# PREFACE

THIS sketch of the social and economic life of the VaLeŋge women of Portuguese East Africa is really an ethnographic study, although my privileged and beloved work as a missionary left me little time to spare for my research until the generous offer of a grant from the Research Committee of Bantu Studies of the University of the Witwatersrand enabled me to have six months' leave to study more intensively the VaLeŋge women, among whom I had lived for many years. My grateful thanks are due to the International Institute of African Languages and Cultures, and to the Research Committee for their financial help; to the Committee of the Society for the Propagation of the Gospel in Foreign Parts, and to the Bishop of Lebombo, who made it possible for me to work among the VaLeŋge; and to Mrs. Hoernlé, Lecturer in Social Anthropology of the University of the Witwatersrand, for help in the preparation of the manuscript.

The Chief of the Division of Botany, Department of Agriculture, Pretoria, and his staff, also the Curator and staff of the Bolus Herbarium, Kirstenbosch, Newlands, have rendered invaluable aid in the botanical determinations of the plants used in native medicines; Mrs. Rishbeth of Southampton has helped in the technical descriptions of string figures; Mrs. A. Hingston Quiggin, of Cambridge, with the baskets and the revision of the text. I likewise remember gratefully those who have given me kind encouragement, especially Dr. Haddon, F.R.S., Cambridge; Professor A. R. Radcliffe-Brown, formerly of Capetown University; and the Director of the Transvaal Museum, Pretoria.

Some readers of this study may say, 'Surely M. Junod's great monograph covers all your field'. To these I would reply, firstly, that M. Junod himself urged that a number of comparative monographs should be written; secondly, that his work is primarily concerned with that division of the Thoŋga tribe known as the BaRoŋga, though he includes valuable descriptions of the 'northern clans'; thirdly, that I have limited myself to a description of the life of the women, which, being a woman, I had special opportunities of studying; and lastly, that the VaLeŋge differ in many respects from the BaRoŋga; being themselves a mixed people, their culture results from the fusion of several tribes.

How closely the work of the anthropologist and the missionary are interlocked is described by Captain Rattray: 'The time when anthropology will cease to be regarded largely as a science whose chief function it is to record the cultures of primitive peoples ere their final disappearance before advancing civilization, or as the collection of data mainly of an academic interest, is, I hope, not far distant. The field-worker will experience, I know, a new thrill, when he begins to regard his task, not as the mere collection of curious facts from which some new anthropological tome may arise, or the gathering of objects as specimens for ethnological museums, but rather as a searching for an elixir which may yet be used to infuse new life into those peoples who appear to droop and flag, or to undergo a change not wholly for the better, as the result of contact with our civilization. As Mr. Edwin W. Smith puts it so finely, the anthropologist's task should be to discover "the idiom of the soul" of the people among whom he is working.'[1]

With this end in view, I have attempted to describe the daily life, the beliefs and aspirations of the VaLeŋge women among whom I lived and worked for thirteen years (September 1917–December 1930 inclusive of furloughs).

E. DORA EARTHY.

TRURO, 1933.

[1] *Africa*, i, 1928, p. 98: 'Anthropology and Christian Missions. Their mutual bearing on the problems of Colonial Administration.' R. Sutherland Rattray.

# CONTENTS

| | |
|---|---|
| INTRODUCTION By Dr. A. C. HADDON | v |
| PREFACE | vii |
| LIST OF ILLUSTRATIONS | xi |
| NOTE ON PHONETICS | xii |
| PROLOGUE | 1 |
| I. ORIGIN AND HISTORY | 3 |
| II. SOCIAL ORGANIZATION AND KINSHIP SYSTEM | 11 |
| III. VALENGE WOMEN. THEIR HOMESTEADS | 20 |
| IV. THE AGRICULTURAL YEAR | 28 |
| V. MATERIAL CULTURE | 33 |
| A. PREPARATION OF FOOD, MEALS, OILS, AND BEVERAGES | 33 |
| B. INDUSTRIES. DOMESTIC IMPLEMENTS. POTTERY. BASKETRY. BEADWORK | 49 |
| VI. BIRTH RITES | 61 |
| VII. EARLY EDUCATION | 84 |
| VIII. GAMES | 90 |
| IX. STRING FIGURES | 95 |
| X. TATUING, SCARIFICATION, AND TRIBAL MARKS | 102 |
| XI. PUBERTY. INITIATION | 109 |
| XII. MARRIAGE, RELATION BETWEEN THE SEXES | 137 |
| XIII. DEATH | 153 |
| XIV. DANCES | 172 |
| XV. RELIGION, MAGIC, AND SORCERY | 182 |
| XVI. FOLK-LORE AND PROVERBS | 226 |
| CONCLUSION | 238 |
| APPENDIX. THE SIBS OF GAZALAND | 240 |
| INDEX | 247 |

## LIST OF ILLUSTRATIONS

|   |   |   |
|---|---|---|
| I. Drawing by a Leŋge schoolboy | facing p. | 3 |
| II. Food-bowls | ,, | 50 |
| III. Ndau women with pots | ,, | 53 |
| IV. Basketry: (a) Plaited winnowing-tray: coiled field-basket<br>(b) Fish-basket: fancy baskets | ,, | 57 |
| V. Basketry: (a) Hand-baskets<br>(b) Stages in making | ,, | 58 |
| VI. Leŋge child's doll | ,, | 87 |
| VII. Doll (ŋwana) | ,, | 88 |
| VIII. (a) Tatuing instruments<br>(b) Facial marking of Leŋge woman | ,, | 103 |
| IX. Body marking of Portuguese East African woman | ,, | 107 |
| X. (a) Mistress of the initiation ceremonies<br>(b) Ntakula drum | ,, | 111 |
| XI. Likhalu girdle used in initiation ceremonies | ,, | 113 |
| XII. Sacred horn, initiation badge, head-dress, ŋkiriŋgwane drum and biological symbols | ,, | 116 |
| XIII. Sacred dolls (mayika) | ,, | 118 |
| XIV. Mayika female doll | ,, | 119 |
| XV. Skirts of bark cloth | ,, | 124 |
| XVI. Beadwork (initiation ornaments) | ,, | 125 |
| XVII. Designs on walls of huts | ,, | 132 |
| XVIII. Aŋgalaŋga dance | ,, | 176 |
| XIX. Divining omens | between pp. | 186 & 187 |
| XX. (a) Thema axe<br>(b) Andoro | facing p. | 208 |
| XXI. Woman making Σiŋgundu | ,, | 209 |
| XXII. Σiŋgundu of man doctor | ,, | 210 |
| XXIII. Σiŋgundu of woman doctor | ,, | 211 |
| MAP |   | at end |

## ACKNOWLEDGEMENT

Plates II, IX, XIII, XV, XVI, XXb are reproduced from the *Annals of the Transvaal Museum* by kind permission of the Director.

Plates VI, VII, XI, XIV, XVIII, XIX, XXa, XXII are reproduced by kind permission of the Director of the Cambridge Museum of Anthropology and Ethrology.

## NOTE ON PHONETICS

1. *e* and *o* have two values each, close and open. These two varieties are apparently used according to some scheme of vowel harmony as in Zulu.

2. *v* can be (labio-dental) *r*, (bi-labial) *v*, or *b*. Whether implosive and explosive *b*—both occur—has not been determined.

3. It has been found convenient to use the symbols:[1]
 ɬ = hl.
 ş = labialized s (formerly ŝ). Cap. Ş. It occurs in the plural prefix şi of which ʃi is the singular.
 ʃ = sh (formerly š). Cap. Σ.
 dʒ = j, except in a few names where j is retained. Dz also occurs.
 ŋ = velar n. Cap. Ŋ.

With these few exceptions, the old spelling of words has been retained, and, for the sake of clearness, hl has been retained in the Thoŋga group name Hleŋgwe.

[1] Cf. *Practical Orthography of African Languages*. Mem. I. Int. Inst. Af. Lang. and Cult. 1930.

# PROLOGUE

A LITTLE Portuguese coasting steamer, wedged between ocean liners, is lying alongside the docks at Lourenço Marques. The time is about 11 p.m. on September 19th, 1917. All is dark on the boat. Two women missionaries, having said good-bye to friends who came to see them off, grope their way along the lower deck, amid little heaps of sleeping humanity—African, natives come from the Rand by train, who have been working in the mines of Johannesburg and are now returning to their own homes for a rest. The missionaries, preceded by a boy with a lantern, find their way to one of the little cabins set apart for white people. They nearly fall over a pig which haunts the passage, accompanying the vessel on all her coastal trips.

At 2 a.m. a sound of pumping engines and other activities is heard, and at dawn the *Liberal* steams fussily out of harbour and prepares for a good tossing on the wide waters of the Indian Ocean.

The human freight on the lower deck endures as best it may. There are about three hundred natives, and they lie closely huddled together. Some are ill. One who has been carried aboard on a stretcher is probably dying of phthisis. Sometimes a wave washes over them and their scattered bundles—such treasure of old tin boxes, dirty blankets, boots, coffee-pots, mugs, native harps, sewing-machines, and odds and ends picked up in musty pawnshops of Johannesburg.

At 3 p.m. a stiffish breeze lashes the long roll of breakers at the mouth of the Limpopo into fury. The missionaries watch their luggage rolling about the cabin. Crash! The *Liberal* strikes sand and quivers, but a great wave comes and mercifully lifts her over the danger spot. For twenty minutes more she poises like a sea-bird on the crests of billows, and then she is 'over the Bar', resting quietly on the broad bosom of the Limpopo, framed in a vivid background of yellow sand and green trees.

Two small boats appear on the river and are rowed alongside. In them are pails of mealie-meal porridge brought from the shore for the native passengers, and supplied from the small red-roofed depot of the Witwatersrand Native Labour Association. The meal ended, the *Liberal* resumes her way along the winding green reaches of the river, the passengers occasionally shouting out chaffing greetings to natives on the banks. About 8 p.m. she reaches the little Portuguese town of Vila de João Belo, called by the natives Chai Chai. Here the native travellers, staggering up the gangway with their loads, are landed, and plunge into the bush on their way to their different destinations. Some remain for the night at Chai Chai, and the next day are carried a few miles farther in a little train of trucks on a light railway. Others walk all night long. But soon they rejoin their families and the womenfolk to whom I am now about to introduce the reader. What memories those miners have to recall, for the benefit of their friends, of the strange sights, sounds, and ways of civilization.

On arrival at Chai Chai, the missionaries sleep on board the boat, enveloped in a cloud of mosquitoes which penetrate the tiny cabin. In the early morning they pursue their way into the bush, travelling in the little train for about ten miles, and then in a donkey-cart for six more miles till they come to the mission station perched on a sandy hill not far from the sea.

A few days later four or five Leŋge women of various ages peer anxiously through the mosquito wire of the veranda of the missionaries' shanty, very eager to see some white women. The clothing of these native women consists of not much more than a loin-cloth apiece, stained by much field-work and by having been washed in lake water without soap. The women are introduced by a young Leŋge, with maimed hands and feet, who is a clever school-teacher. 'These are the women whom you are going to teach', he tells us politely. We might have replied: 'These are the women who are also going to teach us.'

PLATE I

DRAWING BY A LEDGE SCHOOLBOY
Ngoni warriors try to capture a Lenge family.

# I
## ORIGIN AND HISTORY

IN that land of sandhills, spread out like a field of cloth of gold, of marshy lakes, green glades, and fertile gardens, lying between the eastern bank of the Limpopo River and the Indian Ocean, the VaLeŋge dwell in clusters of reed-huts springing up like little mushrooms, on the hills and in the dales.

This part of Gazaland is roughly triangular in shape, the base of the triangle being the Indian Ocean, with the Limpopo River and Chopiland (Tʃopiland) as the two sides (see map).

According to native tradition the VaTʃopi and the VaLeŋge were one race. This was the account given me by Johane Makamu, an old MuLeŋge:

Starting long ago, when the VaȠgoni (Zulu under Manukosi) had not yet arrived, the VaTʃopi and the VaLeŋge had been one race from of old indeed. And also after that when the VaȠgoni arrived, they find all the countries with their own chiefs. And all the chiefs had fortified kraals and their people. The fortified kraals resemble cattle kraals. When the army of the VaȠgoni arrived, then they run, they enter into their kraals. Also those chiefs, they did not join up with another chief, but each one reigned in his own kraal with his people, while they were all one race, the VaTʃopi.[1] Think, the country of the VaTʃopi starts from Choŋgoene and reaches Inharrime. But when they see each other, they call each other by the direction of the winds, like this: on the side of the west, they call it VuLeŋge (West), while all are of one race. Seeing the side of the east, they call it VuTsoŋga, and this means VuTʃopi, while all are of one race, they are VaTʃopi. Their affairs are very much alike indeed.

The story of the Zulu-Aŋgoni invasions and occupations of Gazaland (1825–95) is well known,[2] and afterwards the Leŋge comprised, not only the true Leŋge as of old, but all the new Westerners of Thoŋga, ȡgoni, or Ndau origin. The remnants of that strange race, the VaNdau, whose original home is in the Sabi River district, have left a strong impress upon the culture of Gazaland. The story goes

---

[1] For a list of these chiefs and their districts, see App., p. 240.
[2] The latest work on the subject is that by Sṝ. D. F. Toscano and Sṝ. D. J. Quintinha of Manjacaze, entitled: *A Derrocada do Imperio Va Tua e Mousinho de Albuquerque*. Lisbon, 1930.

that some of the Ndau people, having been taken prisoners by the Ŋgoni, were brought in the train of their conquerors to Gazaland, and settled there. Modern Leŋge speak the Thoŋga language. But, and this is a very important 'but', many of the women among the Leŋge, and some of the older men, speak the old KiLeŋge language, akin to modern Tʃopi, but with marked differences. Thoŋga-Shangaan,[1] the dialect most used by the Leŋge, approximates most to Gwamba, but contains words of Roŋga, Tʃopi, Leŋge, Ŋgoni, and Ndau origin. The successive migrations and invasions have all left their influence on the original language, whatever it may have been. In Bilene one hears conversations interspersed with clicks, and realizes that the Zulu influence has been strong there.

There would seem to be at least three distinct strata of the population among the Leŋge. The oldest is probably of Hleŋgwe origin, represented by sibs[2] such as those of the Manuse,[3] Nyakule, and Kwakwi. It is they who speak the old Leŋge language (allied to old Tʃopi) which is fast dying out. The second stratum is represented by the Ntama and others who are of old Zulu origin. They are represented by the sibs of Vilaŋkulu (probably) and Ŋkumbe (certainly). The third stratum is formed of people of Djoŋga origin (sibs of Ŋwamusi, Masiye, &c.). They brought in the Iron Age with them, by the use of assegais and knives.

The district Chiefs of the Leŋge are five in number. Each chief or *regulo* (*regulo* is the Portuguese word in common use) has a number of petty chiefs called *tihosana* or *tinduna* or *tiŋganakana*, among whom

[1] Shangaan is the name applied to the Thoŋga and all East Coast 'boys' by the whites. For the origins of the names Thoŋga and Shangaan, see Junod, *Life of a South African Tribe*, pp. 14–15.

[2] Among the Leŋge a sib (or clan) is termed a *figava*, and a lineage or siblet *figavenyana*. For a list of sibs see Appendix.

[3] In R. N. Hall's *Prehistoric Rhodesia*, 1909, opposite p. 28, there is a map, prepared by the author, of Macaranga, 1505–1760, showing kingdoms of the Monomotapa, Manica, Quiteve, Sabia, and Otoŋgwe. Just above the mouth of the Limpopo, close to the shore, is printed the word 'Manusa'; just beyond it, 'Inyabuse', and beyond that the 'Inhariŋgiŋgwe River'. At the end of the book (p. 450) he gives 'Mamusa (? misprint for Manusa), a dependent district of Inhapula on the north side of the Rio Dos Reys (Limpopo) near its mouth'. This mention of the old Leŋge sib of Manusa (to-day Manuse) is very interesting. The Manuse people are living now in the Khambana district among the Mondlana, but the Mondlana say that the Manuse are settlers only and not related to them. They are considered to be of Tʃopi origin, but my own idea is that they are old Leŋge, nearly related to the Hleŋgwe. Mamusa may be connected with the Ŋwamusi of the present day, and not a misprint for Manusa.

his country is divided. Each petty chief has his own headmen also. For a list of the petty chiefs of each *regulo*, see Appendix.

The five *regulos* are Σihału, Nyafoko, Mahumane, Makupulane, and Ŋkandze. The two last, although really Leŋge, are now included in Tʃopiland.

REGULO I. *Σihału*. Σihału Ŋwamusi is the first chief of the Leŋge as regards rank. His head-quarters are at Nyampfuŋwini (locative of place, the district being called after a former chief Nyampfumo). On Σihału's death the seat of government will be transferred to the district of which his successor is headman. This will probably be his parallel cousin called 'brother'. In the succession of Leŋge chiefs brothers have priority over sons, but a son may succeed his father if the latter has no eligible brothers or parallel cousins.

Σihału says that his people came originally from Ŋkoseni. The territory of Ŋkoseni is on the other side of the Limpopo. He also said 'the old people of this country were the Nyaviri, the Kwakwi, and the Nyane. Nyahule are very old VaNtama.' He tells the story thus:

A very long time ago indeed, Nyaviri was of the kindred of Σikavele. They ruled long ago and were subject to the Nyampfumo. After some time the Nyaviri find a dead elephant, and they lack a knife and an axe to cut it with, so they kindle a fire there, to heat it at the side, they bend down, they bite the hide, they scrape it with a mussel shell, they skin it there. Then the Nyampfumo arrive, they say, 'Let us leave it'. Then they cut it with an assegai, they sever the limbs and cook them. Then after that the Nyampfumo say 'We are the chiefs, we have assegais'. Then the Nyampfumo fight, are conquered and flee to Mamba ka Mhula and call together a band, and buy the way from the Mambu. They swim across with the force and conquer the Nyaviri.

The clan song of the Va ka Ŋwamusi refers to 'the buying of the road' from the Mamba (sometimes called Mambu).

*Clan Song of the Va ka Ŋwamusi:*

| | |
|---|---|
| *Dimbuli yamisava! Ŋwamusi!*[1] | Dimbuli of the land, Ŋwamusi! |
| *Kunyani* | How then, |
| *nyamatla misiha* | muscles of brawn, |
| *ŋwana vamakwanyeli wamuseka* | son of those huddled up with cold. |
| *Dimbuli hite sodabuta* | Dimbuli who is *sodabuta* |
| *ku muhlaba* | *ku muhlaba* |
| *Reŋgani ndlela akaMambu* | Buy the way from the Mambu. |

[1] On ceremonial occasions, Σihału is greeted by the title of *Dimbuli yamisava! Ŋwamusi!* ( = Dimbuli of the land! Ŋwamusi!), indicating that through him the clan claimed the right to their territory.

*Buya, Makloŋgwe, uzabusa ubukosi nasi iqombo yako bi yindlu yolweŋkosi.*  Return, Maklongwe, and rule the kingdom while it is your bowl, by the chieftainship of Ʃiluvane.

I am told that the last lines are sarcastic, and an addition to the ancient song, and refer to a comparatively recent incident, when Maklongwe, who appears to be of the house of Ʃiluvane, disputed 'the flag' sent by the Portuguese to Ʃihału. The bowl refers to the offerings that are made to the chief.

*Ʃihału (continued)*
The Nyane are an ancient kindred of the VaNtama, while they were living at Nkumini.

The Kwakwi are ancient people who were scattered about the country. They lived in one place after another where a person sees ash heaps. It was they who built long ago, and were very rich. They were scattered by the people who are in the country now.

The sib of the Nyahule. They are Ntama of an old stock which scarcely knew the use of assegais. They fought with the Nyampfumo long ago, were driven away from the country of Nyahuleni and swam across Loŋgwe in fleeing. They make up a song which says: 'We people of the bridge do not swim. It is the people of Ngoŋwani and Nyapondzo who swim. They leave Ngoŋwanini and become subjects of Ʃiluvane Nyapondzweni.' After that Nyampfumo takes the district of the Nyahule and gives it to the Venye. Then the Venye refuse, saying 'It is not a good country, this, with its hills and grass, we shall be pierced.' So the Nyahule return and become subject there and build there now.

One of the Kwakwi women living at Masiyeni told me that the Kwakwi were scattered remnants of the Makwakwa, hence the change in the name.

The Vilaŋkulu are also one of the oldest Tʃopi sibs, probably of old Ntama stock.

Rindela Vilaŋkulu, a woman belonging to the family, gave me Vilaŋkulu's genealogy. She said that Vilaŋkulu was descended from a very great chief who was called Rhee Mambu.

> Rhee Mambu (? Portuguese *Rei*, which means king.)
> Nyankuŋgwane
> Nzuŋwe Ɖwaʃibomu
> Musika
> Mukumbe
> Matsemane
> Vilaŋkulu

When I asked her what Mambu stood for, she said that it might mean 'chief', but others have told me since that it was the name of one of the ancestors of Rhee. In that case the 'Mambu' of Mhula, from whom Σihaɫu's ancestors 'bought the way', may belong to the same stock. On the other hand, if Mambu means 'chief' then it may betoken an ancient Rhodesian origin for Vilaŋkulu.[1]

For a long time I was puzzled as to the exact relationship between the house of Σiluvane Vilaŋkulu and the reigning house of Nyampfumo Ɖwamusi. At the very end, after questioning literally almost every one I came across, wherever I went, and comparing the different answers, my information stood thus:

1. The House of Σiluvane held the premier chieftainship at the end of the Ŋgoni invasions.
2. The House of Nyampfumo Ɖwamusi was also ruling in its own territory.
3. Σiluvane and Nyampfumo were contemporaries; Nyampfumo being called upon to help Σiluvane at times.
4. Σiluvane and Nyampfumo were distantly connected.

But it must be admitted that few people knew anything at all about the matter—'It was all so long ago'.

The connecting link between the house of Vilaŋkulu and Nyampfumo was given me by Σihaɫu himself. It was this: Vilaŋkulu and Nyampfumo could both call Σitsumbuli 'Father'. Now Σitsumbuli does not appear in the direct line of descent of Vilaŋkulu, but if the latter could call him father, then he may have been an uncle (or a great-great-uncle) on the father's side, this relation being called 'father' according to the Leŋge terms of relationship.

The following table has been drawn up as a guide to the genealogy of the chief Leŋge sibs of *regulo 1*. Each name probably represents, not a single individual, but a reigning house. Generations may have elapsed between some of the names.

It will be seen on reference to J. Makamu's list (App. I) that he includes Vilaŋkulu among the VaMhandla. Rindela Vilaŋkulu also said that her forefathers came from Mhandleni, although she could not tell me where this district might be. At any rate, there are now three branches of the Vilaŋkulu sib, one lives at Vilanculos, north of Inhambane, speaking Thoŋga, and the second lives in Tʃopiland, and the third in Bilene.

[1] Rev. H. P. Junod (*Bantu Studies*, 'Some Notes on Tʃopi Origins', iii, 1927, pp. 57–71) found that the old Tʃopi nucleus was formed principally of the two sibs Vilaŋkulu and Ɖkumbe.

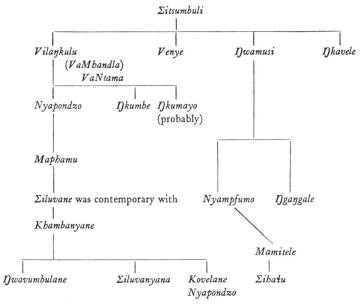

On ceremonial occasions Σiluvane is greeted by this little song:

*Indlu vukosi Siyubaa wadakwe zoyo dakwaa*
The house of the chief, Siyubaa, you were intoxicated yesterday, [really] intoxicated.

I was told that the allusion was to some incident connected with elephant hunting, when Σiluvane lacked iron weapons. The same old story of the elephant is repeated in every sib. It really indicated the coming of the Iron Age in Gazaland. Those who had iron weapons such as knives and assegais remained the conquerors.

Ntete, one of the sibs of *regulo* Σihaɫu, appears to be also connected with the Vilaŋkulu line. The present *hosana* of Nteteni, Maphamu Ntete, had heard that his forefathers came originally from Rhodesia.[1] He believed that one branch of the sib lived in Rhodesia, another in Zululand, and another in Tʃopiland.

An old man of the Ntete family told me as follows:

The chieftainship of Ntete, he who began to reign was Kosa. Then Fene enters, he reigns. Then Duwa enters, he reigns. And now there are ruling his children. When Dumisane died, then Maŋgwiŋgwi reigned. When Maŋgwiŋgwi died, then Duwane entered and reigned. When Duwane died, then

[1] The old man Maphamu said 'Blantyre, Rhodesia', but of course Blantyre is in Nyasaland. This would perhaps connect this sib with the Aŋgoni of Nyasaland.

Laŋgwani ruled. When Laŋgwani died, Zimane reigned. When Zimane died, Nyakanulawe reigned. The origin of the Ntete is this: He who originated the country of the Ntete was Ntete Wapila Tʃigyiwo Mbahokwe. He drove away the people of Nyamphekeni and Seleveni because he was chief, he came from the East and filled the country of Ntete.

'The ethnology of Gazaland and Chopiland (Tʃopiland) is still to be studied. It is a most interesting country, resembling a cross road of peoples ... a most interesting ethnological puzzle.'[1] I agree with M. Junod (*fils*). The longer one lives in Gazaland the more one realizes the complexity of the elements of which the native population is composed. The linguistic definition of a tribe as a people speaking a common language breaks down at the outset where the Thoŋga are concerned. For convenience M. Junod (*père*) uses the general term Thoŋga tribe, divided into the Roŋga,[2] Hlaŋganu, Djoŋga, Bila, Djwaluŋgu, and Hleŋgwe groups, excluding the Tʃopi, as speaking another language, though Tʃopi is nearly related to Hleŋgwe (Tswa), as Sir H. Johnston has shown in his *Comparative Study of the Bantu and Semi-Bantu Languages*, p. 281. On the other hand, the modern Leŋge should be counted in the Thoŋga group as they speak Thoŋga-Shangaan, but the old Leŋge[3] are one with the old Tʃopi, speaking practically the same language. As we have seen, the natives themselves regard VuTsoŋga and VuLeŋge as geographical divisions, meaning eastern and western respectively. VaTʃopi means 'archers', as these people used bows and arrows before they knew the use of assegais. The term VaTʃopi could therefore include the Ntama and some of the Thoŋga as well.

Where then are the Leŋge to find their rightful place? If for convenience' sake, the name Thoŋga is to be retained, the Leŋge may be considered as a seventh group in M. Junod's classification. In his map[4] the Roŋga group is coloured pink, the Hlaŋganu mauve, the

---

[1] H. Junod, *Bantu Studies*, iii, 1927, p. 70.

[2] Pereira Cabral uses the name 'Roŋga' for the whole Thoŋga tribe, whereas Junod uses 'Roŋga' for one group only of this tribe. M. Junod has shown that the names Roŋga and Thoŋga have the same derivation. Cf. Pereira Cabral, *Raças, Usos e Costumes dos Indigenas da Provincia de Moçambique*. Imprensa Nacional, Lourenço Marques, 1925.

[3] To show how relative these terms are I may quote the case of a man at Ngoveni, near Zavala (the eastern end of Tʃopiland), who referred to the VaTʃopi of the Zandamela district to the west of him as VaLeŋge. The Zandamela people, however, will not call themselves Leŋge, but reserve that name for people still farther to the west.    [4] H. A. Junod, *The Life of a South African Tribe*, map opp. p. 16.

Djoŋga primrose, the Bila striped pink and white, the Ḏwaluŋgu green, the Hleŋgwe blue, and my proposed group will be the Leŋge, striped blue and primrose. The modern Tʃopi, speaking a distinct language of their own, can be considered a separate tribe, but as their origins are largely Thoŋga, Vetʃa, and Ḏgoni they might form an eighth group, striped blue and white.

*Surnames*

A consideration of the Leŋge sibs throws an interesting light on the origin of surnames. Their surnames are the personal names of some distant ancestor, but, as the generations roll on, the tendency is to take the name of some more immediate ancestors, such as father or grandfather.

A man is named Jeremiah Madidani. Madidani was his father's name. His real surname is Masiye. He belongs to the Masiye sib, of Masiyeni, who are called after a distant ancestor Masiye. But this ancestor himself had the surname of Mayazi, who had a still more distant ancestor called Kosa. Therefore it is clear that the surnames or *ʃiboŋgo* in this district are in no way connected with totems, though it does not prove that totems have not existed in the remote past.

A Leŋge sib is like a biological cell, constantly dividing until the cellules almost forget the original cell of which they are subdivisions. Perhaps a man named Masiye was called by this name according to the will of the ancestral spirits, as revealed by the divining bones. Masiye settles in a new district by reason of invasion, migration, or conquest. He becomes the headman of the district, which is therefore called Masiyeni, and all the people who are his descendants are called Va ka Masiye. Even people who come to live at Masiyeni, perhaps relations of Masiye's wives, tend to be called Masiye too, especially if Masiye adopts sons of widows or other people who come to be his dependants.

II

# SOCIAL ORGANIZATION AND KINSHIP SYSTEM

AS has been shown in Chapter I, the political organization of the Leŋge consists in the grouping of a certain number of sibs under each district chief or *regulo* (cf. Appendix II). Each sib has its own petty chief (*hosana* or *ŋganakana*), who has a good deal of authority over his own people, but is responsible to, and has the right of appeal to, the district chief, who in his turn is responsible to the Portuguese Government. The people can always appeal directly to the Portuguese Native Commissioner, who when judging individual cases in this way may call up the petty chief, as well as others, to give evidence and to state his point of view in the matter. Each sib is again divided into sub-sibs or lineages, each with its headman, who is generally a councillor (*induna*) of the petty chief, who may be in his turn an *induna* of the district chief in addition to the brother or sons of the latter, if these are old enough. The headman of each lineage will portion out land to be cultivated among his own people. The number of families in each lineage varies very much, some lineages tending to die out, while others are increasing as regards the number of families.

The Leŋge are patrilineal and patrilocal. Women have hardly any authority in legal or political matters, though they accomplish a good deal by the power of the tongue. The *vanyamusoro* (cf. p. 182) have religious influence. Socially the wives and daughters of the chief take precedence of other women, and often have ritual as well as social functions to perform, as for example their offices in the initiation rites. The women of most importance in any family are the father's sisters, the mother, the wives of the sons, especially of the eldest, and the eldest daughter. The sons and daughters of the mother's brothers are also greeted respectfully by their cross-cousins. The child knows that its father's people are all important, and its attitude towards them may be tinged with a little more fear and awe than towards its relatives on the mother's side. The mother's brother is more like a fond grandparent, who spoils the children, while the father's sister often assumes parental responsibility towards them. For this reason young people enjoy much more a visit to the mother's than to the father's relatives. Sisters also look up to their brothers with great respect, and address them as 'Father'. M. Junod in describing the Thoŋga has given in detail the behaviour of the wife towards her husband's relatives, and that of the husband towards his wife's relatives. The Leŋge have practically the same observances. The wife's mother and wife's brother's wife are the people with whom a man must be very circumspect in his behaviour, and with whom he is in a so-called 'avoidance' relationship. The wife's brother's wife will turn aside in the bush, so as not to encounter her husband's sister's husband full face. If you ask why, you are told that this woman has been lobola-ed with the cattle or money which the man has given for his own wife, and which has then been used to lobola a wife for her brother.

*Kinship System and Terms of Relationship of the Leŋge*

The following is a list of terms in common use. The Leŋge being a mixed people, other kinship names occasionally occur:

(*m.s.* = man speaking.  *w.s.* = woman speaking.)

*Nuna* (pl. *vanuna*)  Husband.
Husband of sister, *w.s.*
(Also called *namu*. Potential husband for *w s*.)

*Nsati* (pl. *vasati*)  Wife.
Wife of brother, *m.s.*
(Also called *namu*. Potential wife for *m.s.*)

*Ŋwana* (pl. *vana*)  Child (either son or daughter).
Child of brother, *m.s.*
Child of sister, *w.s.*

*Bava* (pl. *vabava*)  Father.
Brother of father.
Elder brother.
Husband of mother's sister.
Brother of brother's wife, *w.s.*
Father of grandparent (really *kokwane*) may be addressed as *bava*.

*Bava* as a polite form of address can be used by any woman when addressing any man.

*Mamane* (pl. *vamamane*)  Mother. (Also *Ŋwini* = owner.)
Mother's sister.
Wife of father's brother.
Mother of husband (who is really *Ŋwiŋgi*).
Mother of wife.
Daughter of mother's brother.

## SOCIAL ORGANIZATION AND KINSHIP SYSTEM

Sister of every *kokwane* in the direct male line of descent of the mother's brother. (Cf. table on p. 17.)

The term *mamane* can be used as a polite form of address to any woman of suitable age.

*Hahane* (pl. *vahahane*) — Father's sister. See note on pp. 14–18.

*Kokwane* (pl. *vakokwane*) — Grandparent.
Brother of mother.
Brothers and sisters of grandparents and great-grandparents.
Male descendants of males in the direct line of the mother's brother. (See table on p. 19.)

*Ntukulu* (pl. *vantukulu*) — Grandchild.
Sister's child, either son or daughter, *m.s.*
Sister's descendants, *m.s.*
Father's sister's child, *m.s.*

*Ntukulu wa fiŋguha* (or *mukoŋwana*) — Great-grandchild

*Mukoŋwana* (pl. *vakoŋwana*) — Husband of daughter.
Husband of sister, *m.s.*
Husband of husband's sister.
Husband of father's sister, *m.s.* (addressed as *mwane* or *bava*).
Wife of wife's brother, *m.s.*
(In this case the cattle or money paid by *m.s.* for his wife is used by his wife's brother to lobola his own wife just mentioned.)

*Namu* (pl. *valamu* or *tinamu*) — Wife of brother, *m.s.*
(Also called *nsati*.)
Husband of sister, *w.s.*
(Also called *nuna*.)
Husband of father's sister, *w.s.*
(Potential husband for *w.s.*)
Brother of wife.
Sister of brother's wife.
(Also called *ndombe*.)
Brother of husband.
Sister of husband.
Parallel cousin of husband.

| | |
|---|---|
| *Ŋwiŋgi* | Wife of son (addressed as *mamanyane*). |
| | Mother of husband (addressed as *mamane*). |
| | Father of husband (addressed as *bava*). |
| *Mamanyane* (pl. *vamamanyane*) | Wife of son. |
| Form of address for: | Wife of brother's son, *w.s.* |
| | Sister of brother's wife, *w.s.* |
| | (Also called *ndombe* or *namu*.) |
| *Ndombe* or *ŋombe* | Sister of brother's wife |
| (pl. *tindombe* or *tiŋombe*) | (Addressed as *mamanyane*). |

Both the sororate and the levirate exist. A man may marry his first wife's sister during her lifetime, though this is not usual; and he may marry a deceased wife's sister if she is younger than the deceased.

As regards the levirate, a younger brother may inherit his elder brother's widow. A man may inherit his mother's brother's widow, but he may not marry her daughter (his cross-cousin).

*Note on the Hahane.*[1]

The mother's brother plays an important part in the social relationships of the Thoŋga tribe. M. Junod, in his *Life of a South African Tribe*, and Professor Radcliffe Brown, in his address to the Anthropological and Ethnological Section of the South African Association for the Advancement of Science in July, 1923, have described this role very clearly and fully. As yet, however, not much is known about the part played by the father's sister, beyond the information contained in M. Junod's book. It seems, therefore, worth while recording the few facts about the father's sister which I have gleaned during the time I have lived among the Leŋge.

From the tables on pp. 17, 19 it will be seen that all parallel cousins among the Leŋge are called brothers and sisters to each other, but cross-cousins are on a different footing; the children of the father's sisters a man calls *ntukulu*, a woman *ŋwana* (child). The children of a mother's brother a man or a woman calls *kokwane* if they are male, *mamane* if they are female. The reason for this terminology will be clear from the facts disclosed.

The *hahane* ranks as a feminine counterpart of the father, and sometimes acts as such, in conjunction with or in the absence of the father's brothers. When asked why the *hahane* has more weight in the family

[1] Reproduced by kind permission from the *South African Journal of Science*, vol. xxii, pp. 526–9, November, 1925: 'The Role of the Father's Sister among the Valenge of Gazaland, Portuguese East Africa' (E. D. Earthy).

## SOCIAL ORGANIZATION AND KINSHIP SYSTEM 15

councils than the mother, my informants always reply: 'Because the *hahane* belongs to the same family as the father, but the mother belongs to a different family. The mother is not of the same family as her child.' This seems to be one of the proofs that the Leŋge count their descent patrilineally.

The *hahane* calls her brother's daughter *łampsana*, and this girl is almost equal to her father's sister as far as marriage is concerned, for the same man may marry both *hahane* and *łampsana*. That is to say, a man has a right to his wife's brother's daughter. That is why a woman will call her father's sister's children by the same terms as she calls her own children, for they are in fact her step-children, or may become so. That, further, is the reason why either a man or a woman will call the mother's brother's daughter *mamane* (mother), for the father has the right to her as his second wife, and she, therefore, becomes the step-mother. It is, perhaps, noteworthy that the grandchildren, the sister's children, and the father's sister's children are all called by the same name, *vantukulu*, and that they 'eat together', that is, share the same food-bowl, in ceremonial feasts and also at ordinary meals. If meat is portioned out, the father's sister's child is served before the grandchildren.

In the matter of offering sacrifices to the ancestral spirits, the *hahane* may offer a sacrifice (*kupała*) on behalf of her brother's child, in case of illness, in order that the child may recover. She may, however, only do this if one of her own parents is dead. (No one may offer a sacrifice who has not lost one parent, at least.) The child's own mother or grandmother may not offer sacrifice on its behalf. Why? The answer is always the same: 'They do not belong to the same family.'

The *hahane* will also offer a sacrifice on behalf of her *łampsana* if the latter has difficulty in childbirth. If the child's birth is delayed, the *hahane* has sometimes a guilty conscience, and thinks that the fault may be hers for something that she may have done in the past, and that the ancestral spirits are angry with her, and are preventing the birth of her *łampsana's* child. She uses a simple invocation to the spirits: 'You must help me in order that the child may be born.' If, however, the *hahane's* conscience is clear, the expectant mother herself is supposed to have sinned.

It is necessary that the *hahane* should accompany her brother's daughter when she goes to the initiation ceremonies for women. The mother of the girl may go too, but this is not essential. The *hahane* is considered to be the proper chaperone on this occasion.

The *hahane* will also teach the *ṭampsana* to work, and takes a great deal of interest in the career of the child. She can forbid her brother's son's marriage, if she disapproves of his choice. Here, again, her veto is of great weight, and her opinion is considered before that of the intending bridegroom's own mother. She can also prevent her brother's daughter's marriage. If she approves of the match, she is given a present of clothing or money.

The *hahane* has also definite duties on the occasion of the birth of a brother's child, and later on, at the confinement of the *ṭampsana*. She must be present at this event, and assist in cutting the cord, and burying the afterbirth. Sometimes she proposes a name for the child on the name-giving day (a great event), having previously paid a visit to the divination-doctor (*anyaŋga*),[1] who casts his bones to find out if the ancestral spirits approve of the name.

The *hahane* will also help to bury a brother's child. If the *ṭampsana* dies, and leaves a child, the *hahane* takes away the child—it is hers. Sometimes a woman will pounce down upon her brother's *muti* (kraal) after his death, and take possession of some of his belongings—including his wife and child—while the widow meekly begs her deceased husband's sister to allow her to remain in the kraal.

The duties of a *ṭampsana* towards her *hahane* are also specified. The following is a literal translation of what was told me on this matter:

'The father's sister's husband will say to his wife: "Here is £1. You go to your brother and ask for one of his daughters (he names the girl he wants), to come and live with us and be my wife". The *hahane* does as she is bid. Her brother agrees to the match. The *ṭampsana* is still a small child, and remains in her father's kraal till she is old enough to be married. Then another £5 is sent, and the child is properly "engaged" ("*kutembisa*" meaning "to promise", is the word used). The girl goes to her *hahane's* home. Other sums of money are sent by degrees, till the "*akulobola*" is completed, a sum of £25 in all having been paid. When the young *ṭampsana* arrives at her aunt's kraal, she is made to mud the floor of the *hahane's* hut. She must throw away the ashes of old fires and procure wood with which to kindle new fires. She must fetch water from the lake. She sometimes cooks food for her *hahane* and the husband. The aunt will sleep on one side of the hut, on a mat, and the husband and the *ṭampsana* on the other side. Sometimes the two women quarrel. If the man dies, and the *ṭampsana* has

[1] 'Augur', 'witch-doctor', or 'medicine-man' is inadequate as translation of the word *anyaŋga*, so the native title is retained.

# SOCIAL ORGANIZATION AND KINSHIP SYSTEM

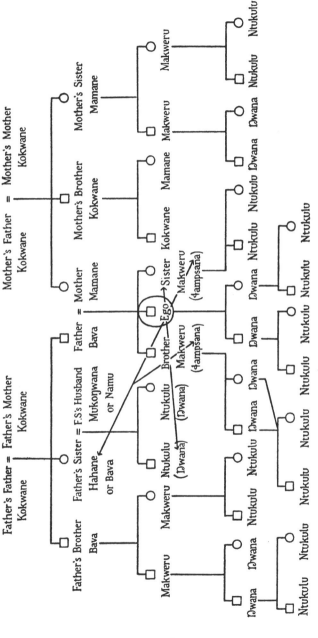

Terms of Relationship among the Lenge

The father's sister's husband is *mukojwana* to a man, and *namu* to a woman

## 18 SOCIAL ORGANIZATION AND KINSHIP SYSTEM

borne him a girl child, she (the *tampsana*) may go away and marry someone else, as she has done her duty to the family by providing a girl to take her place. If the child is a boy, the *tampsana* will probably remain with the *hahane*.'

It is to be inferred from this that the *tampsana* is a very useful person to the '*hahane*' and does a good deal of the domestic drudgery.

A short table (p. 19) showing the relationship of the *vantukulu* to their cross-cousins, the descendants of their mother's brother to the fourth generation, is here given. It will be noted that the direct descendants of the mother's brother in the male line, who never count the descent through a mother, are *kokwane* to the *ego* represented on the table; but when the descent is through a woman, the usual line of descent is followed.

The terms on this table are relative to the *ego* only, and would obviously differ for any other person represented.

## SOCIAL ORGANIZATION AND KINSHIP SYSTEM 19

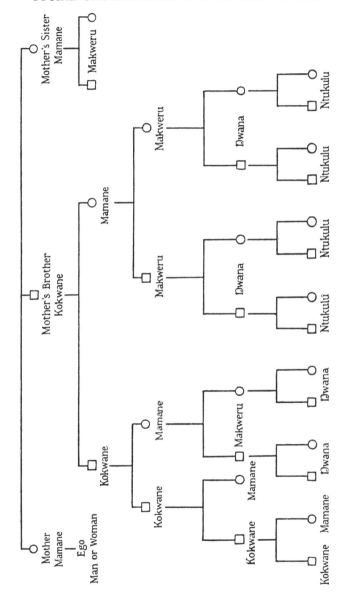

# III
# VALEDGE WOMEN. THEIR HOMESTEADS

*Characteristics of the Women and their Daily Routine*

A TRAVELLER in Leŋgeland would be struck with the variety of physical types among the women. The colour of the skin varies from copper, showing admixture of foreign blood, to a dark brown. The women are mostly tall, some very tall.

As in some other African tribes, there are roughly two main types, one with broad features, projecting lips, and sometimes a slightly mongoloid cast about the eyes; the other small featured, and with well-poised head on a longish neck. There are many intermediate types between these two. All have fine large eyes, a graceful free carriage, beautiful shoulders, generally highly polished, and small, well-formed hands and feet. A colleague of mine once saw a woman who was carrying a baby on her back, and a field basket piled up with vegetables on her head, pick up with her foot something she had dropped.

The figures of young girls are symmetrical, though sometimes very thin. In old age the breasts become pendulous and withered, and constant stooping in the fields seems to cause a lengthened back.

The younger women are scrupulous in their care for their personal appearance, except when they are working in the fields. I have often admired the filbert shape of their toe-nails; and they must be quite aware of their slim ankles, the slenderness of which they enhance by twists of black horse-hair. They keep their skin nicely polished with oil of *Trichilia emetica*, or, when they can afford it, with vaseline bought at an Indian store. The older women sometimes wear old brass anklets and armlets of native make; but the younger ones buy cheap, thin metal ones at the stores, and their fingers are sometimes covered with little brass rings, made by a native smith, three or four rings being worn on each finger. They are also becoming inordinately fond of flashy European ear-rings, which they buy at the stores—the original ear-ring being a tiny metal native-made ring. Strings of modern beads, with small charms attached, are worn by nearly all women.

The girdle is referred to on p. 167 *n*. It might be a relic of the girdle of Isis, judging by the importance which they attach to it.

The Christian women are all extremely anxious to wear a cross. This they call a *fihambano*.

All the women are becoming very fond of clothes, but this is not by any means altogether from motives of vanity, though these play a part. In the first place, clothes have always represented material means, and rolls of material could be used for *akulobola* in the olden days. They are interchangeable with money, and baskets of field-produce can be traded for strips of material at the stores. Women potters living in the bush would rather have as payment for their pots a strip of the dark-blue stiffened print, which is ubiquitous, than money. Clothes are also apt to take on the character of vestments, and form an integral part of some of the funeral and marriage rites and spirit seances. Then again, men returning from Johannesburg and other centres like to see their wives and sweethearts dressed after the manner of the native women in the big towns, and will occasionally send home parcels of clothes by post. How often a woman or girl, especially a prospective bride, would come to me and say: 'I want to be measured'. That meant a tape measure had to be produced and measurements taken and jotted down for print frocks, blouses, skirts, and even shoes. These measurements would afterwards be sent by post to the young man. European garments are gradually beginning to supersede others. Those which have been in vogue for so long consisted (for a best dress) of a tight little Indian bodice called a *fikimawu*, with a strip of dark-blue print or a cotton bed-spread wound round the figure above the chest, and falling to the ankles as a skirt. The head-dress is almost invariably a brightly coloured silk or cotton square of material, called *faduka*, wound round the head in a very pretty fashion in the form of a toque, in a surprising variety of styles, according to the taste of the individual owner.

The women are great chatterboxes, and usually talk a great deal, while they are working, about their neighbours' affairs; the latest fashions at the Indian stores; the cases being tried at the chief's court; the strange things the white people do and say; their own domestic arrangements, and many other things. The heathen women sometimes make their voices loud and mocking; but on the whole, they have pleasing and musical voices. Children's voices, unless raised in exciting play or anger, are low and sweet, especially when they are telling fairy-tales. Singing is a favourite pastime for both men and women. Women sing when at their daily work, in kraal or fields, some of those old, minor melodies and haunting refrains of the East, the topic of the song being generally some death in the family, or some revelations of the spirits in seances, or the machinations of sorcerers. Both men and women improvise the song as they work.

*Daily Routine*

The women are scarcely ever idle. Their manifold work in the fields (including the cutting of wood for fires) and their complex cooking arrangements take up most of their time; and a great many have to walk several miles every day, or every other day, in the early dawn to fetch water. Hence the children are often rather dirty, but oil can be used for cleansing purposes as a substitute for water. How often have I seen women at a kind of well, with small tins hooked on to a long string or stick, scooping up the scanty water which oozes through the sand or mud, and pouring it with great patience into a water-pot.

Needless to say, they have to go very early to the spring, for the water which has accumulated during the night is soon used up. I have often when visiting the villages for a week at a time had to ask one of my women to carry some water for drinking purposes in an old paraffin tin on her head; and I have sometimes had to shut my eyes (and ignore my taste) from the fact that my tea was made with strangely-coloured water.

When the woman has gone to fetch water, the man sweeps out the sandy compound. The women will do this if there are no men about, but it is a man's job. The sweeping is done with a branch of a tree (probably *Mimusops discolor, nyatʃa*) with the leaves stripped off and the branchlets tied together. Some elderly women, late risers, meanwhile warm themselves, if it is autumn or winter, by the fire in a cooking-hut. The women love the cooking-hut. It has reed walls; they like sleeping in it on a mat on the sandy floor, quite close to the fire.

By 7 a.m. the women are returning from the lake or spring, and they have a light meal of food, probably something which has been left over from last night, a stick of cassava or some cold thick mealie porridge. Then women and girls sally forth again for a long morning's work in the gardens.

Very often, in visiting a kraal in the morning, one will find the door locked (with a padlock bought from a store), because all the dwellers in the kraal are at work in the fields; the boys at their task of herding goats, or in school, the girls helping their mothers in the fields by minding the babies, or in weeding and hoeing. The head of the family will be away in an industrial centre, or if at home for a time will be visiting friends, or cutting down reeds to make mats, or cutting poles to build a new hut or granaries.

In the afternoon, after a short midday siesta under a shady tree in the kraal, the women will begin to stamp and pound maize and groundnuts, prepare greens, winnow, and make fires on which to rest their cooking pots. Between five and six o'clock a kraal presents an animated picture, with blazing fires in the cooking-huts, and smoke peacefully ascending in the reddening sunset sky. Children will be playing about or helping their mothers; the men will be chatting among themselves, and the schoolboys will be poring over their spelling-books, slates or catechisms, or making baskets. After the evening meal, the people will sit round the fires and gossip, or tell folk-stories.

The daily routine of the children is practically the same as that of the mothers. They are with their mothers and help them whenever possible. If the work is too hard for them they stop and play instead. A good deal of their time is given to minding younger children and playing with them. If a little girl comes to the mission school she is often accompanied by a fat baby which she carries on her back, and which often cries so that its little nurse has to cease her lesson for a time and take it out to pacify it. It is a choice between bringing the baby to school and taking it out to the fields with the mother. All children are very fond of sewing when they are taught, and they are anxious to learn to read and write. Some of the children have most lovable characters, though quarrels are of very frequent occurrence.

They are extremely fond of games and dances, and attend the latter whenever possible, frequently coming home very late at night.

Leŋge women are very polite to each other, excepting when they are angry. They are punctilious in the matter of greetings. A greeting which can be used at all hours of the day is *feweni* or *fowani*. *Hakulofa* (we greet you) is a respectful salutation. An early-morning greeting is *lifile* (the sun has risen). A midday greeting is *ntikanhi*. *Litfonile* is said in the afternoon, and *lipelile* (it has set) in the evening. The person saluted must always reply '*hm*', or if wishing to be very respectful '*hakulofa*', unless that word has been used by the person saluting.

As regards personal character the women are usually hard-working and devoted mothers. The younger ones are bright and sociable and full of humour. Their greatest failings are obstinacy and jealousy. All are very independent, and can be quite imperious at times.

*Homesteads*

The country is well-wooded bush of a vivid green. The soil is red sand. The lakes, of which there are many, make brilliant splashes of blue in the landscape. The climate is variable. The rainy season lasts from November to March, but there is often a good deal of rain in July, and there are often long periods of drought. The fauna is very rich, especially in birds and insects, and has been only partially studied. The larger mammalia include leopards, hyenas, jackals and monkeys, civet cats, genet cats, and some kinds of buck. Snakes and crocodiles abound. Occasionally a hippopotamus may be seen. The rich sub-tropical flora includes a large number of trees and shrubs of marked interest. The trees most generally found are *Trichilia emetica, Sclerocarya caffra, Anacardium occidentale, Garcinea Livingstonei, Brachystegia venosa*, and species of *Ficus*, also fan palms and wild date palms, all of which are of economic use, and of great importance in native life, especially to the women. Nearly all trees and plants have a magical value. If the women saw me gathering flowers or botanical specimens their curiosity was at once aroused, and they asked me what I wanted them for, the plants being associated in their minds with *tinyaŋga* (medicine-men) and their recipes for magic or medicine.

The women do nearly all the field-work and grow, according to the season, maize, Kaffir-corn (*Sorghum*), ground-nuts (*Arachis hypogaea*), beans, earth peas (*Voandzeia*), pumpkins, gourds, manioc, sweet potatoes, and sugar-cane. Bananas are cultivated near the kraal, and sometimes there are little private gardens for onions, tomatoes, and tobacco. Each homestead has its fields or gardens allotted to it by the *induna* of the chief, and these are generally marked out by rows of pine-apple plants (*maketsa*).

The Leŋge kraals may be large, containing huts for the headman, and his wife or wives, and also huts for married sons and their families. The headman has a good deal of authority, and it is he who will offer the family sacrifices. The tendency now is for the married sons to set up separate homesteads, consisting of one or two living-huts, for which a hut-tax is paid annually, and a cooking-hut, besides the usual curious little wry editions of the larger huts to serve for food storage, fowl houses, and grain bins. The huts in a fairly large kraal are arranged in a circle or oval, round a little compound, the entrance (*paŋgo*) to which is a gateway (*anyaŋgwa*) of two poles. The cooking-huts are usually in the centre of the compound, and the granaries at the side near the bush. Goats have a little kraal of their own, where they are tethered at night. Pigs are kept by some of the more wealthy Leŋge. Fowls are ubiquitous. In the centre of the kraal is the sacred tree under which sacrifices are offered to the ancestral spirits. It can generally be distinguished by a white rag tied round the trunk, and there may be a little pot of beer sunk in the ground by the side. The dwelling-hut is known as *yindlu* (pl. *tiyindlu*) or in Leŋge *nyumba*, and the cooking-hut or kitchen is *findlwana* or *figurumbana*. Where there are two dwelling-huts in a kraal, generally one is a man's hut, and the other a woman's. Very often the mother-in-law lives in the latter. The dwelling-hut has been fully described by M. Junod in his *Life of a South African Tribe*;[1] I will therefore give only a brief description of Leŋge huts in particular.

As is well known, the roof of the hut is constructed on the ground first, and then lifted on to the walls afterwards. It is like a huge cone with a very wide base, in wicker-work. It is built of hoops (*marandzana*) in graduated sizes, connected by poles (*tinhi*). It would perhaps be more correct to say that the framework is of poles, connected by hoops. The top of the cone, where the hoops are very close together, is the *fisuŋgwa*. The work is begun at the top. The poles are made of the branches of *firole* (*Randia dumetorum*), *vumbanye* (*Clerodendrum glabrum*), and *mbała*. Long strips of *kokagwaru* (*Hippocratea* sp.) are used for binding the hoops to the poles.

The huts being of a cone-and-cylinder type the cylindrical walls are formed of reeds (*Phragmites*) placed in an upright position and kept in place by hoops called *timbalelo*. The wall ends at the top inside with two thick rims. Each rim is known as a *mukola*. It is constructed of small poles bent horizontally, strengthened by reeds, and bound with *kokagwaru*. Between the first and second *mukola* is a space, consisting of the tops of the reeds, into the interstices of which the air penetrates, and which allows the encroaches of white ants to be visible and to be stopped. The vertical reeds forming the walls are plastered over with a mixture of sand and water, but this plaster ends with the *mukola*. The doorway is *anyaŋgwa* (Leŋge *gikene*). The outside wall is *kumbe*.

Outside the hut is another *mukola* where the smearing ends at the top. The poles giving an additional support to the hut outside are the *timhanze*. The projecting lintel over the door is the *fikotamu*. The grass which covers the roof is *mutende* (*Imperata cylindrica*). It is generally known as *lułwa* grass. Long strips of thatching are made on the ground with bundles of this grass joined together in the centre by a single row of fitching.

[1] Vol. ii (2nd ed.), pp. 104–10.

The space inside the hut is allotted as follows: At the back opposite the door is the *amfuŋgwe* (Leŋge *magwito ya ɡilawu*). Each side of the hut is a *filawu* (Leŋge *ginyumi*). All round the edge of the floor inside and next to the wall is a little fosse or depression known as *famba khondlo* (Leŋge *kimbi ya khondzo*) (rat-run). As one enters the hut the door opens and is flung back to the right, therefore the right side is the darker, owing to the shadow of the door. Some doors are made of reeds, some of wood, generally the latter. Some are made of old deal boxes, others of thick slabs of mahogany cut from the bush trees. If there is only one hut for a man and his two wives, the first wife and her children sleep to the right of the doorway and the second wife on the left.

In the exact centre of the floor is the circle formed by the *fisiku*[1] or fireplace, outlined by a little fosse. Faggots placed in the *fisiku* are always arranged as radii, the lighted ends being in the centre. On the right side of the *fisiku* is a little depression in the floor, the *fikatu* of the elder wife, where she may rest her pot. On the left side is the *fikatu* of the second wife.

A woman's hut possesses, in addition to the fireplace, a *tsala*, or table, which is so high up that it forms a kind of secondary ceiling. The *tsala* or roof-table is supported on four strong poles driven into the floor of the hut, each pole being called a *fipandzi*. These are the legs of the table, as it were, and they are forked at the top to allow two crossway poles to rest on them, one on each side, called *mihiŋgeku* (Leŋge) or *mitambeko* (Thoŋga). The table is made of a number of withes or rods of *mbaɫa* or sometimes of *mikhandlu* (wild date palm) joined together by simple rows of fitching with *mawuŋgu* reeds. The *tsala* figures largely in folk-lore. A woman climbs up there as in a loft to fetch down her mealies, or whatever else she may keep there. Very often the *tsala* has served as a good hiding-place. It becomes blackened and polished by the fire underneath. Ground-nuts which are to be stored are put in the *tsala* to dry for about a month after they are dug up before being transferred to the *aŋgula*. Earth peas (*Voandzeia subterranea*) are also dried there, then put in another *aŋgula*. Mealie cobs are stored there.

[1] Men do not have a *fisiku* or fire-circle in their huts, and those who have been to the large towns to work have provided themselves with rough hand-made wooden bedsteads. Women never sleep on the bedsteads; they say they are afraid of falling off. A Johannesburg man, showing off his possessions with great pride, said 'Look, there is my bed; and my wife, she sleeps under it'. When the man goes to Johannesburg the bed is taken to pieces and tied up to the roof of the hut, and the women sleep on their mats as usual.

# VALEDGE WOMEN. THEIR HOMESTEADS

New pottery is sometimes placed there so that the smoke may make the pots strong (*umbuluketa timbita*).

Depending from the *tsala* is another much smaller table or hanging shelf. This is immediately over the fire and is called the *fitale* (Leŋge *ndzeratu*). It is made in a mat-like form with reeds or *mikhandlu* palm stems joined by simple rows of fitching with strips of *Combretum* or *Ficus* bark. The framework is also of cross-poles of *foŋge* (*Combretum*) tied to the crossway poles of the *tsala* just above it.

Ground-nuts for immediate use (*sidohe*) and cakes of *fibhehe* and other things, including a hoe and winnowing tray, are kept on the *fitale*.

Each homestead possesses a hut for cooking (*figurumbana*), made on the same principle as an ordinary hut, except that the reed walls are not smeared. Sometimes walls are lacking, and the roof is supported by poles only. The floor is just of the usual sandy ground, not smeared. In the centre is a fireplace made of three inverted pots (*maseku*), each with a hole in it, and the cooking-pot rests on the back of these, the fire being in the centre of the pots. If a Leŋge woman is busy cooking she will express that fact by saying 'I have a pot'. And very carefully she tends that pot. The different kinds of pots will be described under Pottery. The cooking-hut generally possesses another hanging table (*tsala*) for maize cobs, and *sigwa* such as hoes, axes, choppers, field baskets, and winnowing trays.

# IV
# THE AGRICULTURAL YEAR

THE Leŋge do not reckon in months as we do, but rather by the smaller seasons. The greater seasons of summer (*malaŋga*) and winter (*vuſika*) are well defined, but there are no special terms for spring and autumn. I have collected these names of the smaller seasons from the older women. Most of the people have forgotten them.

The New Year, as we count it, comes in at the time of *Pewane*, when the shoots (*mapewa* or *matsuni*) of pine-apples begin to ripen. About the middle of January the season of *Pewukulu*, when the pine-apples have ripened, has arrived. If this season is reckoned as regards pine-apples only, then it may be said to go on till the end of February, though some which ripen late can be had up to April and May. Three kinds of pine-apples (*Ananas sativus*) are grown: *maketsa ya miluŋgu*, planted by means of suckers (*timgakara*), crown generally wanting; *maketsa ya ſinyawane*, of which the crowns (*matsuni*) are planted, ripening quickly, although the suckers are of slow growth; and *maketsa ſilapadzuni*, ripening late in the season, and being propagated both by suckers and crowns. In addition to the fruits (*ſiketsa*) being eaten, a beautiful white thread is made from the leaf fibres of the plants, and an intoxicating drink, to be presently described, from the fruit. Where motor roads have been made in the country they are bordered by rows of pine-apple plants for many miles, a very wise provision for the thirsty native foot passengers.

In the seasons of *Pewane* and *Pewukulu*, pumpkins and gourds also begin to ripen. Beans, maize, and earth peas (*Voandzeia subterranea*) are still being sown. The almonds of *Trichilia emetica* are collected by women. Plums of *Sclerocarya caffra* begin to ripen. New mealies are eaten. Towards the end of January another little season has begun. It is *Nyanyanyani*, when certain wild fruits such as *tindove* (fruits of *Plectronia ventosa* L.) and of *dokomela* (*Landolphia Petersiana* Dyer) begin to ripen. An autumnal ripeness comes. All kinds of vegetable greens are in full season. Beer is being made of *Sclerocarya caffra* plums. The season of ground-nuts, especially of the kind called *ſigoŋgonzwane*, begins. Maize has ripened. The people themselves regard maize as their most important food plant, and except in dry seasons, Gazaland produces fine crops. The first maize of the season is sometimes made into a sheaf, and hung up in a tree. The sheaf may be so large as almost to reach the ground. It is sometimes bent over in the form of a crook (*filodo*), or the sheaf may be made with poles and the maize stored inside. The sheaf is *fikonhu, luŋgelo,* or *mavoŋgwe*. It is 'the wisdom of the people' and is reserved for seed. I was unable to discover any religious or magical rites connected with it. This maize is never eaten, even in time of famine, until all the necessary sowing has been done. The sib name Σikonele is said to be derived from the word *fikonhu*.

The season of *Nyanyanyani* lasts till about the end of February, when the season of *Nyanyanyakulu* begins and lasts for two or three months. Sugar-cane (*mathimba*) is eaten, and the ground-nuts which were sown early have ripened. Mealies are plentiful. In February also begins the season of *Yamułaŋga*, the time of the flowering of lake reeds.

In March begins *Dzivamasoko*, when the grass is so rank after the rains of January and February that the paths are stopped up. Women are weeding in the fields. Maize, ground-nuts, pumpkins, and gourds are plentiful. Earth peas are sown, and some late maize planted. The edible oil (*munyatsi*) of *Trichilia emetica* is made. Runners of sweet potatoes are planted. Food is plentiful.

In April and May *Nyanyanyakulu* is still going on, and this time is also *Ŋgaŋgapambala*, because the maize stands high. *Nyagula*, the end of the *makanye* plum (*Sclerocarya caffra*) season, has come also. It is time to harvest ground-nuts (*kukela timaŋga*). The ground-nut *Arachis hypogaea* (Tʃopi *tinyumi*) harvest is a very important time for the Leŋge. It is in full swing during April and May. Σ*itsululu* plants have darker foliage than Σ*iŋgoŋgonzwane*. Young ground-nuts are known as *madoho*. Refuse of nut-shells and leaves may be used for making a black wash, by burning them and mixing the resultant soot with sand.

In April and May oil of *Trichilia emetica* is still being made, and *vuputso* beer brewed. The foods in season are pumpkins, gourds, cassava root, ground-nuts, and sweet potatoes (*mihambo*). Both the red and white varieties of the sweet potato (*Ipomaea batatas*) are much appreciated in Gazaland. The crop is good. In addition to the potato, the green leaves are cooked as spinach.

May and June begin the season of *Kukuni* (*ŋkokonye* = wildebeest). This is the hunting season, especially for the game in the Sabi district. June is also Σ*iandulele*, because the *Helichrysum* begins to flower, and the leaves of *ntʃene* (*Afzelia*) fall down. The chief cereal to be seen in the fields is sorghum (*fikombe* or *mahila*). Seeds of pumpkins and gourds are planted. The gourds are of six kinds—*Ʃikutso*, which make the drinking-water bottles; *Ʃikalavatla*, the water melon; *Maraŋga*, small gourds, generally spotted; *Makwembe*, pumpkins; *Ʃipaha*, another kind of pumpkin; *Ndzeku*, gourds with elongated necks, making water dippers or drinking cups.

Four gourd seeds are planted in one hole about a foot deep, the holes being about three yards apart. They take about a month to sprout. *Cajanus indicus*, the Congo pea, is being sown now, and again at the time of *Muganu mukulu*. People are making *sopé* (gin of cassava root). Huge bush fires are seen burning off the old grass.

July is *Nſirimelo*, when just a little digging is begun. (Cf. Junod, vol. ii, p. 309, in which *ſirimelo* is given as the name of the Pleiades, the constellation which rises at about the time when digging is resumed.) Manioc planted eighteen months ago is being cut. Pumpkin seeds sown in May are beginning to show young plants.

In August the new agricultural year begins. It is *Purupuru*, time of hot north winds. It is also *Moramora*, time of the fall of the last of the old year's leaves. It is also *Ndiyatse*, time of eagles and kites. Manioc is planted and gathered, especially the kinds known as *ſiginya* and *ſiluŋgu*. *Mbaŋgi* or red manioc is also planted this month. This is bitter and emetic and only eaten in times of famine. The women also sow ground-nuts and all kinds of gourd seeds. A few winter mealies have appeared 'to pacify the children'. Women are making their field baskets in preparation for the coming work in the fields.

In September it is *Rukuruku* or *Hukuri*. The new leaves of the trees begin to sprout. Planting and digging are continued if the soil is 'well', that is, alive, after the winter rains. Food is rather scarce, but manioc and *ŋkaka* and sweet potato greens or tops are to be had. Flowers of the cashew-nut tree (*Anacardium occidentale*) and *muhimbe* (*Garcinea Livingstonei*), and oil tree (*mafurreira = Trichilia emetica*) begin to appear. Pumpkins are beginning to grow and some maize coming up. Palm sap is collected for *vutſema* wine.

October is *Ʃigaŋwani* when the new leaves of *Sclerocarya caffra* begin to show themselves. The work of cutting down the bush (*ku-ſakatsa*) is begun, to make new plots for gardens. Both men and women will do this work. Food in season: manioc, sweet potatoes, and fish caught in the sea by casting hooks. Mussels are collected. *Ʃihaɫu* has dues paid by his subjects with baskets of mussels. Digging operations go ahead. Most of the trees are flowering. Wild fruits of *tinzole* and *tinula* (*Morus mesozygia*) are eaten. Pumpkins are in flower. Ground-

## THE AGRICULTURAL YEAR

nuts are sown, especially *ſiŋgoŋgonzwane*. *Σigema* and *rana* are prepared from dry manioc (cf. p. 33).

November is *Muganu mukulu*. There is much heat, but all the trees have not yet blossomed. It is also *Indyati*—the time of sowing maize in the little gardens. Ground-nuts of three kinds, *ſitsutsululu*, *ndzoŋgomati*, and *ſiŋgoŋgonzwane*, are sown. Many fruits are ripe. Maize,[1] sugar-cane, manioc, gourds, and beans are sown. Four kinds of beans are grown: *tinyawa*, pale red; *ſinyawane*, smaller and dark; *nyabobu*, reddish and very large; and *nyatſeŋge*, white. The rainy season has begun.

Then comes December, *Nłaŋguli*, when the *mahimbe* (fruits of *Garcinea Livingstonei*) are ripe, and the blossoms of other trees, such as *Trichilia emetica*, are beginning to change into fruit, and the first pine-apples appear. Digging, sowing, and planting go on as in November. Harvest of *Trichilia emetica* almonds begins. Food in season: maize, pine-apples, greens, gourds, manioc (*ſiginya*). Quantities of beer made from the fruits of *Garcinea Livingstonei* and *Anacardium occidentale* are drunk.

During the year those people who are supposed to be possessed by spirits will offer to the spirits beer made from *Sclerocarya caffra* in February and March; *vuputso* made from sorghum and maize in June; beer made from *Garcinea Livingstonei* and *Anacardium occidentale* in December.

As the women do almost all the field work, the supply of food depends on their labour and good seasons. Harvests are plentiful when the rainy seasons set in in good time, but times of drought are not unknown, when every resource in the way of food plants must be utilized, for, owing to the isolation of the country, it is dependent on its own supplies, and famine occasionally occurs. If I say, 'Do you eat the fruit or leaves of such and such a plant?' the answer frequently is, 'We do in times of famine.' The rainy season is eagerly looked for. Sometimes when I have been rejoicing in the refreshing coolness of a heavy shower, and have said to a woman 'Now you will be able to

[1] *A fertilizer for maize.* Old cassava root of three years or so is left to rot in the ground. The leaves are plucked, thrown down and left to rot. Bean leaves are also used in the same way. Grass is allowed to grow. This plot of ground is left for two or three years, and then it is called *ſivulo*. After this, it is dug up and mealies are planted. Manioc is planted all round as a boundary (*ndzilaŋkanbu* or *muhiŋganu*). Maize and ground-nuts are planted together, but maize exhausts the soil for itself in two years. The ground-nuts will continue to grow in the same plot for a few years running. It is easy to see when the soil is exhausted. The ground is said to be hard (*kunonoha*).

plant your mealies', she has replied: 'That is not real rain! The mealies would be withered by the heat and drought if I planted them now!' That is why only a few mealies 'to pacify the children' are planted in the winter, a time of scarcity.

In the front rank of food plants of Leŋgeland, those which are perhaps essential to the health of the natives, one must put maize, groundnuts, manioc and *ŋkaka* (*Momordica clematidea*), with pine-apples and fruits containing vitamin C. Oranges, lemons, and small limes are abundant in season. The small limes are believed to be a strengthening medicine for men. Orange (*girosana*) trees have sometimes two magic rings drawn, one in red ochre, the other in soot (*nsita*) on and around the trunk of the tree, to prevent the flowers from falling, and to ensure good fruit. Rain water filtering through orange trees is much liked as drinking water.

*Ŋkaka* is important because the leaves when cooked have tonic properties (slightly bitter) which supply a much needed element in the daily food. It takes the place of greens and also, in a way, of quinine, for the people crave *ŋkaka* when they are ill, and it is the first dish they prepare when becoming convalescent. It is in season almost all the year round.

In the second rank of food plants come pumpkins, beans, and sweet potatoes. Many wild plants such as *dedereka* (*Amaranthus paniculatus*), eaten in times of famine, could doubtless, if cultivated, become valuable.

### *A few Agricultural Rules*

You must never thresh or winnow sand. If you do you will be ill. Neither must you stamp sand unless you are smearing a hut. When you are planting sugar-cane you must not answer if any one speaks to you. If you do, you will not have sugar-cane, only common reeds.

In olden days when women were sowing seeds they must be separated from their husbands.

A good rule is: Never cease work in the fields. When you have dug, then you sow; then you weed; then you reap. When all the harvest is gathered in, then you may rest for a time. But you must do work in the fields every day, if you are well, even if it is only collecting.

# V
# MATERIAL CULTURE

## A. PREPARATION OF FOOD, MEALS, OILS, AND BEVERAGES

### Food

*Manioc*

MANIOC may be called one of the staple food plants of the Leŋge, and as the supply is fairly certain there seems to be no special magical rite connected with its growth. The whole plant is *mitsumbula* (Thoŋga) and *mipau* (Leŋge). The action of pulling up the root is *kutsavula*, separating a tuber is *kukuha*, but when the plant is quite young, and several tubers are separated because food is scarce, it is *kukuhetela*. Roots or stems drawn straight from the earth and scraped ready for immediate cooking are *ʃiginya*. Sometimes the *ʃiginya* is split lengthwise (*kupanzela*) after scraping, and the pieces spread out in the fields for a week or so. When dried they are known as *ʒigema*. The *ʒigema* are stamped in a mortar, and the result is known as *ŋkadaŋga*. This is cooked in boiling water with salt, and the thick porridge-bread which results is known as *vuswa la ʒigema*. Any dish of green vegetables or ground-nuts eaten with this *vuswa* is known as *mutʃovelo* (sauce). The *vuswa* must be eaten hot. It is very hard when cold. Indeed it has to be stirred with a very short stick when being cooked, for a wooden spoon would break. Fresh *ʃiginya* when cut into dice-like pieces, and cooked with the leaves of pumpkins or *Momordica Clematidea*, forms a very palatable dish. Manioc leaves are cooked and eaten in times of scarcity. This dish is known as *mathapa*.

To make *rana* fresh manioc, grated, is added to the pounded *ʒigema* with some salt and the mixed mass roasted in a huge potsherd over the fire. The grater (*ʃitʃindu*) is usually made from a piece of an old paraffin tin, with punched holes.

The Leŋge distinguish several varieties of manioc.

1. *Mbaŋge*. This is so named because the leaves are said to resemble hemp. It is reddish in colour, bitter, emetic, and only eaten in times of famine. *Sopé* gin is made from this kind.

2. *Ziluŋgu*. This is also reddish, and takes eighteen months to mature.

3. *Mbwatane* is whitish in colour and of quick growth. After a

year it is said *kuſuŋgwala*, to be watery. It should be planted at the time of the full moon.

4. *Matubwe* is whitish and of slow growth, and regarded as a great delicacy. Sticks of the root are cooked quickly by being placed in hot ashes.

5. *Tatane* is also whitish in colour and of slow growth, and is highly appreciated.

6. *Nyamazedzane* or *nyampaŋgadzi* is distinguished from the other kinds by the different way in which the knobs or markings (*tiłaŋga*) appear on the stem. This is a bitter variety. The bitter kinds are boiled in two waters, and the water thrown away. The natives do not seem to know of any use for the bitter water, and the amount of potential cassareep wasted during the year must be enormous. Non-bitter kinds are boiled in one lot of water, and the other vegetables added.

*Preparation of Maize*

1. The sheaths enfolding the maize cobs are stripped off. This is expressed by the Thoŋga verb *ku vandla*, Leŋge *gu vanza*.

2. The cobs (*mipumu*) are stamped in a mortar in order that the grains of maize may be separated, *ku hula mavele*, Leŋge *gu hula*.

3. The grains are winnowed to separate the husks, *ku hehera*, Leŋge *gu heheya*.

4. The separated grains are stamped in the mortar, a little water being added, *ku tłokola*, Leŋge *gu łokowa*.

5. The stamped grains are winnowed to separate the chaff (*muhuŋgu*), *ku hehera*, Leŋge *gu heheya*. The wooden mortar is in front of the winnower, and the *ſirundzo* or conical field basket is placed on the top of it to form a receptable into which the chaff may fall, the floury part remaining in the winnowing tray (*ſitelo*). With a very dexterous movement the worker winnows so that the chaff collects on the top of the tray, and is caught in the basket below, that which falls on the ground being pecked up hastily by the pigeons.

6. The stamped grains (*tindzoho*) are pounded again in another smaller mortar, *ku hupa*, Leŋge *gu hupeya*.

7. After pounding, the stamped grains are sifted or winnowed again, *ku hehera*. If the stamped grains are cooked now, without any further preparation, they are known as *tihobe*.

8. After winnowing the stamped grains are soaked in water, *ku loveka tindzoho*, Leŋge *gu loveka dzindoho*.

9. The soaked mass is taken out of the water after being steeped for some hours, *ku tsawula*, Leŋge *gu nuwa*.

10. The steeped mass is pounded again and the resultant flour (*mpupu*) is spread out to dry, *ku kanza mpupu*, Leŋge *gu kanda mpupu*.

11. The hard little bits (*tiłeŋgezi*) which remain after the steeped grains are pounded and winnowed (*ku tsetsela*) are mixed with water in a clay bowl and mashed with a small pestle, *ſimusana*, with a rotary movement, clockwise, then anti-clockwise, until the mixture assumes a creamy colour and consistency, *ku sila tindzoho*, Leŋge *gu kuruŋga dzindoho*.

12. Water is boiled in an iron gipsy pot (*mbote*) or a native cooking-pot. The mashed *tiłeŋgezi* are added to the water with large wooden spoons, and then some of the flour is stirred in. The mixture is cooked very quickly over a big fire, being stirred when necessary. It is then served out into the wooden food bowls, and patted over the top with the spoon to make it round and smooth. It is of the consistency of blancmange, and is generally eaten cold.

To cook, Thoŋga *ku seka*, Leŋge *gu bika*.
To serve in food bowls, *ku phamela*, Leŋge *gu phameya*.
Mortar, *tſuri*, Leŋge *gitudi*.
Pestle, *musi*, Leŋge *mutsi*.

*Sorghum vulgarum*, Pers.

*Ʒikombe* or *mahila* is used to make a kind of malt (*ntsumbelo*) for brewing beer, and also for making loaves of porridge-bread (*ɡivasi*). To make the bread the heads of the sorghum are spread out to dry in the sun. They are afterwards put in a winnowing tray and beaten with a stick, *kutſotſa*, in order that the grains (*manyuŋga, tindzoho*) may be the more easily separated. When separated, the grains are pounded and winnowed many times to free them from the chaff (*mikohe* = eyelashes). Some leaves of sorghum are then placed in a wooden bowl, and the pounded mass (*mpupu*) is mixed with water in the bowl with the hands. It is patted into cakes, wrapped up in the leaves, and cooked in boiling water in a pot over a big fire. The water must be boiling, or porridge instead of bread will result. The cakes must be boiled for at least an hour. When properly cooked they are taken out and put in an old torn field basket. The loaves will keep good for four days. If they become too dry they can be pounded again, and made up again into cakes.

*Ground-nuts, 'Monkey-nuts' (timaŋga) (Arachis hypogaea)*

Before digging up (*kukela* or *kutſela*) ground-nuts the women stamp on the plant (*kukanzihela*) to loosen the roots, they then pull up the plant (*kutsuvula*). With their fingers they dig up the remaining nuts which have been loosened by the pulling, *kukela*, and so a little hole or *keli* is made in the ground. When the last nut is extracted the women pluck off the nuts where they are attached to the stems (*kukatulela*). The underground stem is the *fikoho*, and care must be taken that no part remains attached to the nut. The nuts are collected in a basket and the roots and leaves left to dry in the field.

To shell nuts is *kutlora*. There is a right way and a wrong way of shelling. The right way is to press the nut between the thumb and first finger near the 'mouth', i.e. the little hook where the cotyledons will come out. It is at the opposite end, on the other side of the point of attachment of the nut to the parent plant. When the pod is thus opened the nut is not immediately extracted, but is left with the other half-opened pods in the winnowing tray. After winnowing, the pods fall on the rubbish heap while the nuts remain in the tray. Any remaining pods are picked over by hand. The nuts are then ground in the mortar. The next thing is to sift the pounded nuts so that the little lumpy pieces come to the top, *kuṭela*, and these are placed in the mortar and pounded again. This operation of stamping and sifting is repeated several times before the material is ready for use. It is then put into a basket, and kept to be added to any dish which is about to be cooked.

To take the nuts out of the bin, Thoŋga *ku nusa*, Leŋge *gu nusa*; to shell the nuts, *ku tlora*, Leŋge *gu tſotſora*.

Ground-nuts are most usually added to cooked pumpkin leaves and flowers. The leaves are cut up very finely and put in a pot with very little water and cooked. Hence there is very little waste, none of the water containing the valuable ingredients of the vegetables being thrown away, but being absorbed. Then the ground-nuts are added and a little black salt. When fresh pumpkin leaves are scarce then *mafusa* may be used.

*Mafusa* consists of the dried leaves of bean plants. These are dried in the sun for three days, being taken into the hut at night to avoid dew or rain. If the season is rainy the leaves may be dried in the smoke of the hut. *Mafusa* will last for a year if properly dried. Pumpkin flowers can also be dried. These take three days to dry properly. *Tihaka* (the unripe fruits of *Momordica clematidea*), when dried, are kept in a gourd. All of these are cooked with stamped ground-nuts. Edible fungi are also dried. They are known as *fibohwa*. The kind growing among fallen decaying leaves of *Brachystegia venosa*, called *didiŋghwe*, must be dried before being eaten, and the *ndzevendzeve*, growing on the dead wood of *Afzelia*, may be eaten either cooked fresh or after drying.

*Salt*

Salt (*munyu*) is a very precious commodity. A rough blackish kind can be bought at the Banyan stores. Field work is done willingly with salt as payment. Some of the Leŋge prepare their own salt by evaporating sea-water in pots placed over large fires, but this is a lengthy process.

## Meals

The evening meal is the chief meal and is served about 7 p.m., when that great mass of bubbling white mealie-porridge in the pots will be portioned out into the various wooden or enamelled food bowls. The food is taken in the open air in summer-time and is very appetizing. It usually consists of two main dishes, mealie-meal porridge stiff enough to be called bread or *vuswa*, and pumpkin-tops or other greens (*matsavu*) cooked with ground monkey-nuts. Or there can be alternative dishes of mashed sweet potatoes and roasted sticks of manioc. The men usually eat with cheap metal spoons, the women with their fingers or with mussel-shells. If the bowls are large, two or more persons will eat from one bowl.

The Christians say grace before a meal.

When there is a meat dish, which is not often, the distribution is as follows:

A woman named Sarah said she would hand a bowl of meat first to her younger son, Lazaro, who would hand it to his elder brother, Jacob, who in his turn would hand it to his father. The father will say, 'Jacob, you must divide the meat.' Jacob replies, 'Oh no, because I am the eldest. Let Lazaro do it.' So Lazaro divides the meat into portions, and then hands it back all ready cut up to Jacob, who gives his father some first, and afterwards his mother. Jacob and Lazaro eat together and then hand over the rest to the mother who will give it to the daughters in order of age. The men always get their portions, whether of beer or food, first. A child does not eat with its parents but with its grandparents.

With regard to game killed in hunting, the distribution is not quite the same. Suppose that Jeremiah, the father of the family mentioned above, has killed a rooiebuck, he will take a fore-leg and a hind-leg and give them to his wife, who will give them to Eva, her husband's brother's wife. Then Jeremiah will hand another fore-leg to Sarah, who will give it to her eldest daughter, Stephania. Jeremiah and Joseph (his brother) will eat together; and Jacob and Lazaro likewise. Stephania will share her food with her second sister Rebecca. Sarah gives her younger daughters Monica and Ruta a bit of the back (loins). Jacob gives Jeremiah the tongue, 'because the tongue is sacred to the father'. The mother Sarah should have a hind-leg, and the eldest daughter, Stephania, a fore-leg. If there is a daughter-in-law, especially the wife of the eldest son, she generally serves out the meat and porridge.

*Food Prohibitions among the Leŋge*

Any food prohibitions which have held good in the past are fast dying out. None of the women will take cow's milk if they can help it, especially at the time of the menses. Neither will the younger ones eat eggs. The reason they give for this is that such food will cause them to suffer very much if they have a child. It is said that the Tʃopi boys will not eat eggs for fear of failing in the initiation rites. All the Tʃopi and Leŋge are forbidden to eat crocodile's flesh, except when used in special medicines. The reason given is that the stone which the chief swallows at his accession is found in the crocodile. Some people are forbidden to eat turtle, probably because the Tʃopi chiefs consider turtles as their special property. The Ŋgoni in olden days did not eat fish, fowl, or pork. They may do so now. The Vandau of the *Va ka Simaŋgu* sib may not eat a monkey of the name of *simaŋgu*.

Some women during pregnancy will not eat *madoho*, young groundnuts. Children are not encouraged to eat honey or bananas, because the teeth of those who eat them will not be strong.

## OILS

In the life of a primitive people oil has two main uses. The first is religious, for anointing, which has a derivative secular use, the cosmetic one; the second is economic, the use of oil as food.

It is to be expected that when any natural product plays a great part in the life of the people, and is necessary to their existence, especially if the supply is precarious, that it is hedged about with rites to ensure a good and constant supply and to ward off the dangers and accidents which might threaten its diminution or loss.

*Trichilia emetica* Vahl (*ukuɫu*, pl. *mikuɫu*)

This beautiful tree flourishes in all parts of Gazaland. It attains a great size, and its abundant foliage makes a pleasant shade. It is often the sacred tree in the centre of a native kraal under which sacrifices are offered to the ancestral spirits. The tree loses most of its leaves in the winter, flowers appear between September and October, and the fruit may be gathered from December to March. The outer husk of the fruit is tri-locular, the chambers having two divisions in each of which rests a kernel covered with a thin layer of white pulp and an outer skin of a bright orange-scarlet. The thin white pulp produces a very valuable oil used in cooking, called *munyatsi*. The kernels inside are bitter and oleaginous; the oil obtained from them is non-edible and is known simply as *mafura* (oil or fat). It is this *mafura* which has religious and cosmetic uses.

Three varieties of *Trichilia emetica* are distinguished by the natives. *Ɖyatʃotʃwa*. In this variety the black 'eye' is very small. *Makanete*, in which the skin is orange-red. *Mwakanane* or *madʒavane*, in which the skin is whitish. This is said to be *Dʒa! I dʒa*, 'it is very white'. The red kind is *ya tsu*, 'it is very red'. The owner of a *mwakanane ukuɫu* is paid £5 if his tree has been cut down by some one else, who is fined for doing so. Sometimes a girl will play the *ʃigoriyu* under the tree to let people know that the oil-seeds are ripe, and that no unauthorized person must gather them.

The tree is a very valuable one to the natives, who use every part of it. From the strong roots the handles of the hoes are made. From the wood of the trunk are carved large spoons, wooden food-bowls, and the sacred goblets (*magombe*) used in offering libations to the ancestral spirits. The bark when burnt produces a clear blue flame without smoke, and its white ashes, mixed with the ashes of *Eugenia cordata* (*muɫu*), make a whitewash indistinguishable from the commercial wash. The dead branches of the tree make good firewood, and smaller branches are used as the sacred brush which is dipped into the magic mixture with which the *anyaŋga* sprinkles the huts to drive away evil spirits and sorcerers.

But the most valuable parts of the tree are the fruits, which provide both food and oils. To make a dish the fruits are gathered; those which have fallen on the ground are collected, all are put into a pot and cold water is poured on them. The water is then warmed. It must not be too hot. The inner kernels (*tihuɫu*) are taken out and put into a bowl, leaving behind the red skins and the white pulpy part, called *tsoma*.

The kernels are put on a mat outside to dry in the sun for three months. These will be used to make *mafura* oil.

The cooked leaves and unripe fruits of *Momordica clematidea* (*ŋkaka*) are boiled, drained, squeezed in the hands and put into the *tsoma*, all mixed together, and the dish is eaten hot. The mixture is called *nyaſitupwe*. Small pieces of cassava root cut up and cooked may be added to the *tsoma* instead of *ŋkaka*.

The edible oil *munyatsi* is made about March or April. Before making it a visit is paid to the *anyaŋga* of the divining bones which indicate the member of the family who is to carry through the operations. The bones may indicate a young girl, one of the daughters of the house. The others will help her, but she must light the fire (it is tabu for others to do so), and must keep it going. Sometimes the *munyatsi* oil is made all night long. If a married woman makes oil she must not have intercourse with her husband, or the oil 'will refuse to come', i.e. will not turn out satisfactorily.

When the oil is to be made the oil maker runs about to her neighbours borrowing their biggest pots if she has not enough of her own.

The dried fruits are steeped in a large pot with cold water (*kuloveka*) for a day or so. On the morning of the third day *tsoma* is prepared from the pulp and skins, strained off through a reed basket (*mbusi*), and placed in another large pot, while the residue is taken out and spread out to dry. A big fire of logs blazes away, and the pot containing the *tsoma* and water is placed on it. The mixture boils all the morning, the scum (*ŋkuve*) being skimmed off occasionally with a leaf of *Garcinia Livingstonei*. The scum is placed in a wooden bowl, and when it has melted into oil again is put back in the big pot. If the fire has been lighted at about ten in the morning, the *munyatsi* can be skimmed off with the *ndzeku* dipper or with a large wooden spoon, and poured into another pot at about 2.30 p.m. But it must be cooked again in a second pot, which is much smaller than the first, for about half an hour. It is then cooled and the next day poured into a gourd (*ŋkupa*) by means of a funnel made of a large leaf of the Tʃopi bark cloth tree. The mass remaining in the pots is then subjected to an intense heat till it becomes very thick. It is skimmed occasionally and the skim placed in a wooden bowl (*ŋgelo*). The last drop of oil having been extracted, the *tsoma* is cooled, patted into cakes (*ſibhehe*), and smoked for a couple of days, when it is ready for food. It will keep for a long time.

Everybody who makes *munyatsi* must give a present of it to the chief in a small gourd. The petty chief has to send some of it to the big chief of his district. *Munyatsi* is used for cooking. If people use it for cosmetic purposes they are supposed to get *wuhalala*, which is said to resemble leprosy.

To make *mafura* the kernels are stamped in a mortar in the third month. This stamping must be done on a hot dry day or the oil will not ooze out. The ground mass is placed in a large basket (*firundzo*). Some grass is taken from the roof of the hut, and the pestle wiped with it (*ku ɬaŋgula musi*) and the grass placed with the ground kernels, and all left for the rest of the day and the following night. In the morning the basket is turned upside down and the hard mass shaken out (*kukuɬula*). This mass is called *loŋghe*. It is set aside for a month before being cooked. It is so hard that it has to be cut in pieces with an axe. The pieces are put in a pot of boiling water early in the morning, and the oil is strained off about midday. The oil is taken off in a little gourd (*findzekwana*) and poured into a rather large gourd (*fikutso*) known as a *gutsa*, leaves of bark cloth tree being used as a funnel. The residue of the kernels after the last of the oil has been extracted makes good fuel or candles (*makandela*).

*Tragia cordifolia* Benth. (Σ*ikhumbakhumba*), is called 'medicine' of the oil tree. It is worn twisted round the wrist, and when the *tsoma* has been prepared, and is ready to be boiled to make *munyatsi*, then the little twist is taken from the wrist and put into the pot of *tsoma*. Why? Because as it makes the skin smart when worn, so its prickles will act as a charm to prevent the sorcerers (*valoyi*) from taking the oil. A tree parasite on the oil tree called *siɬafana* or *fimanyu* (*Ficus* sp.) is used in one of the most important of the birth rites, the *ŋkandlu*. The *siɬafana* is supposed to have the property of regulating the motions of the child. The *firhema*, an epiphytic orchid which is capable of killing the oil tree when it grows too profusely, is also considered to have magical value because it is stronger than the tree.

Another plant, *fiupfaupfa*, is also called *fakubohaŋkuɬu* because it binds the tree.

It is tabu to place the fruits of *Eugenia cordata* in the pot with the fruits of *Trichilia emetica*. The oil will not appear. The children sometimes put some in. When the fruits of *Trichilia emetica* are being steeped, preparatory to making *tsoma*, the pot is covered with the leaves of the tree, before it is put on the fire. This is 'medicine' to help the oil to be extracted.

The forked branch which supports the branches of the tree drooping with their oily burden, and which is made of *mbesu*, *ŋkaɫu* (*Conopharyngia* sp.), or *ſiɫaŋgwa* (*Cassine* sp.) wood, is called the *banzi* (Leŋge *bandi*). The *banzi* seems to have *mana*, for women have a tatued incision representing a *banzi* on their back or ribs.

The *ſilodo* or crook by which the branches are pulled down so that the fruits may be gathered is made of *maŋgwa* wood. The *ſilodo* also has a magical value. Some women have a tatued incision made on the forehead, which represents a *ſilodo*.

The *fuŋge* (receptacle for ground-nuts or beans) and the *ſikonhu*, (sheaf of mealies for seed), are often hung up in an *ŋkuɫu* tree.

Those who are possessed by spirits of Ɖgoni or Ndau origin begin to *lumela* (*kulumela* = to thank the spirits for first fruits) the oil tree in November, because the children will be sure to gather the fruits or play with them if the *lumela* is delayed too long. Five little bunches (*mabanza*) of young branches with fruit (*ṣiɫoŋgoleti ukuɫu*) will be gathered for preparing the *tsoma*. The *tsoma* is then mixed with cooked leaves of pumpkins, &c. (*matsavu*), and also with the *maɫuŋgu* or soot-medicine of the spirits (charred and ground leaves of *dzimaŋgoma* (*Tricalysia sonderiana*), *ſitomane*, &c.). The little medicine gourds, *tinoŋgovane*, must never be empty of this *nsita* or *maɫuŋgu*. The bowl containing the offering is placed at the *ſipandzi* of the hut. Then thanks are given to the spirits: 'Help us, give us life, we give you the new fruits'.

A wife is associated with her children in this offering. If it is the woman who is 'possessed' she will offer the sacrifice. The food in the bowl is afterwards given to the children in the kraal. If a neighbour is also possessed by a spirit and lacks the necessary medicine to perform this rite, she will beg a little from her friend. The penalty for omission of the rite is illness, because the spirits will be angry if they are not told that the first-fruits have arrived. Beer of the fruits of *Garcinia Livingstonei* is also offered as *lumela*, and *matsavu* of all the species of *Cucurbitaceae*. *Nɫaŋguli* is the usual time for *akulumela*, because the flowers and the little fruits begin to appear (November and December).

The Leŋge have some stories about the tree. There was once a woman who was cutting away the short branches of the oil tree with great energy. She made some wooden dolls, and some fibre thread, and procured some red ochre to make a head-dress for the dolls. She took them to the nearest Native Commissioner in a field basket (*ſirundzo*) and he gave her money to make the dolls dance. She brought them home again, and because she refused to give them clothes they

## MATERIAL CULTURE

went back to the tree from which they had been cut. (Told by Lydia Nyahule, wife of Lazaro Mukavele.)

During the annual harvest dances a reference is made in one of the songs to the oil tree, *Σitukutwane ſiwile ŋkułweni; ſiwile ka Matamane na Musipane*, 'The angel fell from the oil tree. It fell upon Matamane and Musipane.' Σitukutwane is a spirit which lives in the sky. If it falls down from heaven and speaks with a person that person will die.

### Castor seeds (*Ricinus communis*)

This plant grows everywhere like a weed. Oil from the seeds is prepared by the women as follows:

The beans are dried for a week, then are roasted in a potsherd (*kukatiŋga lomu ka ſireŋgele*). When they are sufficiently roasted they are ground in a *tſuri*. The crushed mass is then placed in a pot with cold water, which is brought to the boil. Then the pot is placed aside, and the oil collects on the top when the mixture is cold.

The oil (*mafura yanłampfura*) is used for mixing with red-ochre for hair dressing, and for dressing the Tſopi bark cloth in which often a baby is carried on its mother's back. It is also mixed with 'medicine' which is plastered on the fontanelle in order to 'strengthen' it.

The seeds, when the capsules burst open and scatter them, are sown almost immediately in holes in the ground in summer-time.

An oil, called *zende*, is sometimes made from ground-nuts. The nuts are pounded and the mass is put in boiling water. It boils for a short time, say about three hours, and the oil collects on the top, and when the mixture has cooled it is skimmed off and put into bottles.

### BEVERAGES

#### *Palm-wine (vutſema)*

The top part of the wild date palm (*mintſindzu*) is cut off and a slit made about six inches below the cut. A *Strychnos* shell (*sala*) is tied just below the slit. Leaves are inserted in the slit, and as the juice oozes out it runs down the leaves into the shell. This juice fermented is palm-wine.

Minala palms are tapped in the same way.

#### *Pine-apple beer (gwala la ɡiketsa)*

This is made in January and February at the height of the pine-apple season. The pine-apples are cut up and thrown into a mortar. The pieces are stamped (*kukhuvuta*), a little water being added. The remains (ʃikaphi) are taken out from time to time as more fruit is added. After two hours the liquid is dipped out with a wooden bowl and poured through a strainer. Grass is placed in a field basket, which has a hole at the conical base, resting on the top of a pot. The liquid filters (*ku tsurudeta*) through the grass and a funnel of *Ficus* leaves into the pot. If the beer is made in the afternoon it may be drunk the next day. After three days it becomes too alcoholic.

## Mahimbe beer (*gwala la mahimbe*)

This is made from *Garcinia Livingstonei*, a beautiful tree, which has somewhat the appearance of holly owing to its stiff glossy dark green leaves, and its very vivid scarlet-orange plums. It is widely spread in Gazaland. The spikes of little green flowers are heavily scented, and literally drop honey. The juice of the fruit is greenish-yellow, of a rubber-like consistency.

Those people who have ʃikwembu to propitiate, i.e. a woman who is possessed with a Ndau or Ŋgoni *ʃikwembu*, will '*lumela*' *mahimbe*. A couple of fruits will be placed in a little wooden bowl at the *ʃipandzi*. Sometimes the juice of the fruit is squeezed into a bowl of cooked pumpkin tops and soot-medicine prepared from many sacred plants. A large party is invited, men, women, and children. Everybody takes a pinch of this mixture. Even the babies get some of it, for a little is smeared on the mothers' breasts.

To prepare the beer a field basket is filled with the fruit and brought home. The fruit is squeezed with the hands into a pot, so that the skins and stones are separated from the pulp (*kuɫukuta*). These are thrown away and water is added to the juicy pulp which remains. This mixture is cooked in a pot but not boiled, the scum being taken off (*kuwuŋgula*) when it collects. This scum is filtered through a fish-basket (*mbusi*), and the liquid (*ʃindzoʃa*) added to the beer. The pot is placed aside till the next day, when the beer will be drunk. A small quantity is poured into a little gourd (*ʃikalaviso*) and offered to the spirits. If there is a child in the kraal it will drink the libation; failing a child, the woman will drink it herself, but a little residue will be left in the pot for the spirit.

## Cashew-nut beer and gin

Two kinds of fermented liquor are made from the fleshy part of the fruit of the cashew-nut, *Anacardium occidentale* (*ŋkandʒu*). The beer is called *dʒamborawu* or *mpebwe*; the gin is *sopé*.

To make the beer the ripe fallen fruit is collected, the nuts are nipped off and put aside for later use. The fleshy parts are divided into small pieces, being torn with the fingers. This mass is kept in a pot, and the juice oozes out during the night. The next day a final squeeze is given, the pulp and squeezed skins (*ʃikampfi*) are removed, and the juice is put into another pot. A fresh lot of fruit is then squeezed and set aside in another pot. On the morning of the third day the second brew is added to the first. *Dʒamborawu* is not offered to spirits. It does not keep well and is best drunk fresh.

The gin or *sopé* is made from the squeezed skins and pulp in the primitive distillery described below, in the same way as manioc gin.

*Manioc gin (gwala la mipau, sopé)*

The making of this gin is prohibited by law, but it is still carried on illicitly. There are certain magical rites connected with the process. Woody stems of the manioc are selected, and the outer sandy skin (*madziva*) is loosened by friction between the palms of the hands and taken away. The stems are then spread out on a layer of grass in the fields to dry, and covered with more grass. After a fortnight the manioc begins to rot. The upper layer of grass is then taken away and the rotting stems are dried in the sun. When quite dry (after about a month) it is thoroughly stamped in a mortar. Some large clay pots are sought for, and a trough (*tsevele*) of the bark of *Sclerocarya caffra* (*makanye*). The ground mass is put in the pots and trough; cold water is poured on, and it is left for a month or so. The mass so steeped is called *rida*. Then some huge pots standing two or three feet high are set up, and the *rida* is put into them and a big fire is lit round. The mixture is stirred constantly. The action of stirring when the stuff is thin is *kuhakasa*, but as the mixture boils and becomes quite thick it is *kuwonzela*. The stirring is done with a huge wooden spoon (*kombe*).

After being boiled, and while it is still hot, the mixture is doled out with the large spoons into the first set of pots and the trough, where it cools and remains for three days. Then *ntsumbelo* (malt) of maize is added to it, after which it ferments for another three days. It is next put into an enormous clay pot, the mouth of which is closed with a kind of lid, which is really a very large old potsherd of a *ʃeku* pot, fitting snugly. Any crack is plastered over with mud so that no air can escape. A pipe (*lambikwa*) proceeds from a hole in the side of the pot, also tightly sealed, and passes through a wooden trough or *ʃigovolo* filled with water. This trough rests on forked branches driven into the ground called *mabanzi*. A small stick (*liwatʃado*) is connected with the pipe and the other end is inserted in a bottle, which is to catch the drops of gin. Enormous fires are lighted. The steam issuing from the closed pot is condensed into drops of liquid in the cold pipe under water, these drops falling into the bottle.

The distilling process may go on for three days. Magic rites are associated with the manufacture. The owner of the kraal will pay a preliminary visit to the *anyaŋga* and his omens. The omens declare which member of the family is to be mistress of the rites, i.e. conduct the distilling. The woman has then to pay a visit to another *anyaŋga* to find out if the venture will be successful from her point of view, if she consents to act. If he replies in the affirmative she will probably ask him to tell her what 'medicines' she must use to ensure success. This information has to be paid for. She will probably also ask the *anyaŋga* himself to come and start the business. He asks the owner where the distillery is to be. Then when shown he makes a magic circle round the pots by scratching little holes in the sand (*kuyimbela*) and putting his medicines in the little holes and covering them up. The medicine may be a root of *Senecio deltoides* or the seeds of *mbuŋga* (*mapiki*) or something else which will prevent any black magic being used by sorcerers to spoil the gin. Once, when I was at Σilumbelo, I asked the reason for the huge blazing fires in the kraal, and was told that a certain family was making *sopé*, the first lot having turned out a complete failure owing to sorcerers.

The mistress of the distillery calls upon the other members of the kraal to come to help her to light the blazing fires. The distilling may go on for three days, but the responsible person never leaves her work.

Before the gin is poured from the small bottles into a large *garrafão* the *anyaŋga* tastes some in a goblet (*gombe*), sprinkles the apparatus with a few drops, and throws a few more into the fire, as an offering to the spirits. The mistress of the rites and the helpers all taste solemnly, but only just a drop. The Leŋge have a very expressive word which they use in this connexion, '*kuminyeta*', to measure drops.

*Sopé* is made all the year round, but more in the winter, June to August, because the 'beer of trees', i.e. the beer made from fruits, is lacking then. A *garrafão* of *sopé* is sold for £1.

*Beer of Sclerocarya caffra (gwala la makanye)*

This stately tree, standing in the centre of a kraal, has sometimes a white rag tied round its trunk, showing that the primitive altar (*gandzelo*) to the ancestral spirits is there.

## MATERIAL CULTURE

About the middle of October, the fresh young leaves of the tree are sprouting, and by the end of the month the flowers are out. Early in November the tree is of a vivid new green colour, but the branches are not yet all covered with foliage. In December the green plums are ripening to fall in heavy showers at the end of January and in February. To make the beer great baskets of windfalls of the fruit are picked up and make a heap (*mumbu*) outside a hut. If the fruit is nearly ripe the heap remains there for a week. Then the housewife begins to make her beer. She sits in front of a heap of plums and pierces each one with a metal arrow-head (*mpafwa*), severing the hard skins from the stones covered with pulp, which are collected in a bowl (*fihiso*).

The pulp is scraped from the stones with a little branch with two prongs like a fork (*ravi la fihimbiti*). This action is *kutluva*. The stones (*tipfula*) are spread out somewhere in the kraal to dry. The pulp is put into a trough (*tsevele*, made of *ŋkanye* bark), water is added, and it is left to ferment. After about six hours a white frothy scum (*bubhitlu*) appears on the top. Fresh pulp is added the next morning and the third morning. At noon on the third day the beer is ready. The scum is not skimmed off (*kuwoŋgula*) but only pushed aside (*kukupula*) in order to draw the beer. The beer if very fermented is called *mpalwa*; if not very fermented, *ndzova*. If in February one passes through a kraal and notices a strong fermented smell like that of decaying fruit, it will be found to proceed from a trough full of *gwala la makanye*, and a heap of rotting skins and drying plum-stones.

The stones are dried for about a year. They are cracked (*kubanza*) to obtain the kernels (*timoŋgo*) when these are needed. The kernels have a delicate flavour and form a good substitute for ground-nuts. Many people use the stones when smearing the floor of a hut to strengthen it.

The scum was formerly used as a kind of cement for mixing with sand to mud the floors, but its use has been discontinued because it was found that it caused cracks.

To make the trough a deep incision is made in the outer bark of the *ŋkanye* tree, then a stick of the oil tree (*ŋkułu*) is carved, and used as a lever to raise the bark from the tree. Cross-way rods of the *nsumbi* tree (*Brachylaena discolor*) skewer the sides of the bark together to make the trough.

People possessed with Ndau or Ŋgoni spirits offer libations of this beer about the end of January, when the plums begin to fall. The beer is mixed with a little soot-medicine which has been prepared thus:

At a seance, when the spirit is about to reveal its identity, leaves of the trees *manoŋwa* and *sasa* are spread out on a mat and cut into small pieces with a knife. These pieces are heated in a potsherd, and put aside till the early morning, when they are ground, and the powder is put in the little gourds, to be afterwards mixed with the beer at the time of *lumela*. The pot of beer will be placed at the *ſipandzi* inside the hut, with some such words as these:

> We beg of thee, spirit, to give us life!
> We cook fruits, that you may guard us well!

The libation is then usually drunk by the person who offers it, leaving a little residue for the spirit.

*Malt (ntsumbelo)*

Malt is usually made from sorghum (*mahila*). The grains are separated and put into a pot (*ndzomeya*) with a little cold water, steeped for a day and taken out (*kutsavula*). Then a little pot (*ſimbitana*) with a hole in it is searched for. The hole allows free passage for the air. The top of the pot is covered over with castor-oil plant leaves (*kuvimbela*). The grain remains four days in the pot. On the fifth day it is taken out and placed in an old winnowing tray. It has sprouted indeed (*kumila*). It remains in the winnowing tray until it is dried, about three days. It must be thoroughly dry before it can be stamped (*kukanza*). The *ntsumbelo* will last good for three weeks. After this time, if the housewife has been lazy and has not made enough *vuputso* beer to use it all up, it must be thrown away.

*Vuputso*

Every wife has to prepare *vuputso* for her husband's early morning drink. It is food and drink combined. Warm (not hot) water is poured on the sorghum (*mahila*) grains, and, a few hours afterwards, the steeped grain is pounded and sifted (*kuƚela*) many times. The flour (*mpupu*) is put into a pot (*liduwa*), cold water is added, and the mixture is stirred with a wooden spoon (*kuhakasela*). Meanwhile some water has been boiled in a *mbita* pot over a big fire, and some of this is dipped out with a gourd (*ndzeku*) and added. This is stirred and assumes a very thin porridge-like consistency. The mixture is then transferred by the dipper to two other pots (*ſibiso*) and spread out as much as possible over the sides (*kuandlatela*) to cool it (*kuhuŋgulela*, to cool by airing). The maker then washes her hands and feels if the mixture (*vuswa la vuputso*) is cool enough. Some malt (*ntsumbelo*) is pounded, and when the temperature of the mixture is right the malt is added

# MATERIAL CULTURE

(*kupatseka*) and stirred in, and the pot is covered over. The next morning the woman takes off the cover and looks. She takes the wooden spoon, washes it with cold water, and stirs the *vuputso* to find out if it is fermenting. Then she gives a little in a wooden goblet to a man or child to taste it, to see whether it is all right or not. It is tabu for her to taste it. It lasts good for two days.

### *Pepeta Beer*

Maize is steeped and taken out of the pot of water the third day (*kutsalula*). It is then spread out on the ground in the hut, covered over with leaves, with sticks to keep them in place. On the third day a fresh supply of steeped maize is added. When it begins to sprout (*kumila*) the leaves are thrown away. After a month the malt (*ntsumbelo*) will be quite dried. Then fresh maize cobs are taken and pounded (*kutłokola*) and the grains are steeped in hot water, and taken out on the fourth day. Some fresh sorghum is taken and pounded with a little warm water (*kupanzeka*), and mixed with the maize. The next morning it is pounded and sifted. The flour is put into *tipfuko* pots, cold water poured over and the whole is stirred well, and then filled up with boiling water. Malt is added the next morning. This stands for a day, and in the early morning of the next day it is boiled over great fires. After boiling for a considerable time it is put into big pots and spread out to cool (*kuandlatela*). More malt is prepared, and the process is repeated three times. It is finally strained and ready for drinking. The remains (*mapundupundu*) are eaten.

*Pepeta* or *vuputso* are the only libations offered to the ancestral spirits among the Leŋge at the present time. The other beers are offered to Ndau and Ŋgoni spirits. An extremely intoxicating drink is made from crushed sugar-cane, called *aʃitʃimelane* or *ʃwayiwayi*. This is probably of foreign origin.

## B. INDUSTRIES. DOMESTIC IMPLEMENTS. POTTERY. BASKETRY. BEADWORK

### Domestic Implements

These may be grouped together under the name of *ʂigwa*. Among the most important of these are the wooden mortar (*tʃuri*) and the pestle (*musi*).

A new mortar (*ʃigwaŋgwanana*) is not used for a year to pound anything but steeped maize (*tindzohe*) because, the wood being new and slippery, anything else would fly over the top and be lost. Therefore a woman will borrow her neighbour's mortar to stamp ground-nuts and maize off the cob, and the neighbour will help her by using the new mortar for her steeped maize. This will help to season the new mortar.

Mortars are usually carved from the trunk of a *ntſene* tree (*Afzelia*) or from the *nyatſa* tree (*Mimusops discolor*). The pestle (*musi*) is made of *nyatſa*, sometimes quite plain, but often with two distinct ridges formed of two grooves at the thicker stamping end. The *musi* is used with the wooden mortars. A shorter pestle (*ſimusana*) is used with the mashing bowl (*ſihiso*). It is tabu to sit or stand on a mortar or pestle.

## Hoes and Axes (*ɡikhomo and ɡiłoka*)

These can be bought at Indian or Portuguese stores, but most of them are made by native smiths (*vabheti va nyundu*). In olden days, before old metal could be bought, the hoe was made entirely of wood, carved in a trowel shape, and called *mpalala*, pl. *mipalala*. This was inserted in the handle (usually of *Trichilia emetica*) as the iron blade is now.

The metal-smith uses skin bellows (*misaŋgi*) made of goat or ox-skin with horns of some animal like the *mhofu* (eland). The tips of the horns are hollow and are inserted into a tuyère made of pot clay, and the bellows are worked up and down by means of handles. He has generally a native-made hammer (*nyunzu*) and a pincers-like tool (*ntlawu*). A mass of iron (*dhombo*) embedded in part of an old tree trunk serves as a forge. The smith makes arrow-heads (*mipaſwa*), hoe and axe blades, awls for basket making, copper and brass slave bangles (*masindza*), brass finger rings, and many other things, including the cylindrical brass bead described on p. 212.

The remaining *ɡigwa* to be noticed are the wooden food-bowls, the gourd water-jars and bottles, the gourds for oil, and the carved wooden goblets or drinking cups.

## Wooden Food-Bowls (*tiŋgelo*)

These are usually carved from the wood of *Trichilia emetica*, are circular in shape, sometimes oval with four little supports or legs and a handle. The oval bowls are supposed to represent a pig. The outer surface of the bowls is blackened with a hot iron, and oil is rubbed in to preserve the colour. Designs are cut by a chip-carving process, making incised triangles, which represent native modes of hair dressing, the bowl turned upside down representing a human head. The hair is arranged with little partings (the incised lines on the bowls) grouped

PLATE II

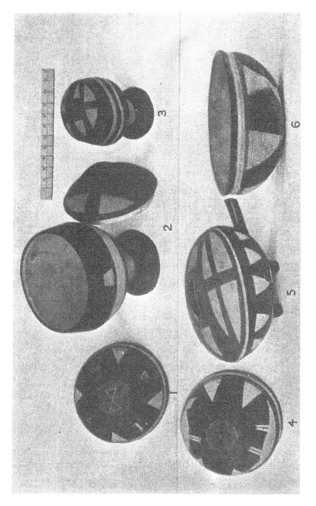

1, 4, and 6. Wooden food-bowls used as service plates.
2. Wooden food-dish with pedestal.
3. Wooden vegetable-dish with pedestal.
5. Wooden food-dish (Pig-bowl).

together in a triangular shape, constituting a *ſidokwe*. There will be one in front of each ear and two at the back of the head, and four are usually represented on a bowl. Women and children specially affect this form of hair dressing. Men and boys used it in former days, but owing to the ridicule showered upon them by the Ŋgoni invaders the practice was gradually discontinued.

At the base of the triangular *ſidokwe* is often seen a notched arrangement of blackened wood, forming a series of lozenges. These lozenges are made in the hair as well, and are called *ſipakane*. Sometimes the lozenge pattern is replaced on the bowls by a chevron pattern in black. If there are no lozenges or chevrons the hair pattern is that of either widows or uninitiated girls. The lozenge pattern indicates that the woman's husband is alive and well. The chevron pattern indicates that he is alive, but not well, perhaps a confirmed invalid, or it may indicate the recent death of the husband. If the lozenges are very small they indicate an uninitiated girl or one who is ready for marriage.

On the bowls the *ſidokwe* usually lie with the base towards the mouth or top of the bowl, while the apex aspires to reach the centre or bottom part, but never does so. On the covers the triangles either lie horizontally with bases facing one another, or with bases parallel to the edge of the cover, and apex pointing to the top.

Besides the triangles, there are also square patches (*miphama*) carved in the blackened wood, and circling bands. The *mphama* represents a shaven portion of the head made above the right ear of Leŋge and Tʃopi boys and girls. The *ndodoma* is a broad hair parting, which may encircle the head, varying according to the age of the wearer. The older women have longer and broader *mindodoma*, while those of the younger women and children are narrower and shorter. These are represented on the bowls by white bands encircling the top or middle of the bowl.

It is a well-known fact that the Tʃopi were head-hunters in olden times and thus the *mindodoma* might be regarded as a vestigial representation of a line of scalping or decapitation. This view, however, only one native, a woman, confirmed. The term *mindodoma* means generically hair partings, and is applied to the hair partings within the *ſidokwe*; a group of small *mindodoma* arranged in triangular fashion constitutes a *ſidokwe*. The incised lines on the bowls are sometimes reproductions of incisions on other parts of the body made for decoration purposes.[1]

[1] *Annals of the Transvaal Museum*, vol. xi, pt. 2, plate xix.

## Gourds and Spoons

Water dippers are made of gourds (*şindzeku*) with long necks, which are used as handles. Water and all kinds of beer are drunk from the *şindzeku*.

*Şikutso* are gourds of a different kind. They are used as water-jars or bottles, with a stopper made from a mealie cob. The surface may be decorated by singeing with a hot iron in patterns to represent triangles, the damarela lizard (*Homopholis Wahlbergi*), or they may be covered with beads. Small gourds (*şiqokwana*) used as cosmetic pots have designs of eyelashes, lizards, and objects of magical interest. The gourd is prepared in this way: the top of the neck is cut off and a knife inserted into the fleshy part to loosen it. It is then slightly heated in a fire to improve the colour (*kukaŋgulela*). The gourd is then buried in the earth for a week, after which it is taken out and scraped and the rotting inside removed. It is thoroughly washed both inside and out, the designs are made with the hot iron, and the whole surface is rubbed with oil.

If a gourd is to be used as an oil bottle (*ŋkupa*) a little outer case or frame of minala palm or *minzombe* is made for it, with a handle of the same by which it can be hung up. Beautiful wooden goblets with tripartite handles are carved from *Trichilia emetica* or from the harder *Markhamia acuminata* (*ndani*). Exquisitely carved head-rests (Thoŋga *muqamelo*, Leŋge *gikyelo*) are also made of *ndani*. Although they are of orthodox shape they show a surprising variety of design. Small wooden spoons (*şikwana*) are used for stirring food in a pot or serving it out, but not to eat with, unless it is tabu to touch the food with the finger, as for instance when a woman is in a state of ceremonial separation, when her baby has died, or during her monthly periods. She may not then use her fingers to take food from a bowl when she is eating with others but, failing a spoon, uses a mussel shell or the stiff leaf of *Garcinia Livingstonei*, though she may use her fingers if she is eating alone.

## Out-of-door Chattels. Bins and Granaries

There is a wicker bin (*fuŋge*) hung up in a tree of *Trichilia emetica* which is generally used for beans. It is made in this way. Two branches of *fisiŋgazi* (*Dathergia obovata* B. Meyer) or of *ntsave* (*Rhus incana*) are crossed and tied together. The four ends are then bent over downwards and driven into the ground, so that the point of intersection of the two branches becomes the apex of the *fuŋge*. The spaces are filled up with a sort of rough netting (*kubaŋgela*) of minala palm. The

PLATE III

NDAU WOMEN WITH POTS

receptacle is then thatched with grass, turned upside down, filled with beans, stopped up with more grass, and hung up in the tree.

The preparation of the beans for storing is as follows: On returning from the field the beans are spread out on the floor of the hut without shelling them. They will dry for a week, and then they are brought outside, and left in the dew for a night to soften the shells, so that they may not be brittle or break easily. In the early morning they are put in the *fuŋge*.

A tiny reed hut made for fowls is called a *fihalu*, and a *sakaselo* is an out-door granary resembling a small hut standing on a platform of reeds. In it are kept maize cobs, unshelled beans, or ground-nuts.

## Troughs

The *figovolo* is a large fermenting trough carved out of a solid tree-trunk, usually *Sclerocarya caffra*, and resembles a somewhat square boat. More commonly smaller troughs (*tsevele*) are made of the bark of the same tree, folded over and skewered at the ends to make them water-tight. There will be several of these of various sizes, smaller ones being used as drinking troughs for the domestic animals.

### POTTERY

Pots and potsherds play an important part in the domestic science of the Leŋge women. All the pottery is hand-made without the aid of the wheel. The potters are all women. They do not form a special class, but in a district where suitable clay is found all the women will make pots. The clay bowl (*fivumba*) of the pipes for smoking hemp (*mbaŋge*) can be made by either a man or a woman. Clay is not found everywhere so that women needing pots have to pay visits to the native potteries at Ɖguzeni, Buŋgana, Mbaŋgu, Malahisi, Mpalaneni (near Nyokweni), and the Barra district at the mouth of the Limpopo. The buyers carry back the wares on their heads, or in the hands if they have several pots to carry at a time. Payment is usually made in pieces of print (*tiŋguvo*), mealies, sorghum, and sometimes money.

I have been unable to discover any traditions or legends about the origin of pottery but there are interesting allusions to pots and their makers in folk-stories, which are mostly of Ndau origin.

At Malahisi the potters are mostly of Thoŋga and Ndau origin. All the women are potters, and the children too. The clay (*wumba*) is found abundantly in a swampy part of the lake, known as *kwava*,[1] and

[1] These words are used in all the localities mentioned.

the pots are of a rich red terra-cotta colour. The favourite designs round the neck are series of incised triangles, each pair being placed apex to apex. At Nyokweni the potters are Ndau. The clay is black. At Barra (Σilawuleni), near the mouth of the Limpopo, the potters are Thoŋga of the Va ka Mula and Va ka Σilawu sibs. The clay is black, but the pots are not very strong.

At Buŋgana the potters are mostly Khambana or Ndau. Here they make all kinds of pots, especially the open bowls (ṣihiso). The clay is of a pretty pale colour, and the bowls are noted for their strength.

The various kinds of pots in use among the Leŋge are these:

*Σihiso*, pl. *ṣihiso*, a large open bowl. This is used as a kind of mortar for mashing, the pestle being of wood used in a rotary manner while the women sit on the ground. The *ṣihiso* have a secondary use when they have a hole in them caused by the *ṣimusana* or little pestle. Three together inverted make a kind of stove, on which a pot may rest for cooking purposes, the fire being lighted in the space between. They then cease to be *ṣihiso* and are *maṣeku*.

*Liduwa* (pl. *tiduwa*), a large water or beer pot with a smaller mouth and a pronounced neck.

*Pfuku* (*tipfuku*), also used for water or beer, has less neck.

*Mbita* (*timbita*) is a pot without a neck, used for cooking, or if small for medicine. *Timbita* are also sometimes used like the *maṣeku* above, to support a cooking-pot. These pots have no necks, so that it is easier to stir the food when it is being cooked.[1]

*Σitolelo*, a small *mbita* pot used for oil and red ochre.

*Σikhambana*, a shallow food-bowl.

*Khamba*, a rather larger kind, is used as a washing-basin.

*Ndʒomeya*, a pot for drinking beer, said to 'follow' the design of a woman's hand-basket.

*Σikalaviso*, with a larger mouth also used as a goblet.

*Galaŋgu*, a large pot used in distilling gin (*sopê*). Said to be of Thoŋga origin (Inhambane).

*Σigalaŋgwana*, a diminutive of the *Galaŋgu*.

*Σikutso*, a water-pot made to represent a gourd and (in some cases) a large Portuguese wine-bottle called a *garrafão*. This *ṣikutso* is of Ndau origin. Pots resembling gourds are made with the hand, as far as the neck, then, when the hand can no longer be inserted, a stick is twisted round inside the neck.

Pottery is made by the lump method. The pot clay (*wumba*) is put

[1] The Leŋge word for *mbita* is *ngadi*, and the Tʃopi, *khadi*.

## MATERIAL CULTURE

in the shade and covered with *Ricinus* leaves to keep it moist. When needed it is first stamped in a mortar with water to make it pliable. It is then taken out of the mortar and small fragments (*tisira*) of old potsherds are ground to a coarse powder. The fresh clay and the old bits are stamped together with a little water until the substance is of the right consistency.

The dough-like mass is then taken out of the mortar and kneaded with the hands in a large wooden bowl, more water and sand being added as desired. An old potsherd is then fetched and large green *Ricinus* leaves are placed on it. The lump is put on these and patted into the shape of a jampot with the hands or a little slat of wood.

Keeping a little water by her in a bowl, and using a little triangular piece of wood as a shaper, the potter makes a hole in the middle of the clay and flattens out the sides of the hole, drawing the clay upwards very gently and adding water as required.

Sometimes the potsherd on which the clay rests is twisted round while the clay is manipulated with the wooden slat. Sometimes only the fingers are used.

When the pot is fashioned enough to please the maker she covers it over with a large inverted pot for five days or so, in order that it may not dry too quickly from exposure. Now and again she takes it out and polishes the surface with a large flat bean picked up on the sea-shore.

Very large pots are made by means of placing rings of clay one above the other to form the sides and neck.

For firing quantities of wood are collected, and the pots are placed on the wood, covered with other faggots. The fire is lighted and burns for some hours. I watched Vaŋgueya, a Ndau woman, firing her pots at Mahumaneni. She made a shallow pit in the sand, and there the pots lay like eggs in a nest, as if the earth had taken lovely shapes of delicate shades of red and yellow ochre. The wood fires burn out and the pots are flecked with grey ashes, with here and there a touch of smoke black.

Pots are sometimes coloured red with a surface layer of red ochre (*tsumane*). This is found on the roots of rotting grass in marshy ground when the water of the lake is drying up. It is mixed with reddish clay, stamped in a mortar, and patted into little cakes with the hand. The cakes are dried in the sun for about a month and then roasted in a hot fire until they are of an intense red colour.

Before the pots are used they have to be tested. When cooking-pots are tested a little thick maize porridge (*vuswa*) is put in the pot and cooked, and given to old people who are no longer able to have children. Water must not be heated in a new pot until it has been used for cooking something more solid or it would break.

To make the water-pots non-porous boiling water is poured into them. Then, after one or two journeys to the lake, in which they are filled with cold water, they become sufficiently non-porous to be used. Water-pots are never put on the fire, or they would be blackened on the outside.

Food-bowls may be put on the fire for a short time to warm up food.

Washing-bowls are supposed to be properly fired by the potter, but they must be 'strengthened' by roasting husks (*muhuŋgu*) of maize in them before they are used. If the bowl should break the maker will not give another to replace the loss.

Designs are made with a thorn or a shell. They represent the 'handwriting' of the potter, her trade-mark. The designs are round the neck and mouth, and almost always are said to represent body scarification. On some pots, about where a handle would come, there are knobs called *tiłaŋga*, keloid scars, but these are rare. The Malahisi designs of superimposed incised triangles round the neck have been mentioned above.

Potsherds (*şireŋgele*) are used in medicine. A sherd fetched from a former old home, rubbed with oil on the back and warmed a little in the fire, is pressed on a swollen limb to reduce the swelling. A potsherd from the present home will not have the same effect. Most people, when moving, leave a potsherd or two behind for this purpose. A potsherd is slightly warmed and used to allay irritation of the skin, which is gently scraped with the sherd (cf. Job ii. 8). The clay itself is believed to have remedial properties. If a child is undersized when born, a plaster of the clay is put on its chest to cool its body, so that it can breathe properly. When the women go to the lake to get the clay and carry it in a basket, they must never make their head-ring, or little crown of leaves to rest it on, of the leaves of *Momordica clematidea* or *Merremia angustifolia*. If this rule is broken the pots which are made of the clay will be broken also. Pots are not used for divination among the Leŋge. A pot may be seen on the apex of the hut roof, but the reason given is that it is protection from rain. If a woman dies, her little medicine pot and cooking-pot are sometimes placed on the grave or buried with her, but more usually these are thrown away. 'Her daughters do not wish to see their mother's own little special pots again when she is dead, to remind them of their loss.'

PLATE IV

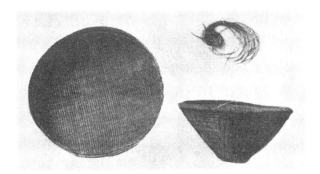

(a) PLAITED WINNOWING-TRAY : COILED FIELD-BASKET

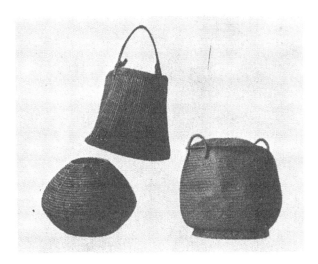

(b) FISH-BASKET (*MBUSI*) : FANCY BASKETS

## Basketry

Basketry, plaitwork, and matting are crafts in which the Leŋge excel, but, with the exception of a few special articles, the industry belongs essentially to the men. The women say that they would not like to take the men's work away from them. 'We fail to do it', say they, meaning, 'we are not clever enough'. But some of the more enterprising of the women will take the trouble to learn how to make a basket which is ordinarily made by the men.

The basket which is the most important and useful to a woman, the *firundzo*, or field-basket, the woman's constant companion in her work at home or in the fields, is made by women only. Women also occasionally make the winnowing tray, *fitelo*, the basket bin, *aŋgula*, and the fish-basket, *mbusi*, but rarely the latter.

There is no general term for baskets among the Leŋge. Each basket has its own special name, though all baskets may be grouped together with pots, bowls, and gourds and other articles of domestic use as *ɟigwa*.

### The Field-basket

To make the field-basket (*ku tlhava firundzo*, i.e. to pierce the *firundzo*) the materials are the leaf segments of a fan palm, *Hyphaene* (*filalane*), and some long stems of *Tecomaria capensis* Sprach. (*nyuŋguluti*). The tool required is the piercer (*lisuŋgunye*).

The strips of leaf are soaked in cold water which is brought to the boil and boiled for about ten minutes, and then spread out in the sun to dry for about three days. The basker-maker winds a coil of the flexible *Tecomaria* stem round her waist and she has her leaf strips in a clay pot filled with water by her side. She uses the piercer to trim off the rough edges of the strips. The base of the basket is begun with a special *firarawu* knot, the strands of which are used to coil over the foundation of *Tecomaria*, in simple oversewn coil. The basket is finished off at the mouth by double strips of the foundation, making a firm edge. It is strengthened on the outside by bands (*mabambe*) of the inner bark of *Brachystegia venosa*, which, after being dried in the sun for three days, and steeped in water for two, resembles leather. This is stitched on the outside of the basket in the form of a cross, with fibre of *Ficus* thread. These strips are rubbed with oil (*Trichilia emetica*) to make them soft, and often coloured red.

A very large *firundzo*, almost as large as an old-fashioned cottage clothes-basket, but of a conical shape, is used for beer. The beer is poured into the basket and the dregs settle and the beer is poured off into a pot.

When a woman is making a field-basket, no one must put food in it, or take it up and carry it on her head, or the maker would forget the way to finish the basket, or even forget that she has begun it. Stepping over the bark strips (*mabambe*) when in the middle of making the basket must also be avoided.

*The Hand-basket*

No account of a Leŋge woman would be complete without a description of her *ndzava* (dim. *ſindzavana*) or hand-basket, her pocket and hand-bag combined, her constant companion wherever she goes and whatever she does, which is buried with her at her death. This is her most useful possession, and much care and labour are lavished upon it, but the work is always done by the men.

The basket-maker starts at the base of the basket, with little bunches of prepared minala palm, kept moist and cool in damp sand, sprinkled with water. Each bunch of wefts is made into a knot (*ſifunzo*) and the ends are plaited in various twills up to the mouth. Here the shape decreases in decorative patterns 'to kill the way', *kufaka ſitlhava* or *kudlaya ndlela*, and finishes off in doubled-over fringes, which are cut off closely below the rim. The knots are turned inwards at the base which is stitched along firmly on the outside. A strong handle is added, being made either of a plait of minala palm segments or of the fibres of the young branches of Tʃopi bark cloth tree.

The women use the baskets for carrying a little food when they go on a visit; or to keep their snuff-box, ornaments, and head-kerchief in.

The *anyaŋga* keeps his divining bones in a little basket of this kind, with a cover which is made in the same way. The handles pass through holes in the cover which slides up and down. The covered basket is called a *ſirava*. It is often, like the *ndzava*, completely covered with skin or with beadwork. A larger kind of *ſirava*, not covered with beads, is used by men for carrying letters, meat, &c.

*The Winnowing Tray*

The winnowing tray (*ſitelo*) is also made of minala palm segments, double for the warp and split for the twining wefts. The warps are connected by a row of twining down the centre of the tray, and the twining is continued on either side, in slightly decreasing rows towards the edges, to form a circle. The tray is bound to a hoop of *Trichilia emetica* wood on the inside, and a wider strip of the same on the out-

PLATE V

(a) HAND-BASKETS

(b) STAGES IN THE MAKING OF A HAND-BASKET

side, this being pierced with a red-hot arrow head, for the stitching of minala strips.

*The Basket-bin*

The basket-bin, *aŋgula*, is occasionally made by the women. It is for storing ground-nuts or earth-peas, and it stands on a little reed platform in the hut, supported on short poles driven into the ground. These baskets may be three or four feet high, bottle-shaped or globular, and are made in coiled basketry (simple over-sewn coil) on a foundation of grass (*luɫwa* or *belele*, *Cymbopogon* sp.) or minala palm, sewn with minala palm strips, an extra thick coil finishing off the neck. The *aŋgula* is sometimes worked in a pattern named the *magwava* pattern, resembling scars of that name. If a young Tʃopi in olden days went to seek a bride and in passing through the kraal saw an *aŋgula* made in this *magwava* pattern, he would take it as a good omen that he would soon find a beautiful bride, all covered with *magwava* scars. The *aŋgula* is also the home of mischievous sprites, *gigono* of the folk-lore.

## Beadwork

Beads figure largely in Leŋge life, being valued both for decoration and for magic. Specially noteworthy are the bead ornaments worn in the initiation ceremonies, the girdle (*likalu*), the neck pendants (*gidzimaŋkolwane*), bracelets and anklets (*gibombiso*), and the bead vanity bag (*ʃindzavana*); while beads also decorate the dancing skirt (*ʃidokola*) of bark cloth. The girdle is of heavy strings of white or yellow beads, wound round and round the waist. The necklet is more elaborate and consists of two pendants of black and white beads, one falling from the neck in front and the other at the back. These beads are believed to be ancient, and they are usually covered with red ochre. The same white beads form the bracelets and anklets, being simply wound round ankles and wrists. Girdles (*madevetʃi*), covered with beads, are sometimes worn by women under their clothes. The girdle is a flat band of netted vegetable fibre, decorated with blue and black beads in geometrical designs. From the flat band depend a number of tails made of wool covered entirely with beads. At the end of each of these tails is a seed-case, hollow and filled with 'snuff', stopped with a tiny wooden stopper (*ntoŋgwane*). This girdle (of Ŋgoni origin) protected the wearer when on a journey, and was only taken off at night. These are seldom worn now, the fashion being to have simple girdles of trade wire. Mothers sometimes put a thick circular collar, resembling a rope covered with beads, round a baby's neck, to strengthen it, and to help it to keep its head up.

Bottles, gourds, and women's small hand-baskets are often covered entirely with beads. I suspect a Zulu origin for the more elaborate forms of this art. It is said that at first the Leŋge could not do this work, but the young people taken captive by the Ŋgoni, when they escaped to their homes, brought back the knowledge with them. The patterns are usually zoomorphic or phytomorphic; tracks of a turtle in the sand, tracks of a kind of marine animal (*fisaŋgaguŋwa*), or a bean leaf, for example. Triangles are common and are said to please the spirits. Large triangles are *tinzalama* or *mabamuza*, small ones are *ʒinamana*. Lozenges are *kwahu*. Large beads, especially old ones, have a magical value. *Mabuwa*, large red beads, probably medieval Venetian, are very rare, and are worn as health charms. Dark-blue ring-shaped ones are also rare and much prized. A large white bead, *kudari*, is worn to please a 'possessing' spirit. Dark-blue cylindrical beads, *mavatlwane*, are worn by old women, and were formerly used in initiation ceremonies, sewn to the bark cloth skirts. These are believed to have come from the Barberton district. Bright-blue beads are worn by witch doctors round the ankles. These were the kind formerly used for *akulobola*. *Tikota* are large dark-blue beads of Ndau origin. Black beads with white stripes are *matotoviyane*.

The same word, *kutotoviya*, is used for the magical asperging of a new hut (cf. p. 223, n. 1). Can the stripes represent the sprinkling water?

# VI
# BIRTH RITES

CHILDREN are very much desired by the Leŋge. Women who have no children are sometimes despised and put away by their husbands. A woman wishing to have a child will pay a special visit to the *anyaŋga* of the divining bones[1] (*ya titolo*), or more usually her father or mother will go on her behalf, and the *anyaŋga* will declare that a sacrifice must be offered to the spirits (*ʃikwembu*). The divining bones reveal this fact. Women who have not wished to go to a heathen *anyaŋga* have sometimes asked me if there is any *muri* (medicine, in this case, drug) which they can take for the purpose. It may be that some ancestral spirit is angry and must be appeased by an adequate sacrifice; or if the woman herself is 'possessed by' spirits of Ndau or Ŋgoni origin, they may be preventing conception, or if she is pregnant, delaying the birth, because some act of sacrifice is lacking.

If the divining bones reveal that some ancestral spirit of the woman's own line of ancestors needs propitiation, then it must be her father or father's sister, or elder brother, who will offer the sacrifice on her behalf. But if the offended ancestor is on her husband's side of the family an offering must be made by him, or his father or father's sister or some near relation.

If the woman is 'possessed' by a spirit of Ŋgoni or Ndau origin[2] (quite a common occurrence) she may herself perform the act of sacrifice. She will take a mouthful of water from a little gourd (*ʃikutswana*) and spit it out again, uttering the magic word '*Psu*'. Then she addresses the spirit (or spirits, because there may be one of Ndau and another of Ŋgoni origin) and pours the water on the ground. The water is the sacrificial offering. She entreats the spirits thus:

'*Ŋkomo! Ndauwe! Hikolaho, ŋwina, ʃikwembu, vaŋge matsuva, hi leli lihiki laminambu ndzihanyiseni, ndzinyikeni avutomi leʃaku ndziŋgahikwi himunhu, ti, ti, ti, ti, hikuva ndzitemba hiŋwina, mindzi londzovotaku.*'

'Lord! (to the Ŋgoni spirit), Lord! (to the Ndau spirit). They say you are **angry**. By this offering from the rivers, save me, give me life, that no-one may make me barren. Ti, Ti, Ti, Ti (sound expressive of **coolness**, and therefore of good health. Cold water is *mati*

[1] See p. 182.   [2] See pp. 196 ff.

*yakutitimela*). Because I trust in you, who are protecting me, Lord.'

A second visit to the *anyaŋga* is made to find out if this sacrifice has been acceptable. The bones may reveal that the offering has been pleasing to the spirits and performed in the right way. If so the *anyaŋga* tells the supplicant to go home and wait patiently and that she will see what will happen.

Sometimes the bones declare that the spirit desires a piece of print for a garment. In this case the husband of the woman will buy the print, and put it on his wife, addressing the spirit as he does so, saying: 'We thank you with this garment.' (Has the *anyaŋga* seen that the woman's garments need renewal, and is this an artful way of getting a new dress?)

Although the ancestral spirits can be instrumental in bringing about or in preventing conception of child-birth, the idea of reincarnation, if it ever existed among the Leŋge, seems to have quite died out. Neither do the Leŋge think that a woman can conceive without the aid of a man.

And here I must describe the strange concept of *Nyakwadi*.

*Nyakwadi*

Most of the Leŋge women, especially the older ones, believe in *Nyakwadi*. This is what they say:

Inside every person lives *Nyakwadi*, in the form of a snake. *Nyakwadi* lives in front (apparently just above the abdomen). If *Nyakwadi* leaves the front and goes round to the back of a person, it is a sign that both will die. Also if *Nyakwadi's* eyes look to the back instead of to the side of a person *Nyakwadi* dies and the person too.

In marriage it is the woman's *Nyakwadi* who receives the *ſidumbi* which the man gives her, and who moulds the child from the day of its conception. It is *Nyakwadi* who pushes the child out when it is ready to be born. Each child is born with its own *Nyakwadi* inside it. Sometimes the mother's *Nyakwadi* comes out of the mother with the child, licks the child all over, and returns into the mother. If perfect silence is kept by all present during the time that *Nyakwadi* is outside the mother licking the baby, a silence which must not be broken even by a sigh of pain, while the women cover their faces with their hands, then *Nyakwadi* will return into the mother and she will live. If the silence is broken, then *Nyakwadi* will not return and the mother will die. During the little time, at the moment of birth, if *Nyakwadi* comes out, then the mother is like a corpse, lifeless. She is said to be with *tsane*. If a child cuts its upper teeth first, or if its legs come first, then also the mother is said to be with *tsane*. I was unable to discover the exact meaning of *tsane*, but it evidently describes an abnormal and sometimes unconscious state.

Banyane, a woman now living at Masiyeni, has a younger sister living at Nyokweni. When this sister was about to give birth to a child, the midwives saw *Nyakwadi* coming as well. They all hurried out of the hut with fear, excepting one, a near relation. This woman said that *Nyakwadi* came partly out of the woman's body, a white snake with large black spots, and licked the child all over. The mother lay as if dead, but as soon as *Nyakwadi* returned she began to show signs of life. The other women were called back, the cord was cut and the child washed. Ḓwa Mbowa, a rather old woman, told me that if a child's skin is patchy in colouring, it is because *Nyakwadi* has been licking it. The same woman told me that *Nyakwadi* arranged the menses, and the general opinion seemed to be that *Nyakwadi* was ruler of all the vital functions. When I asked if *Nyakwadi* lived in animals the women said that they did not know, but they thought not. The young people are not usually taught about *Nyakwadi*, though they overhear their elders talking. If a person dies his *Nyakwadi* dies and is buried with him.

*Pregnancy*

A woman may tell her husband that she is expecting a child after two months of pregnancy, not before, because if she has made a mistake about the matter, the husband may accuse her of practising abortion, and beat her. She may also tell her husband's sister, who will inform her husband's mother. And of course she will tell her own mother. She will not so soon inform her husband of the expected child if it is not his, if she has been unfaithful while he has been away working in the Rand mines or elsewhere. She is afraid that he will kill her if he knows the truth.

If, during the early months of pregnancy, the woman has internal pains, the sacred medicine of unborn children (*muri wakuḻauleka watinyimba*) is used. The husband will procure dried crocodile flesh, perhaps years old, and a bundle of stems of a plant called *fisaŋga* (*Asparagus plumosus* Bkr.). Then he will make a strong thread of pineapple leaf fibre, and will thread on it five small pieces of the crocodile flesh, with pieces of the stem tied on the thread at intervals. The girdle thus made is cooked in a little pot with water until the water has boiled for some time. The woman drinks the water when it has cooled a little, but is still warm. Then the husband, kneeling back to back with his wife, stretches out his arms behind him, and ties the girdle round her loins. This rite is supposed to strengthen the unborn child, and prevent miscarriage. The name of the medicine is *ŋgweto*.

*Abortion*

Abortion is practised for one of three reasons: first, because the pains of child-birth are feared (not a very strong reason); secondly, to conceal adultery (much more usual); or, thirdly, to vent spite upon the husband if the woman is angry with him. Medicine used for abortion is known as *bhaka*. The plants used are of three species: the fresh roots of *Pupalia atropurpurea* Moq., *mbuluvati*; the roots of a bitter variety of *Momordica clematidea* Sond.; the cooked leaves and roots of *Helichrysum* sp., *firembwati wamatsuni*. The first two medicines are inserted internally. The third is eaten. To ensure sterility a decoction of the leaves of *Olax dissitiflora* Oliv., *nyamutana*, is taken internally every morning.

*Tabus and Prohibitions*[1] *during Pregnancy*

During the period of pregnancy the woman is subject to very many tabus to prevent injury to her child, and also to the crops. The prohibitions show that the people see a close connexion between nascent life in the fields and that of human beings; they realize an essential unity underlying the varied outward manifestations of life.

The mother-to-be must not work in the fields with her garment (*ŋguvo*) tied above her breast in the usual fashion. A loin-cloth only may be worn. If she disobeys this rule, the pumpkins, mealies, and ground-nuts will rot in the fields. 'Clothes will squeeze or press upon the child.' The idea seems to be that if the child is squeezed or pressed, so will the pumpkins, &c., be strangled in their growth.

The woman may not light a fire in the fields or roast mealies in the fields. If she overheats herself the mealies will die. She may kindle a fire at home, but she must not take one of the sticks in the fire to use as a kind of poker to scrape the embers of ashes together (*kuhanzakasa makala*). Should she do this the insects will eat the seeds and cut through the young shoots of the growing plants.

Before she begins to sow seeds in the fields she must take a little

[1] It is rather difficult to draw a hard and fast line between tabus, prohibitions, and avoidances. The two former are usually expressed by the verb *ṣa yila* = it is forbidden; and the last by some such expression as 'it is not done'.

earth in her right hand, and a little earth in her left hand. With the right hand she presses some earth on the right side of the abdomen and with the left hand on the left side. This rite is called *kualaha*. The omission of it will cause the seeds to die, because she has come into the fields while pregnant. If the woman is about to help a neighbour in sowing seeds the rite must be performed again. She need only perform the rite once in the season for herself, but for every new neighbour she helps it must be repeated. If she is about to climb a sacred oil tree (*Trichilia emetica*) to gather the fruits, she must first put a little earth in her loin-cloth, tie it up, and climb up with it. When once she is aloft, then she unfastens the loin-cloth, and lets the earth drop to the ground. Also, if she happens to be in the fields when the labour pains begin, she will take a little earth, tie it up in a garment, and place it on her head and go home. This is to enable her to reach home safely before the child is born.

If the woman pays a visit to her friends or relations, she must travel with her own sleeping mat. She may not use the mat of any one else, except that of a child who 'does not know anything' (i.e. is ignorant of the subject of sex and its tabus). The idea seems to be not that the woman may defile another person's mat, but that the woman herself may incur the risk of ceremonial misfortune (*khombo*) by contact with a mat which is tabu for some uses, having been used for other rites. A child's mat is not likely to have been used in this way.

As her time draws near, she has to be increasingly careful not to incur this subtle danger, this *khombo*. She must not wear other people's clothes (borrowing clothes is otherwise common), for fear that some danger lurks in them. But she may wear new clothes, and also a child's old clothes, because they have not been used ceremonially. The woman herself does not seem to be in a state of ceremonial defilement while pregnant, though she has to undergo rites of purification after she has borne a child.

She must be careful with regard to diet. She may not eat cooked pumpkin leaves, *matsavu*, in the fields. She may eat it at home, but not when it is hot, for if she does the seeds in the fields will die. If, however, she is near the time of birth she may eat it. *Ijkaka* (*Momordica clematidea* Sond.) must not be taken hot, or the foetus (*nyimba*) will kill the mealies in the fields. Some varieties of manioc or cassava are avoided at this time, not by reason of any magical ideas, but because they act as an emetic if taken too freely. They are known to have poisonous properties when rather old.

The expectant mother must not play with a monkey or the child might resemble it. Women generally are afraid of monkeys. They believe that they are degenerate human beings.

If the woman goes to the lake with her water-pot, she must not place the pot on the spot on the margin of the lake where another woman has recently placed hers. She can see the spot by the traces of occupation (*ṣikato*) in the sand. A water-pot is one of the symbols of the womb. (A woman always tries to keep this rule of the water-pot, whether pregnant or not.) If the woman transgresses this rule, she will be punished by having *filumi* (biting pains, sometimes menstrual). If any married woman is suffering from *filumi*, she must not lend her garment to any other woman, or she might suffer from *filumi* in consequence (*kuluma* = to bite).

*A Prenatal Rite*

Some of the Leŋge practise this rite. When the *nyimba* is a few months old, the expectant mother goes out into the rain with a little gourd, and fills it with water from the lake. She then goes to the huts of her relatives in turn and washes herself with the water, and sprinkles it on the seeds in the fields. The seeds will grow abundantly after this. She then takes a tiny piece of rag, torn from her garment (*ŋguvo*), and hangs it on a tree or bush. There will be one little piece of magic rag for each friend's garden. The rag will catch the rain drops, and fertilizing drops will fall from it on the field (*mabota madwana*, the drops fall). The little *ŋguvo* and rain drops running from it will 'bless the seeds in the fields'.

During the last month of pregnancy, not before, a woman will take *tsatsiso* medicine (*Senecio deltoides*, or *Tricalysia sonderiana*, or *Viscum nervosum*) every day in order to facilitate the birth. If the birth is delayed, it may be that there is something wrong in the family life. The woman herself may be in trouble or anguish, or may have committed some sin which is not known to her circle. The *anyaŋga* must be called, as she is not well enough to go to him. The divining bones may reveal some deep-seated jealousy between the mother-in-law and the daughter-in-law, or some other sin which is displeasing to the family spirits. A sacrifice must be offered to the spirits, and the mind of the patient eased by confession to the midwives. The *anyaŋga* decrees a *libiki* sacrifice. He stands outside the door of the hut. He must not enter. He brings with him the skin of a buck or other small animal disgorged by a python killed when in the very act of swallowing. This magical skin is called *piki*. The *anyaŋga* orders the midwives to procure some *makukuri* (short grass dried by being trodden underfoot in the paths). One of the women then pinches up delicately with her fingers some hot ashes from several spots in the circular hearth, *fisiku*, and places them in front of the patient. The little bit of *piki* and the *makukuri* are put on the ashes, and as they sizzle the smoke is waved to and fro before her eyes. (Fanning the smoke is called *kukuputela*. *Dzikuputela* is the secret word for wind in the women's initiation rites.) The sizzling mixture is placed in a little wooden food-bowl filled with water, and so extinguished. This is the regular *lihiki* sacrifice. The woman sips from the bowl, and spits out a little of the frothy mixture, uttering the magical syllable, '*Psu, Psu*'. The sipping of the mixture is called *kunusa aŋkuma*, 'to take ashes.' Then the woman invokes the ancestral spirit, using the usual *lihiki* invocation '*Ndzipfune, Bava* (or *Mamane*, whichever of her parents is dead) *legaku ndziŋgahikwi himuŋwani munhu; ndzipfune legaku ndziveleka ginene, tani hi legi uŋgaveleka mina, na wena*', 'Help me, Father (or mother and grandparent), that I may not be bound by any other, that I may bear well, even as thou didst bear me.' As usual the woman herself may not offer the sacrifice, unless one of her parents is dead. If it is the spirit of a grandparent which is angry, a woman of the same descent will perform it for her.

The *lihiki* sacrifice is primarily to avert sterility,[1] caused by the anger of some near ancestor at some disturbance in the family life, probably the woman's own fault, or her husband's. The woman is urged to confess her sins to the women attending her, usually her husband's mother and father's sister. They say 'the child asks the sins of the mother'. If the mother confesses everything the child will be born quickly and well. A little water mixed with medicine is sometimes sprinkled on the ground in front of the mother when childbirth is delayed. This will help her, because 'it calls to the child within'.

A very strange rite which was practised on a girl I knew, and which seems to be of common occurrence, is as follows: A woman who knows of some 'medicine' which will help children to be born in the right way (but who will not divulge the secret of the plant from which she prepares the medicine to another native woman, unless she is paid half a sovereign or its equivalent) makes a little incision in the arm of the mother-to-be some time before the confinement, and inserts the

[1] *Σihikwa*, a barren or sterile woman.

'medicine' (which resembles soot, being made from the charred and pounded leaves of the plant) into the incision (*fitlhavelo*). Then, when the child is about to be born, if there is fear that the child may come in the wrong way, this woman is summoned. She inserts her hand into the patient's body, holding the same 'medicine' in it, as that which she used for the incision, and makes a clucking noise, repeatedly, just as if she were calling fowls to be fed. I naturally asked if she were summoning the unborn child or a spirit, and my informant said 'No, she was calling to the medicine which she had previously injected into the arm, and had put more medicine on her hand to attract it' (perhaps as a kind of a magnet). This confirms my theory that the 'mana' of the 'medicines' used for injections by these natives is absorbed by, and remains with, the person who undergoes the injection.

My informant while talking to me about the midwives also said that there are women who are clever at turning a child round if it is thought that its legs are coming first, and who know how to break a ligament (*ku tsova khoto*).

Labour is often very protracted. A poor girl I know began to feel the pains on Friday and the child was not born till the following Tuesday morning. She was often in great pain owing, it was thought, to some obstruction. She was massaged by the midwives in different ways. I noticed that one of the women used her own head to massage the patient, kneading the abdomen with it. I was told that this was to cause the head of the child to appear. The husband of the woman, perhaps thinking that some delinquency of his had caused his wife to suffer, sent for our native deacon in the absence of the priest, in order to make a confession of his sins. The deacon obeyed the request, although not being a priest he could not give the absolution.

A husband during his wife's confinement must not use bad language or revile people, or commit any flagrant sin. If he does the child may fall ill, and perhaps die. If he has been in the habit of scolding his wife and the birth is delayed he will offer a sacrifice in repentance. If a turtle or some large animal has been killed by a man at the time of his wife's confinement, the part which is usually given to the chief as his due is retained by the man for his wife. He has the prior right to it instead of the chief.

### *The Birth*

The birth usually takes place at the back of the hut outside (*ama-hoseni*) in the day-time, or in the hut, if it is night. The name of the actual spot is *fisakeni*, 'in the nest'. The woman does not take any food. If she does the child 'will not appear'.

The mother is in a sitting position, leaning on a mortar or supported at the back by her husband's mother. It is tabu for the husband's mother to be in front of her daughter-in-law at this time. If the woman's own mother is present she may face her daughter and support her knees. But the usual two women in front are the woman's father's sister (her *hahane*) and the husband's sister. However much the woman is suffering she does not utter a sound unless she has some small request to make. Some one outside, perhaps some man, might hear her crying out—that would be shameful.

Sometimes the *masuŋgukati* scold her. She is 'afraid' to give birth. It is her own fault that the baby does not come.

Owing to the medicine which the mother has taken, the placenta comes away almost immediately after the baby is born. If there is undue delay one of the women will take the end of the cord which has been cut, and wind it round a stick and draw it gently. 'There are women who know how to bring away the afterbirth', my informant told me.

The umbilical cord (*likavana*) is cut with the native razor (*likari*) first by the husband's mother, and then by his sister, and then by the mother and *hahane* of the woman if they are present. An end of the cord is inserted into the child's mouth, so that the baby shall be fed with the blood, *va mugyisa ŋgati*. The object of this is to prevent the child from having convulsions or epileptic fits in later life.

If the confinement has taken place in the hut, the husband's mother will dig a deep hole, in which the *likavana* and the placenta (*kulu*) and the *vazanyana* (or *tindali*) are to be buried. But the hole is not filled up until a little rite called *kuhatamisa ndzilo* has been performed on the mother. The same grandmother of the newly born babe takes a handful of grass from the lintel (*mutendu*) of the hut, lights it at the fire, and gives it to the mother, who waves the lighted bunch in front of the child's eyes. She then waves it before the eyes of the other women present, and rubs her upper and lower eyelids with the ashes. The remains of the grass and ashes are then placed in the hole with the afterbirth, and the hole is filled up. Some people just put the remains of the grass by the wall of the hut, and it is then thrown away when the hut is smeared.

The women present will suffer from misty eyesight, their sight will become dim (*kupuma*) unless they have undergone this rite. The light of the flame is symbolical of giving light to the baby's eyes, that it may not go blind because it has seen its former 'house' and its blood.

The new-born babe is washed by the husband's mother to help the mother, and then handed to another woman to have a rag wrapped round it. The water polluted by the blood of birth is thrown away inside the hut if the birth has taken place inside. It is tabu to throw it away outside if the child has not yet been taken outside the hut.

When a woman has borne a child outside the hut (*amahosini*) she must before entering her own hut step over a pestle placed in the doorway as a barrier, and when she comes out of the hut again she must again step over it. One of the midwives has previously treated the pestle by chewing the root of *ndzau* (*Juncus* sp.) and spitting the chewed portion on it.

*Notes on Cases*

Σitazawu was one of our catechumens, and I went to visit her before her baby was born. She began to feel the pains coming on on Sunday morning. All day Monday she was suffering at intervals. She lived some miles away from our house, but I went to see her on Monday afternoon. Nothing happened on Monday, and on Tuesday morning I went to see her again. She was then sitting outside the hut at the back in an exhausted condition. A stretcher was brought from our Mission in order that we might take her back with us, to have proper attendance by our doctor. She was quite willing to be carried, but the stretcher was heavy, she herself was a very heavy woman too, and with the exception of the two women who had brought the stretcher all the others in her kraal flatly refused to help, as they believed that if a person is carried anywhere that person is sure to die. At last, with help from our Mission, the stretcher was carried with the patient lying on it through the bush for about a mile to a sandy road where our old Ford car was waiting. The road was rough and the patient nearly fainted. However, we reached the Mission at last, and the poor woman was put into one of our hospital huts. The doctor examined her and reported that he thought that matters were proceeding normally. Two women from her own kraal had come and were in attendance on her. The doctor went to see her in the evening and she seemed sleepy. Then, a little while afterwards, she died. The doctor was surprised, as she did not die in giving birth to a child, and he thought that she might have been poisoned. Then I remembered that when I had reached her kraal on the Tuesday morning, and had stayed with her for some little time waiting to find some one to carry the stretcher, she had been very sick, and had vomited green matter like crushed leaves. She had probably been given an overdose of the native medicine which is given to women to hasten the birth and to bring away the placenta at the same time. This medicine is almost invariably taken, and, as another woman told me long after the case which I have described, if too much is taken the patient will die. I, of course, tried to find out what the poor woman had been given, but they said it was the secret of the native *anyaŋga* who supplied it. I know that they take *Senecio deltoides*, but I do not know if an overdose would be poisonous.

We have a little burying-ground attached to the Mission and poor Σitazawu, being a catechumen, was buried there. The heathen women relatives asked the priest if they might cut open her body in order to take away the unborn child or children (they thought she was going to have twins), as it was their custom to do this. They think that otherwise all the family of the woman, and also of her husband, will die. The priest naturally could not allow this, as the woman was being given a Christian burial.

Curious little incidents sometimes happen at the birth of a baby. When Muneŋwasi's baby was born, it did not cry. The *masuŋgukati* said that the child's head had been squeezed, and they all clapped their hands singing *Hilava ŋwana, hilava ŋwana*, 'We want the child, we want the child'. They said that they clapped their hands in order to make the child breathe. This clapping and singing has a special name, *kugusela*, while the usual expression for clapping hands is *kutʃayela mandla*.

On April 15th, 1928, I saw the birth of the child of A., a woman, partly of Tʃopi origin, whom I liked and had known for some time. It was the second child. The amniotic membrane (*ʃisaŋga*) had been broken for some time and it was thought that the baby would soon be born. It was about three o'clock in the afternoon, and A. was at the back of the hut outside. She was resting her back on part of an old recumbent tree trunk. Her legs were drawn up and covered with an old garment thrown lightly over them. One of the *masuŋgukati* was standing behind, leaning over A.'s head and clasping her sides with a firm pressure of her thumbs on the waist. Two other women, one of whom was A.'s mother and the other the aunt of A.'s husband (he was in Johannesburg at the time), each clasped a knee, but the mother occasionally let go the knee that she held and stood astride right over A., clasping her body from beneath and massaging it with her head, in order to make the head of the child appear. The baby was slow in coming and A. lost hope and kept repeating '*Ndzifile nyamuntlha*', 'I have died to-day'. The chief midwife went to fetch some native medicine which she had brought with her in a little hand-basket. She went to the cooking-hut, took a little clay pot, and the green leaves from the basket, and prepared the medicine. I afterwards asked A.'s mother what plant she had used, but she said she did not know. 'It is known to her, the *nsuŋgukati*, she will only tell if she is paid. It is her work.'

When the *nsuŋgukati* came back with the medicine the patient had quite given up hope. She localized the pain, saying it was 'too high up and not far enough down', which remark made the other women look very anxious. A. really looked ghastly. I felt her pulse, which was very feeble, though it had been fairly steady a short time before. The chief *nsuŋgukati* then took matters into her own hands. She put the little pot to A.'s mouth and made her drink some of the medicine. She sprinkled some more on her body; she stood over her and made passes with her fingers over the stomach, and pressed it, and then poured forth a harangue which I thought unequalled for eloquence, but it was in the Tʃopi language which I do not understand so well as Leŋge. I had the impression that she was addressing the patient in kindly scorn and adjuration, and it certainly had a tonic effect, as A. began to revive and look brighter. But one of the women present, the faithful Tʃopi woman who was my constant companion, said that the speech was addressed to the ancestral spirits of the midwife, entreating them and ordering them to help her in her work, so that the medicine she was using might be efficacious. She entreated: 'You and you and you (mentioning the names of the spirits) help me, you know how well this medicine has worked in other cases, help me now, that it may not fail', and much more to the same effect.

I went to my hut for a short time. I could not have been there for more than five minutes when I heard excited cries and ejaculations from the women, and then, to my great relief, the sound of a baby's cry. I went back to find the newly born child lying in front of the mother, resting on one of her legs, while the placenta was on the ground near the child, the cord not having been yet severed. They begged me to give the patient some medicine which was in a little gourd in a hand-basket. It consisted of pulverized charred roots and leaves of plants, apparently looking like soot. As A. was eagerly looking for the medicine, and the midwife, who was massaging her 'that nothing should be left behind', said that the medicine would help to bring away anything that ought to come, I gave her a little of the powder in the palm of her hand. She hastily put it in her mouth and her tongue and lips were black with it. The grandmother (A.'s mother) fetched a native razor and one of the aunts tied the umbilical cord twice tightly with a fine thread, and then it was cut through, about two inches of it still adhering to the body of the child. The grandmother then took the end of the cord, which was covered with blood, and put it in the child's mouth. The baby moved her little tongue about the blood. Then the same process was repeated on the child's forehead and chin, and she presented a most curious sight. She had a whitish face (native babies are always lighter at birth than afterwards) surmounted by tight black curls of hair, rather more silky than in later life, and whitish hands and feet. With the dabs of blood on her face, she was a black, white, and red baby, and really looked for all the world like a miniature circus clown. This rite was the *kumugyisa ŋgati* one just described. If a child is subject to convulsions this rite will help it.

Then a very curious performance took place. One of the women took the placenta and plastered it down on the baby's head, in the shape of a cap. When I asked why this was done, I was told that the baby had passed water on the placenta, which was a sign that she would have 'big moons' later on and this act was to prevent these. I wondered if they were referring to the menses, but was told definitely that if the child has a big moon it means that it will suffer from convulsions or epileptic fits during the time when the moon is big (full moon or later).

The next rite was *kuhatamisa ndzilo*. The grandmother took some pieces of dried grass, and lighted it, and gave it to the mother, who waved the lighted grass before our eyes and her own. Why? Because we had seen the 'house' of the child (i.e. placenta), and the 'blood', and that having seen these sacred mysteries our sight would become dim unless light were given to us by the light of the brand. Two burning logs had been brought and put by the side of the baby's mother. The grandmother then washed the baby, holding it up. One of the women held a gourd of water, and poured some of it at intervals on the grandmother's hands, who used one hand as a washing glove. I fetched a piece of old white linen which I had with me, and they placed the baby, dripping wet, on the linen and gave her to me to hold. By this time the mother was able to stand up and wash herself and her loincloth with cold water. I gave her the baby and she went and sat in the cooking-hut by the fire there. The women congratulated me, because they thought that I had brought good luck. 'It is your child', said they, and they proceeded to call it 'Missa' (Miss) after me. The newly born baby seemed most intelligent. She looked as if she were quite used to this old world and the sunshine and the wind and the faces smiling at her.[1]

In less than an hour after her birth the mother was trying to suckle her, seated by the fire in the cooking-hut, quite contented and happy. After a little while, when she felt inclined for it, some thin mealie-meal porridge was given to the mother. Then the grandmother brought 'medicine' in a banana leaf and dabbed it on the child and the mother. I was told that this was to prevent the baby from being sick too much at the time of her 'big moon'. Meanwhile one of the women dug a hole at the side of the hut outside, and placed the placenta which had previously been covered with sand in the hole. She covered it with more sand but did not fill up the hole just then.

On the day of birth the cord was touched with the caustic juice of *ntuma*, the fruit of a species of *Solanum* (*S. panduraeforme*), very common in this country. On the second day the *ntuma* juice was superseded by the juice of a gourd called *fikagala*. The top of the gourd was cut off and a little of the fleshy inside scraped out and a feather dipped in the oozing juice. This evidently had a caustic effect for I was told that this would cut the rest of the cord effectually, if done twice a day on alternate days.

For the rest of the week after the birth the mother took up her abode in the cooking-hut, only coming out when necessary. She wore her old clothes, wrapping the baby in one of them, and putting it to sleep on a reed mat by the fire. A cooking-hut is not exactly a comfortable place to spend a week in, as the floor is of rough sand, not smeared, and the debris of the cooking is scattered about. But still, there is a fire there, and the woman can put her pots on the fire without even troubling to get up. All round her on the floor were pots and wooden bowls and perhaps an old tin or two. A miserable little kitten warmed itself at the fire, but if a dog came in, and attempted to steal some food, as often happened, he was soundly whacked and driven out. Fowls were frequent visitors; one broody hen was a resident, sitting on the *fibaka*, a ring made of leaves and grass, inside which were the eggs. This hut was the baby's nursery.

The child was born on Tuesday, and on Friday the remains of the

[1] The baby has since been baptized, and I am her god-mother. She will probably never know of the strange things which happened at her birth.

cord came off. Then the child's hair was all shaved off. The tight black silky curls were occasionally dabbed with water, to make the shaving easier, but the poor infant cried all the time, and no wonder, for the native razor was not very sharp, and every particle of hair was shaved off until the head was quite bald. The hairdresser was the father's father's sister. The father being absent in Johannesburg this *hahane* was ubiquitous to uphold the rights and dignities of the family in his absence.

The cut hair and the remains of the cord were 'moulded'[1] together into a little ball and buried in the ash heap. When I asked the reason for this I was told it was to prevent the child from having convulsions. On another occasion I was told that the ball is buried in the hole of a *nyantukenyane* (a small mammal that I do not know) because it will then never be seen again, the little beast takes it away. A baby of three weeks old will have a bracelet of the *nyantukenyane's* skin as a health charm. The rule is that after the mother has buried the navel cord and the hair she returns without looking behind her.

If the confinement has taken place in an ordinary hut, when the mother returns from burying the little ball she will smear her hut, the mother-in-law providing the sand and water.

The baby's hair is generally cut again during the second month after its birth, and the hair buried in the shade. If the hair is buried in a sunny place the child will get fever.

*Ceremonies on Emerging*

After the burial of the navel cord and the smearing of the hut the mother performs the little rite of *kupora ndzau anyaŋgweni*, the purification of the hut after childbirth. She takes some of the root of *ndzau (Juncus* sp.) and chews it. Then she bends down and puffs with her breath in the doorway and on the spot where she and her husband have slept. After this her husband may enter the hut for the first time, though she may not share his mat for a month after. Probably the father has wanted to see his child during its first week, and he has managed to do so, because his mother, its grandmother, has held the baby in her arms near the door of the hut and he has peeped at it. He has not been able to talk with his wife for the first week. She speaks very little and only with the women.

When that little rite is finished the wife collects the cosmetic pot (*ſitolelo*) and other utensils which she has been using during her period

[1] The verb *kuwumba* = to mould was used, the same as in pottery, pot-clay being *vumba*, and the act of moulding it *kuwumba*.

of seclusion, such as her wooden food-bowl, wooden spoons, and little water-pot or cooking-pot. She pulls a little grass from the roof of the hut and kindles a fire with it. Taking a handful of the lighted grass she waves it over the little collection of pots. This is the second rite of *kukaŋgulela*. It takes away the *khombo* of the *mułezane*, the ceremonial defilement of childbirth. Then she cooks herself a formal meal of mealie-meal porridge and when she has eaten she anoints herself and her baby all over with a second daubing of bright red ochre and oil.

The first anointing with the red ochre is done by the husband's mother, while the woman is still confined to her hut. But after she has appeared in public she does it herself twice a day, morning and evening.

*Naming*

The giving of the name, *akutsula kavito lafiłaŋgi*, is a significant rite. A child is usually given a name on its birth day, after the cord has been cut. But this is not its important name. An old Leŋge woman gave me this description:

They begin by going to the divining bones; they say: 'From whom is this child's name coming?' They try to say the name of the father. If the bones refuse, they cast them again, saying, 'We will give the name of the grandparent who is dead.' If the bones refuse, they ask the names of the other relatives. If the bones refuse all, they remain, they think, they seek the names of the grandparents of the grandparents (*yavakokwane yavakokwane*). If the bones consent, they will arrange that they call the child by that, because the owner of it died long ago. When they have returned, they take a fowl, they make a promise of that name, the fowl being a gift of surety that they give thanks for the name to the owner of it. Even if he or she is dead they stand and say 'We pray that this name may be for the welfare of the child, for the sake of you, the first owner of the name, that you will protect him all his life. Therefore this fowl is a promise to tell you that we have taken your name, we give it to this child.' The day the mother comes out of the hut they do it, because all the people will come asking 'What is its name', therefore they will tell them 'It is *nasike*'.[1]

If baby is ill the first few days after the name has been given it will be changed, but as a rule the name is not changed after illness. The fowl that has been dedicated to the ancestor whose name has been chosen is allowed to go free. If it is killed afterwards another must be choosen to take its place. If it dies in the bush without being killed it is tabu for any one who sees it to mention the fact.

[1] *Nasike* (*nakise*) is a colloquial word in great use, meaning 'What's his name' or 'such and such', used for place, time, or person. It is *nasikeni* in the locative.

## The Milombyana Medicine

On the third day after birth the *anyaŋga* of the divining bones arrives at the woman's hut. He and the father of the child arrange matters outside the hut. The *anyaŋga* procures a little calabash (*ſikutswana*) of cold water. Then he, or the father, finds a little lizard on the outside walls of the hut, and drowns it in the calabash. There it remains until it is dissolved. The mother must provide some crushed leaves of *ſimurintima* (*Cordia caffra* Sond.) which are added to the decoction in the calabash. This is then filled up with water and stoppered with a part of a mealie-cob. The child's nails are cut—the nails of its two thumbs, two little fingers, two great toes, two little toes—and the pared nails are put into the calabash with the lizard decoction. Every morning the child is given a little of this mixture, and some of it is used to wash its face. When the water is exhausted more is poured in. This medicine is supposed to prevent the child from having convulsions (*ſinyokane*). For every succeeding child a fresh lizard is added.

The rite of the broken pot,[1] into which are put pieces of the skins of all the wild beasts of the bush, so that they will not harm the child, is not unknown to the Leŋge but 'a big doctor' would have to be summoned, who would ask the equivalent of £1 in payment.

At the end of a month the mother performs the ceremony of *akuseŋgela tſisa*. She takes a lighted brand from the fire and squeezes milk from each breast on it, and then throws it at the new moon when she sees it, telling the baby 'Do not be afraid, your moon has arrived'. The baby's hair will be shaved off again after this rite.

On the second month after birth she will *halata ſiłaŋgi*, i.e. throw the child up towards the moon in her arms. She will say again '*Uŋga-tſavi, anyaŋga yawena yifikile*', 'Do not fear, your Moon has arrived'. She washes herself ceremonially and puts on new clothes. Then, and not before, she may wash her husband's food-bowl. She will also cut her hair, and her hair and her old garments will be buried in the bush for fear that the sorcerers should get hold of them and work magic with them. When her monthly periods begin again she must not handle food at the time, or wash her husband's bowl. This is a rule for all women, but it is not strictly kept.

The child's hair is cut very often. It is believed that if its hair is allowed to grow it will get thin, and also it might get parasites (*tiŋwala*).

---
[1] Junod, *loc. cit.*, p. 42.

## Miscarriage

After a miscarriage a woman remains outside the hut, near the wall, but she may go inside to sleep. She simply sits outside all day and does nothing. They give her water in a broken gourd (*fikambasi fa fikutso*) and use another gourd for her food. She must on no account use one of the wooden food-bowls. She sleeps in the hut of her husband's mother. At the end of the first week her mother-in-law cooks *ŋkaka* (*Momordica clematidea* Sond.) and while it is still warm she presses it on her breasts. This poultice is supposed to squeeze out the milk. Fresh applications are applied every day until they are no longer necessary.

If the girl has relations who can feed her her period of separation will be five weeks, but if she is destitute and obliged to prepare her own food one week will suffice. She will smear the hut on the day of miscarriage if there is time before dark, even though she feels weak. If her husband's mother is there she will do the smearing for her.

She will not be united to her husband again until she has had menses again, perhaps for two or three times. The day following the renewed union she will give a special medicine to all her relations, her husband and herself partaking of it. This is called the *uvisi* rite. Even if some of the relatives live four or five miles away she will take them some of the medicine. After this rite she may use the food-bowls again.

## Other Rites

If a baby dies the mother has to be very careful when she is expecting another child. She keeps by her a Kaffir orange (*sala*, *Strychnos* sp.) and rubs each breast with the soft pulp surrounding the pips of the fruit before she nurses the child. This will take away the *khombo* of the first child's death.

If the mother herself dies in childbirth the *masuŋgukati* will try to save the baby by giving it to another woman, a relation, to nurse. Still-born children will be rubbed and shaken for about twenty minutes (*kupfufa muhefemulo*) to awaken the breath. A clay pack of lake-mud (*ndzope*) is put on the chest and legs, and then the baby is wrapped up and put at the side of the hut. They say this is in order to keep the child 'cold'. The idea is to place the child under similar conditions and in the same position as those in which it was born.[1]

---

[1] Cf. M. Junod, *The Life of a South African Tribe*, vol. i, p. 40. The premature birth rite as described by M. Junod is not performed by the Leŋge, who prefer the clay-pack treatment.

## BIRTH RITES

If a baby dies at birth or soon after, its grandmother (father's mother), about a fortnight after the burial, will collect *maraŋga la desa*, the bulbs of *Crinum forbesianum* Herb. She pounds them with a stick and places the mass in a winnowing basket. Then a hoe (*fikhomo*), is heated in the fire and placed on the crushed bulbs. The mother of the child and all present will rub the 'medicine' over their hands and legs to purify themselves from the *khombo* of the death. When I asked why the hoe is used I was told 'Because the hoe is sacred. We work with it'. This rite permits the women to nurse other children or carry them without contaminating them.

### Twins

If a woman has twins, two Kaffir oranges (*Strychnos spinosa*) growing together on one stem are buried with the afterbirth. This acts as a charm to prevent the woman having twins in future. If the twins should die the mother must procure a special medicine, *phasa*, made of pounded charred mealie-cobs mixed with mealie-porridge bread. This mixture is put in dabs on a *fitelo* winnowing basket, and afterwards rolled up in maize leaves and put on the hanging shelf (*tsala*) where it will dry and not rot. The mother keeps some of the *phasa* medicine all her life. If she feeds other children she first gives them some of this medicine. If she herself has another child she must take a little of the *phasa*, dry it, roast it, pound it, and put a little on her breasts, so that the baby may swallow some of it. Or she may take a little in each hand and let the child bite it. In this case the mother's hands must be crossed, each hand representing one of the twins.

A child is usually given a name on its birth day (as stated above), but if there are twins the first child is named immediately after birth, and then the second child likewise. On the second day the father makes a special visit to the divining bones to find out what the real names of the children are to be.

Albinos (*ǧdʒiaha*) were killed in olden days. At the present time no one seems to mind them. There were three or four in our neighbourhood. An abnormality (*muhuku*) was formerly killed.

### Further Notes

The mother has to be careful about her diet during the first week after birth. She must not eat pine-apples, young ground-nuts, or mealies. She may eat mealies after the first week if she ties a single grain of the maize round the baby's waist to act as a charm to prevent the child from being upset because its mother has eaten mealies.

To increase the flow of milk a mother will take the stems of *neta* (?*Pentarrhinum*) and let the milky juice flow from the stems, adding it to roasted ground earth peas (*tigoŋgo*). She then eats the mixture. A species of *Euphorbia* is also used in the same way.

The baby is carried about by the mother tied on her back in a piece of bark-cloth, though nowadays she uses a piece of dark-blue print, or even a cotton bedspread used by Europeans, which also serves at times as a garment for the mother. This is provided by the father of the father of the child.

If the mother has to leave her child for a short time when she returns home it is tabu to feed it unless she first sits upon the wooden mortar (*tʃuri*). It is difficult to see the origin of this prohibition. At other times it is tabu to sit on the mortar. If you do you will invite troublesome affairs to come to you.

If a Thoŋga woman is leaving her baby for some time she will squeeze some drops of milk on its neck, to prevent its feeling thirsty. This is not unknown among Leŋge. Also a Thoŋga woman will scratch the child's forehead if it bites her. An old Leŋge woman added, 'Yes, she may scratch the child's forehead until it bleeds.'[1]

There is a minor rite, which is supposed to stop bleeding at the nose (*moŋgola*). The child is fumigated with the smoke of burnt *vondo* skin (*vondo* = nestling?). The charred remains of the skin are put into a little bit of reed, which is then closed at both ends. The child wears it until the end of the nursing period, when it is taken off and hidden in a little basket (*ʃindzavana*) because 'as it is medicine they do not like to throw it away'. It will be kept for many years until it crumbles away. If it happens to get lost the mother must inform the *anyaŋga*, who strictly enjoins her not to tell any one, for fear the child should die.

A charm is worn to prevent illness through bewitchment. When the baby is ill the mother pays a visit to the *anyaŋga* of the divining bones, and the bones say, 'You must seek a big doctor who knows how to *tsuŋgula*' (*ʃisuŋgulu* = charm, rather a strong word). He pares all the nails of the child (*ku senza tiŋwala*), he cuts the eyelashes, and also a little of the child's hair. He adds 'medicine' and puts all in a *liłaŋga* reed. The ends of the reed are closed with black wax (*muhula wa tani*) or a kind of tree gum (*pemba*) or a wax deposited on the ground by insects. The little reed is hung on the child's neck, and the charm prevents the little wearer from being bewitched. To strengthen the

[1] Cf. Junod, loc. cit., pp. 45–6.

fontanelle the baby's hair is all cut off and a sticky black plaster of honey mixed with charred leaves and roots is put on the *fipanzi* or fontanelle.

Maria Ɗwamusi's baby girl was born one day about 3.30 a.m. When I went to call about 9.30 a.m. she was sitting up, already covered with oil and red ochre. The baby had also been rubbed all over with red ochre and had had its ears pierced for ear-rings. A week and a day later the baby had a sore on the umbilicus (*ŋkava*). The mucous membrane of its lips inside was covered with black 'medicine' which had been prepared from *dzimaŋgoma* (*Tricalysia*), *nyamapfwane* (*Euphorbia*), and *kubandundu*, roasted in a potsherd, pounded and added to the small leg-bones (*minȡonȡoro*) of a dog, ground. This mixture called *nsita* was mixed with oil of *Trichilia emetica* (*tihuɫu*) and dabbed in spots on the child's arms, legs, and sides. The baby was also given a little to swallow, hence the black lips. '*Vakanzeta fiɫaŋgi vafigyisa nsita*', 'They dab the baby with *nsita* and give it some to eat.' This medicine was supposed to strengthen the child.

*Aggregation Rites*

Two special rites are performed to recognize the admission of the child into the community. The first aggregation rite, *kufuya fiɫaŋgi*, takes place on the day of birth. This is the *ŋkandlu* rite because no married person may take the baby to nurse it or to play with it until the rite has been performed. The second part of the rite takes place later on.

The *ŋkandlu* is carried out thus. The *kokwane*, the baby's father's mother, procures the leaves of *fiɫafana* or *fimanyu*, a parasitic tree, and grinds them with 'medicine' and Kaffir-corn (*mahila ya fikombe*), and the mixture is put in a winnowing basket (*fiɫelo*) and winnowed. The grandmother 'writes on the body of the baby with the medicine', i.e. draws a straight line with it upwards over the body and the head, and then round the shoulder and under the arm. If the baby is born late in the day the rite takes place early the next morning, before the mother eats her porridge. This rite is supposed to aid the family 'to take possession of the child', *ku fuya fiɫaŋgi*. It is an aggregation rite. The medicine is then thrown out of the door of the hut. It remains on the threshold, and cocks and hens must come and peck at it. The fowls 'stand for' the child. There is supposed to be some intimate and subtle connexion between the fowls and the child and its parents, because (said my informant) 'the mother is not yet washed and not able to have intercourse with her husband', but the fowls may have intercourse. If a hen arrives without a cock it must be driven away and not allowed to peck at the medicine (*kudʒokotela muri*). The old woman, after 'writing' on the child, looks out of the door to see if the fowls are approaching, a cock and a hen. The rite is repeated again the same day in the afternoon, and the 'medicine' again thrown to the fowls. The corn is added because the fowls are then eager to have it.

At the end of the week after the birth the mother will perform her ceremonial ablutions at the lake, to end the period of her seclusion. She must do this washing privately and not where there are any other women bathing or drawing water, otherwise the baby will incur *khombo*, ceremonial misfortune, and perhaps die.

The second aggregation rite, the tying of the string,[1] by which the baby is strengthened in its position as a member of the family, takes place when the child is able to crawl. Before these two rites have been performed the child is *tula*, a doll. 'Its parents do not know it', said one informant. This rite consists in the tying of a girdle round the baby's loins. The girdle must have been in intimate contact with the parents during their ceremonial union (they must have intercourse, but in such a way that the mother will not become pregnant), and must be smeared with their '*tʃaka*'. If the child's father should die before this rite is performed the mother must do it with another man.

After this rite the parents may again have intercourse, though the mother must avoid conception till the baby is weaned. If she break this law she must take medicine to cause abortion. But it may be that the father prefers to take a second wife, which he may not do until the rite just described has been performed. If he breaks this rule the child may die. If he has money he will lobola the second wife in the usual way, but if he takes another woman without *akulobola*, when he does so he gives a sign to his first wife by standing outside the closed door of her hut and rolling a blade of a rank kind of grass between the palms of his hands so that she may see. This act is called *kususa ʃihunze*. *Punzi la ʃihunze* is a blade of the grass *ʃihunze* (*Panieum maximum* Jacq.).

*Dentition*

It is tabu to call the first four teeth by the name for teeth, *matinho*. It is said that the baby '*ʃi humesa ʃilala*' or '*ʃilala ʃi suŋgula kuta*', 'the baby brings forth *ʃilala*' or 'the *ʃilala* begins to appear'. When asked

[1] This is also called *ku fuya ʃilaŋgi* by the Leŋge. The Roŋga say *ku boha puri*.

why the first teeth are known as *filala* (*sing.*), my informant replied 'because they are painful'.

When the first tooth is slow in appearing the mother will take one bean, *nyawa*, of any kind. She rubs the gums on the place where the tooth ought to appear. Then she sows the bean among the ashes on the ash-heap. When the bean begins to sprout, then the child's tooth will appear. This is also a charm to prevent the upper teeth appearing before the lower ones.

The Leŋge say 'The baby has cut a tooth' if it can eat *tihobe* (pounded maize). The first teeth of a child to fall out are hammered into the *ŋkanye* tree (*Sclerocarya caffra*) or put in the ashes.

# VII

# EARLY EDUCATION

*Suckling, Child-feeding, Weaning*

A MOTHER will try to suckle her baby very soon after birth, and if the flow of milk is delayed she gets alarmed. When baby has started sucking then she will feed it irregularly, at all hours, trying to pacify it in this way if it cries. The baby often gets more milk than it can digest and is sick in consequence. Babies are fed at the breast for quite two years, and generally much longer, the rule being that at least two years should elapse before the birth of another child. Before they are weaned babies will be given a cooked stick of cassava root or a sweet potato to suck, or a little mealie porridge. When weaned they eat almost anything. Mothers generally bring a little hand-basket to church or to class with some food for the child to keep it quiet. The shells of ground-nuts, bits of cold porridge, and other scraps are often left scattered about on the floor of the church. Children are often spoilt, and their mothers let them scream with passion as long as they like. We have often considered the advisability of having a crèche outside for the babies during the hours of service.

When weaning the child (to wean, *kulumula*) the women often rub their breasts with *sabori*, a species of *Capsicum*. The pounded leaves and scraped roots of a tree named *vuriva* are mixed with portions of a cooked fowl and given to the child to eat. This tree (*Commiphora* sp.) is supposed to cause forgetfulness. The child is often sent away for a while. If a family has adopted a child it becomes of the sib to which the family belongs, and its marriage is arranged accordingly. The marriage prohibitions are the same as for a real child of the family, with the added prohibition that it may not marry into the sib from whence it came. The adopted child is also given a medicine made from *vuriva* in order that it may forget everything about its former life.

One often sees little girls carrying about babies nearly as big as themselves. These little nursemaids are known as *ɡikhoŋgi*, those who pacify the baby. They are not necessarily relatives, but usually belong to the same sib as their charge. Their duties are to wash the baby and keep it clean, to try to keep it quiet, and to take it to its mother if it cries too much. They must tie on its little rags and look after it generally. Pieces of its mother's old garments are used as napkins, but these are not tied round the child. For sanitary purposes leaves of *Vangueria infausta* and *Waltheria indica* are used. If the baby has a cold, a very frequent occurrence, the mother or nursemaid wipes its nose with her fingers. As the child grows older it will learn to blow its nose in the proper way by pressing it between the thumb and first finger and blowing the mucus on the ground. If the babies are sore in tender parts the leaves of a plant called *kokonho* are cooked in water and the decoction is sprinkled on. This is said to be very effective. A little of the mixture is also given to the baby mixed with a little thin porridge.

*Learning to Speak and Walk*

To teach the child to sit up the mother makes a little depression in the sand and puts the baby there. Or she may take the *nsiŋgu* in which she carries the infant, twist it into folds, and place the baby in the middle. When the child can sit up it begins *kusula nyoŋga* (to polish the buttocks), i.e. to fall over on its side.

At the end of the first year the baby can probably say '*Tate*'—Father, after beginning with the syllables '*Ta, Ta, Ta.*' A little later the child will say '*Ma, Ma*', and end with saying '*Mamane*'. '*Ka, Ka*' ends in '*Kokwane*' much later. The next step is to make baby familiar with the little nurse's name. One day the infant coos. The mother says 'Oh! the baby is calling *Ruta*'. Baby was not calling *Ruta*, only cooing. The mother calls again '*Ruta! Weh*'. Baby looks again, and one day on seeing *Ruta* approaching will try to say *Ruta*. Gradually it will learn the names of other people in the kraal, but it will be about four years before it can say '*ha-ha-ne*' (*hahane* = father's sister). Although the word *mamane* is used as a form of address, and otherwise, the actual word for mother is *ŋwini* (owner).

When the child is a year old it is taught to toddle. The mother catches it by its wrists, saying, '*Dhe! dhe! dhe!*' Hence *kudheda* is to toddle. Then, when it is taught to run, the mother or nurse catches hold of the three middle fingers of each hand saying '*Tetela! tetela! tetela!*' The next month the mother sings '*Tsutsuma, tsutsuma*', and the baby runs.

A charm is used by a nursemaid who has let a baby fall, evidently to prevent future falls. The nurse presses her hand on the ground three times in succession so that it is covered with sand, and then places her sandy hand on the baby's head.

*Early Training*

When the little girl can run about by herself, she is taught to take a small basket (*ſindzavana*) and to go out *kukaya ŋkaka*, i.e. to pick the leaves of *Momordica clematidea* Sond. Then she takes a lesson in collecting firewood. She gathers little sticks and breaks small branches. She is given a strip of palm leaf: she places the little sticks in a row first, and then in a pile, and binds them with the strip of palm leaf. She ties it once, then she takes a little piece of wood (*ſisoko*) and turns it two or three times round the knot to make it firm. Then a little head-ring (*ſisimbwane*) is made of grass and put on the child's head, and the tiny bundle of faggots is lifted on. When the little daughter has seen her mother make the head-ring for two or three weeks she is at last able to do it herself.

The next thing is to teach the child to draw water. The mother and some big girls and the little girl go to the lake. The mother shows the child how to dip her gourd into the lake and fill it with water. At first the child puts it on her forehead instead of the top of her head. Her mother gently shows her how to put it right. The child puts the little gourd on her head-ring. Sometimes it falls off and breaks, and the little girl cries. When the child reaches home the first water that she has drawn is always given to her father.

The mother teaches the child that she must not mix grass and the stems and leaves of a certain plant (*Helichrysum argyrosphaerum*, *nyatſitſetſembwáne*) when she is making a head-ring. Otherwise, when she grows up and gets pot-clay from the lake for some one who is making pots, the pots will break in the process of being fired. When I asked the reason of this I was told that the plant forms an ingredient in a powerful secret medicine used by a 'big doctor' when he offers a sacrifice. When using the 'medicine' he repeats the words *Nyadimbwane* (*nyatſitſetſembwane*) *aŋgakuŋgi tsimbu ntſombeni akukali vanhu.* '*Nyadimbwane* does not coil a head-ring. At the lake people are not scarce.' Others say that a woman will have twins if she uses this plant for her head-ring. Children begin to twist the grass or leaves (*kukuŋga*) into the head-ring when they are about four years old. About the same age a little girl will be taught how to shell ground-nuts (*kutlora timaŋga*). She begins by using her fingers, but as sometimes the little fingers are not very strong she breaks the shells with her teeth. Also she cannot lift her own little wooden mortar, a small edition of the big one used by her mother, so she rolls it over (*kuwumbuluza*) until she finds the right spot for it. Then she takes her little pestle (*ſimusana*) and at her mother's command, '*kukanza*', she begins to pound. She is taught to sift the ground-nuts in her own little winnowing tray, which

PLATE VI

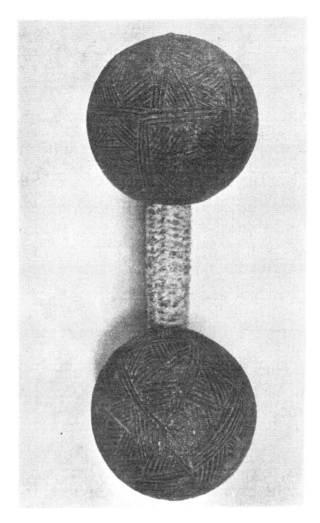

LEDGE CHILD'S DOLL
Two shells of *Strychnos spinosa* connected by a maize cob.

is also a small edition of her mother's large one. When she has sifted a little the lumpy bits (*madʒota*) remain on the top. These must be put in the mortar and stamped again and then sifted. Now her little cooking-pot must be put on the fire in the cooking-hut. At the mother's bidding to pour water (*kutſela mati*), she dips her little drinking gourd into the big water-pot. She pours a little and peeps to see if it is enough. 'Pour a little more', says the mother. She pours a little more and peeps again, '*Hiṣona*' (That is all right) says Mamane. She brings the water to the boil (*kutlaleka mati*). She picks over the *ŋkaka* leaves (*kutaula ṣilavi ṣaŋkaka*), adds them to the boiling water, and later the ground-nuts are put in and a little salt.

When the child is a little older she will accompany her mother to the fields to dig up the ground-nuts. She can help by separating the young scarcely ripe nuts (*ṣidoho*) from the big ones (*kuteŋgeleta ṣidoho*).

*Dolls*

The little girls make their own dolls.

The baby girl begins to want a child. She gathers two Kaffir-orange shells (*Strychnos spinosa*), she takes a mealie cob, and puts a *sala* shell at the top and bottom. She seeks for clothes, she wraps them round the cob. She says 'This child is my child'. She gives it a name. When she has given it a name of another person she will prepare food, she carries it, she goes with it to the owner of the name. She arrives saying 'I thank you for your name because I have used it. I have given it to my baby.' Also after that the owner of the name will bring out a gift, perhaps a fowl, perhaps five shillings. If another person catches hold of the baby she must pay perhaps a shilling. If one lacks this, she will catch a fowl because if they catch hold of the baby (doll) and have not given presents they will inflict misfortune on the child who owns it, because when she grows up and bears a child her children will not be strong.

Mothers teach very little girls the way to carry these dolls on their backs. If they fail to do it nicely the first time they will try again after a month. If a girl takes another girl's doll and breaks it they think that when the owner of the doll has a real child it will die. So the child who has broken the doll has to pay a large fine, perhaps as much as a pound or more. If a child plays with another child's doll she must pay a shilling and take great care of it.

After the child has had a doll for about three months she thinks of giving it a name. She cooks ground-nuts and puts them in a basket. She takes a little *vuputso* beer and goes to the sponsor (suggested by the child's mother, who accompanies her), carrying the beer and the doll. She says, 'I have given your name to my child, I will show you my child'. The sponsor and his wife drink the beer, but the ground-nuts must be given to an old couple who can no longer have children.

*Home Work and Discipline*

Gradually the little girl learns to lift and to carry the heavier domestic utensils (*kutlhakula ɡigwa*). She may become a nursemaid to a younger brother or sister, or to a neighbour's baby. She learns how to clear out the ashes of old fires and re-light new ones. When she is about fifteen she begins to learn how to smear the hut and to make the hearth (*ſisiku*).

When cooking or serving out food she must never scrape the spoon with which she is stirring the pot with her fingers to eat the scrapings until she has finished serving the food. If she does this when she is married and has to serve her mother-in-law with food she will be beaten. When serving food she spreads out the food (*kuandlata ɡakudla*) in the bowl, patting it to make it smooth and to cool it. She is strictly enjoined to wash the bowls before serving food in them. When giving food to men and boys she must always kneel down in front of them when offering it. If she has been taken by *akulobola* she must kneel to her father-in-law and mother-in-law. Her husband would beat her if she offers food to even a small boy without kneeling. A mother will not kneel before her small son, but before her big ones. The obeisance is *kuguqa*. It was practised of old by Shangaans and Ŋgoni.

Children will be beaten with a stick for telling lies, stealing, immorality, and fits of anger. The father generally does the beating, but the mother will do it in her husband's absence. The mothers are the chief educators in the case of girls. They always wish to see tears when scolding a child. The child will be tested in many ways, and if she cries and is 'sad at heart' (*afaniseka ambilwini*) her mother will know that 'she is able' (*aɡikota*).

The daughters of chiefs are brought up in a bad way because they are allowed to take other people's food and, if visiting, may order the host to kill a goat to provide something to eat. They will be given a mat, while other girls often have to do without.

Girls are taught to dance and sing by their mothers and grandmothers. The mothers also teach them to count and play games and make string figures. Stories are told in the dark. If they are told in the day-time the narrator will grow bald (*kurundzuruka misizi*).

The mother teaches the very little girl to tie her cloth (*ŋguvo*) round her waist, and another round her chest. It is a pretty sight to

PLATE VI

DOLL (ŊWANA)

# EARLY EDUCATION

see the air of importance with which tiny girls twist their *ŋguvo*, tucking in the folds round their little chests.

She is taught to wash her face and hands, and the use of the cosmetic pot. This is a tiny gourd, filled with oil (*mafura*) with which she rubs (*ku tota*) her head, her face, her arms and body, her feet and her back. This softens and beautifies the skin. The women generally rub themselves over with this when they return from the fields and rest at midday. The cosmetic pot (*ſitolelo*) is a very important possession.

The somewhat painful process of taking out the eyelashes (*kutsivula mikohe*) is supposed to be a beautifying one, but there is also a practical reason given, as if an eyelash gets into the eye it causes pain (*kutsunya tiło*). Red ochre mixed with fat (*tsumane*) is first rubbed on the eyelids and acts as a depilatory, and it is then easy to pull the eyelashes out.

A child of thirteen will be taught to cut the hair of a baby of three. She will learn to make partings and patterns (*kuboſa ʒidokwe ni kuboſa mindodoma*) and also shave all round the head in a straight line (*kukeŋgenza ntsenzela*). Hair-partings in olden days made patterns which were tribal marks. Mothers teach the children to pluck out superfluous hairs when they see them coming. Before going to the initiation school girls practise depilation of the whole body.

# VIII

# GAMES

THE three first are games by which the mothers teach the children to count.

1. *Ʃambala*

Counters: grains of maize, arranged in numerical order in the sand, as below. The children are told to look very carefully at the arrangement, and then to turn the head and repeat from memory the following:

| | |
|---|---|
| ● . . . | *i Nyaʃakwane* = It is Nyaʃakwane, the one. |
| ●● . . . | *Ʃotambiri* = It comes two. |
| ●● . . . | *Ʃotambiri* = It comes two. |
| ●●● . . | *Ʃotambiri ŋharu* = It comes two, three. |
| ●●● . . | *Ʃotambiri ŋharu* = It comes two, three. |
| ●●●● . . | *Ʃotambiri ŋharu mune* = It comes two, three, four. |
| ●●●● . . | *Ʃotambiri ŋharu mune* = It comes two, three, four. |
| ●●●●● . . | *Ʃotambiri ŋharu mune ntlhanu* = It comes two, three, four, five. |
| ●●●●● . . | *Ʃotambiri ŋharu mune ntlhanu* = It comes two, three, four, five. |
| ●●●●●● . | *Ʃotambiri ŋharu mune ntlhanu ni yiŋwe* = It comes two, three, four, five, six. |
| ●●●●●● . | *Ʃotambiri ŋharu mune ntlhanu ni yiŋwe* = It comes two, three, four, five, six. |
| ●●●●●●●●●● | *Ṣitahela ni masiku muni? Khume!* These will end in how many days? Ten! |
| ●●●●●●●●●● | *Ṣitahela ni masiku muni? Khume!* These will end in how many days? Ten! |

●●●●●●
●●●●●●
●●●●●
●●●●●     For the remaining lines of maize grains,
●●●●      repeat as above, for each line according
●●●●              to number.
●●●
●●●
●●
●●
● . . .  *i Nyaʃakwane.*

This form of counting is probably archaic, as it is ungrammatical at the present day. *Ʃotampiti*, a still older form of *Ʃotambiri*, is sometimes used.

2. *Nyaŋguriŋguri wa Teketa*

Two people play, perhaps the mother and child. The counters

(maize grains) are arranged as below in the sand. This we will call the 'plus pool'. A 'minus pool' will presently appear.

Plus pool (no native name was given)

```
16   17   18   19   20   21
 •    •    •    •    •    •

10   11   12   13   14   15
 •    •    •    •    •    •

 4    5    6    7    8    9
 •    •    •    •    •    •

           •    •    •
           1    2    3
```

I have numbered these grains in the order in which it is necessary to know them, in order to play the game. But it must be remembered that the child has to carry the number of each in her memory. She is allowed to look at the arrangement of the grains for a minute or so, and then she must turn her head away for the rest of the game.

*A* (the mother), touching grain No. 1. 'Who is this?'
*B* (the child). 'It is *Nyanguringuri wa Teketa*' (meaning not known).
*A*, touching grain 2. 'And who is this?'
*B*. 'It is *Ganga Khukudi wa Sigono Samilambini*.'
*A*, touching grain 3. 'And who is this?'
*B*. 'It is *Teka Mabota*.'
*A*, touching grain No. 4. 'And who is this?'
*B*. 'It is *Teka Σikona*.' (Take It-is-there.)

*A* then takes No. 4 grain and places it in the minus pool. She then returns to No. 1 grain and begins again 'Who is this?' The same answers are given by *B* as before, until *A* touches No. 4 grain which is now in the minus pool, saying 'And who is this?' *B* will then reply '*Ku hava*' (there is not one).

*A* touches No. 5 grain. 'And who is this?'
*B*. 'It is Take It-is-there' (*Teka Σikona*).

*A* then places No. 5 grain in the minus pool and starts again. *B* should remember correctly the number of grains in the minus pool, and this is where *B* sometimes makes a mistake.

To proceed with the game. If we suppose that *A* has reached the ninth round of repetition, the counting will stand thus:

*A* touches grain No. 1. 'Who is this?'
*B*. 'It is *Nyanguringuri wa Teketa*.'

*A* touches grain 2. 'Who is this?'

*B*. 'It is *Gaŋga Khukhudi wa Şigono Şamilambini*.'

*A*. 'Who is this?'

*B*. 'It is *Tata Mabota*.'

*A* touches grain 4. 'Who is this?'

*B*. '*Ku hava*' (there is not one).

*A* touches in turn grains 5, 6, 7, 8 which are now in the minus pool and gets the same answer each time, 'There is not one'. But when *A* touches grain 9, which is still in the plus pool, the answer is '*Teka Σikona*' (Take It-is-there).

In fact each grain which has been taken away and put in the minus pool is called *Ku Hava*, and each grain which is still in the plus pool is called *Teka Σikona*. This game is evidently a subtraction one. No one appears to know the meaning of the names of the first three grains. '*Şigono Şamilambini*' should mean 'elves or spooks of the rivers'.

3. *Dzinyaŋgalatani*

This game is very similar to the one just described. The first two counters have the names of *Dzinyaŋgalatani* and *Davazakayiwa* respectively. In addition to these two there are four rows of six counters each. Instead of *Teka Σikona* the player will use the expression *Tava Tebeta* for the counters in the plus pool, and will say '*Hu-Whee*' instead of '*Ku Hava*' for the counters in the minus pool. The players say they do not know the meaning of the words used. *Dzinyaŋga* is a word often used in spook-language in folk-lore.

4. *Maŋgadi or Manzadi*

This game is for dexterity in throwing and catching. Any number of children may play. They sit in a circle with a little pool scraped out of the sand in the centre. In this hole are a number of fruits of *Solanum* (*tintuma*). The girl who begins has one counter in her hand. She throws it in the air, but before catching it she must take another counter or two from the pool, and place them on the ground before she catches the first. If she is successful in doing so the counters taken from the pool are set aside and called her children. She may go on catching children till all the counters in the pool are exhausted if she is successful every time. The first time she fails to catch the descending counter she loses her turn, which is taken up by the next player. The player who has the largest number of 'children' has won the game.

As the mistress of the initiation ceremonies plays this game with the money which is given her at the rites it may have some magical force.

5. *Mutembere-lini, Hau! Hau!*

The children range themselves as for a tug-of-war. The foremost child clasps a tree-trunk with her arms, but each succeeding child catches hold of the player immediately in front of her. One girl acts as a mother. She passes up and down the line of children singing: *Mutembere-lini, hau! hau!*

All the children join in the chorus, singing *hau! hau!*

The mother sings a song to a very pretty little tune:

> Who is it?
> Knocker of knockers
> Be quiet, I will tell you,
> There is anger (or a kind of medicine) on the neck.
> *Dho! Dho! Pfumani! Dho!*
> We do not doubt the *Makariŋge*.
> They are silent—*tsi—tsi*.
> Who remains to stand?
> *Yo-weh! yo satsagambu*
> *Satsa wee. Dzo!*

She passes up and down the line as she sings, touching each child and singing a few words of the song to each, but when she reaches the word *Dzo!* then the child to whom she sings it has to get up and go away and begin a new row, bending from the waist downwards. She is soon joined by another child whose fate has been *Dzo!* and then by a third, until all the children form a horizontal line. The mother takes some sand and puts it on the back of each child, singing: 'This is your food, my child.' She then pretends to go away to work in the fields. When she has gone one of the children brushes all the sand off the backs of the others. Then the mother returns singing: 'Who has eaten my child's food?' The one who confesses is beaten and driven away, and the game is ended.

Some children at Ŋkumbeni, using the old Leŋge language, played this version of *Matembere-lini* one day as I was watching them. It was called *Balambelani*. The children sat on the ground, and the one who acted as mother beat their legs, tapping them between the knee and the ankle, singing a little rhyme for which I was unable to find a satisfactory translation, as it appears to be in an archaic form of the language. The mother taps the legs of the children one after the other, after the fashion of: 'It isn't you! it isn't you! it is you!'—because the child to whom the last word falls gets an extra hard tap, and has to go away and form a new circle. In this circle they all touch the ground with their foreheads, scraping together a little pile of sand in the centre. Mamane puts three little pats of sand on their backs, saying: 'Sand to smear Father's (hut)—sand to smear Mother's (hut)—sand to smear Aunt's (hut)—indeed!'

Then the mother goes to the fields, and they all sing: 'Mother is returning, Mother is returning!' The mother returns and begins to sing: 'Who has eaten my baby's food?' She taps one child on the shoulder, and this child points to the next, saying: 'It is not I! It is she!' When the culprit is found, she is beaten and driven away. Then they all go to a tree, the foremost clasps the tree, and the others clasp her.

*Nyapembe*

This is a toy common to both girls and boys. It is a little disk, usually made of a piece of *sala* (*Strychnos*) shell, through which are passed strings by which it is pulled, rotating rapidly. One loop of the string encircles the left thumb, and one the right finger. Sometimes a gladiolus bulb takes the place of the little disk, in which case the toy is called *ſikuluyimbwa*.

While the *nyapembe* is being twirled, some little song like the following may be sung:

> *Nyapembe! weh!*
> Resound well! little *Nyapembe!*
> Resound well! little *Nyapembe!*
> Thou shalt eat oil and honey
> Resound well! little *Nyapembe!*
> *Nyapembe! weh!*

## IX
## STRING FIGURES

THE Leŋge make various kinds of figures with a string made of a vegetable fibre known as *vuſolwa*. The fibres are extracted from the bark of the branches of the shrub of this name ( = *Grewia occidentalis* Linn.) and rolled in the usual way to form the string. The general name for string figures in Leŋge and Tſopi is *vuſolwa*, but amongst the Thoŋga they are called *vatſaka* or *tſakata*. The word *gu-tſaka* in Leŋge means to throw the dice (or bones) for divination. According to the statement of an old Leŋge woman, 'the mothers make string-pictures of everything, and teach their little daughters to make them, in order that the little girls may be wise, and may play by themselves when their mothers are in the fields'. While this is so there seems to be something more than mere play in the string figures. A native once told me that he thought they were connected with divination, and that to know too much about them was to show that you were well instructed in witchcraft. I have noticed that the majority of girls whom I ask about them are very eager to disclaim any knowledge of them, or perhaps reluctantly admit that they know one or two.

The figures here described were shown to me by Semende Ndima, a woman of about thirty years of age, whose mother is a Leŋge, and her father a Ḍwanati of Khambana. She says they have been handed down from mother to daughter for many generations.

*Tſaka*

This figure, which seems to have no name except the general name given to all string figures, is identical in every respect with the figure called 'Calabash Net' by the Yoruba of West Africa, recorded by Parkinson (*J.R.A.I.*, xxxvi, 1906, p. 132).

*Masaŋgu (mats)*

This is identical with the 'Parrot-Cage' of the Yoruba. Parkinson (*J.R.A.I.*, xxxvi, 1906, p. 131). And also with 'Ghosts' beds' of the Lower Congo. (Prof. F. Starr.) Cf. *Among the Primitive Bakongo*, by John H. Weeks (to face p. 160).

*Ɛiwonzelotana (The Reversal)*

Pass string twice round the left index finger (from radial to ulnar side) so as to form a distal and a proximal loop. Insert the right index

96  STRING FIGURES

finger into these loops from the proximal side and draw the hands apart. There will now be two loops on each index finger with the two radial strings running straight across, while the ulnar strings cross.

Twist the right index finger downwards and outwards (clockwise), making a complete circuit with the finger so that the loops are crossed in the.middle of the figure.

Pass the thumbs distal to the proximal radial index strings and take up the proximal ulnar strings from the proximal side.

Pass the thumbs distal to the distal radial index strings and take up the distal ulnar strings from the proximal side.

Pass the little fingers distal to the distal radial index strings and take up from the proximal side the proximal radial index strings.

Each little finger is now in a triangle. Pass the middle fingers from the distal side into these triangles, and by turning them up towards you, pick up on their tips the oblique strings, i.e. the distal radial index strings.

The first position of *ſiwonzelotana* is now completed and is supposed to represent the repose of a lazy girl who does not want to get up to work.

The 'reversal' is formed as follows: Turn the left hand, with its strings, down away from you over the figure and then up to the left over the figure, at the same time swinging the right hand away from you towards the left. The figure is now displayed with the wrists crossed (the left wrist nearer you) and the hands back to back. As the figure is extended, the loops slip off the thumbs, but the thumbs still remain within the figure.

The 'reversal' represents the *refusal* of the girl to get up when she is called. My informant explained that the girl would get up to take her food, but would go back to her mat if called upon to do some work.

### *Timbila.*[1]  *Xylophone or 'Tſopi Piano'*

First movement of 'The Reversal'.

Pass the left thumb distal to the proximal radial index string and take up the two ulnar index strings from the proximal side.

Pass the right thumb distal to the proximal radial index string and take up the proximal ulnar index string from the proximal side. Pass the right thumb distal to the distal radial index string and take up the distal ulnar index string from the proximal side.

[1] The *Timbila* or TSopi pianos are quasi-sacred instruments. The TSopi used to think that if a person breathed into one of the sounding-boxes, that person would die.

# STRING FIGURES

Pass the little fingers distal to the distal radial index strings and take up the proximal radial index string from the proximal side.

Pass the middle fingers from the distal side into the triangles in which each little finger is enclosed, and lift up the oblique strings, i.e. the distal radial index strings.

Release thumbs and take up with the mouth the loose string passing between the thumbs on the radial side, and extend the figure downwards.

The string held in the mouth represents the handle of the xylophone by which it is carried.

## *Titolo* (*Divining Bones*) (*Tsopi*)

Hold part of the string between the thumbs and index fingers, the hands being about six inches apart; make a small loop by bringing the

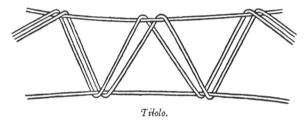

*Titolo.*

right hand towards you and to the left. Hold the loop between the thumbs and index fingers so that both loops hang down, and pass both index fingers towards you through the loops. Draw the hands apart and turn the index fingers up. There should now be two loops on each index, with the two radial strings running straight across, while the ulnar strings cross.

Pass the thumbs between the two radial strings, i.e. distal to the proximal string and proximal to the distal string; take up the proximal ulnar index strings and return.

Pass the thumbs distal to the distal radial index strings and take up the distal ulnar index strings.

Pass the little fingers distal to the distal radial index string and take up from the proximal side with the backs of the fingers the proximal radial index string and return.

Each little finger is now in a triangle. Pass the middle fingers from the distal side into these triangles, and by turning them up towards you, pick up on their tips the slanting string, i.e. the distal radial index string.

Release the thumbs and extend the figure by throwing the hands in a downward direction, palms facing one another and fingers fully extended pointing downwards, in imitation of the action of a witch-doctor throwing bones for divination.

*Note.* This figure differs from the Little Fishes (*Tup*) from Murray Island (*Expedition to Torres Straits*, vol. iv, p. 326) only in being extended on the middle instead of the index fingers.

*Mukumbe (A Boat resembling a Trough)*

This figure is made in the same way as *Timbila* except that the figure is extended by using the thumbs instead of the middle fingers to

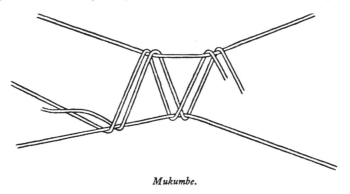

*Mukumbe.*

take up the oblique strings of the little finger triangles, the original thumb loops having been previously slipped off gently.

*Σisaka ſa nyamoŋgonzwane (Nest of a certain bird)*

Opening A.

Release little fingers. Pass the thumbs distal to the radial index strings and pick up the ulnar index string from the proximal side.

Pass the little fingers distal to the radial index strings and pick up the proximal ulnar thumb strings from the proximal side.

Release the thumbs. Pass the thumbs distal to the index loops and take up the radial little finger strings from the proximal side.

Do Opening A with the palmar strings.

Keep the figure in a vertical position, and the string to the distal end of the index fingers.

The nest is in the centre of the figure. The *nyamoŋgonzwane* is a small reddish bird much sought after by *tinyaŋga,* who make medicine from the nest.

*Mukeli wa tiko (A Boundary Trench between two Countries—figure of Thoŋga origin)*

Opening A.

Transfer the little finger loops to the ring fingers, index loops to the middle fingers, and thumb loops to index fingers.

Lift the loops off the middle fingers and tie them loosely together in the middle of the figure.

Pass the thumbs proximal to all the strings and take up the ulnar ring finger strings.

Pass the thumbs distal to the radial index string and take up the ulnar index string from the proximal side.

Pass the little fingers distal to the radial index string and take up the proximal ulnar thumb strings from the proximal side.

Pass the thumbs distal to the index loops and take up the radial little finger strings from the proximal side.

Take up with the thumbs the radial index strings close to the index fingers.

Navaho thumbs.

Untie the two loops tied in the middle of the figure, taking care not to disarrange the figure.

There is a triangle near the base of each thumb. Into these triangles insert the index fingers from the distal side, release the little fingers and extend the figure by straightening the index fingers away from you.

This figure represents a boundary trench made in time of war, or as a line of demarkation between lands of neighbouring chiefs. Finished figure same as Cunnington's 'Pit, or Large Hole' from Ujiji.[1]

*Antana waŋgwenya (Crocodile's Back)*

Opening A.

Transfer the little finger loops to the ring fingers, index loops to the middle fingers, and thumb loops to the index fingers.

Pass the thumbs proximal to all the strings and take up the ulnar ring finger string. Release ring fingers.

Pass the thumbs distal to the index loops and into the middle finger loops from the distal side. Pick up the ulnar middle finger strings from the proximal side and return.

Pass the little fingers distal to the index loops and pick up the proximal ulnar thumb strings from the proximal side.

[1] *J.R.A.I.* xxxvi, 1906, p. 128.

Slip off the loops on the thumbs and extend the figure. The loops are now on the index, middle, and little fingers of each hand.

Pass the thumbs distal to the index and middle finger loops and pick up the radial little finger strings from the proximal side. Take up also with the thumbs from the proximal side the radial index string (as near as possible to the base of the finger). Navaho thumbs.

There is now a triangle at the base of each thumb. Take the side of the triangle nearest the middle finger of each hand (i.e. the string running on the top of the figure) and raise it gently with the middle fingers.

Release little fingers and extend.

*Phasi (A Flash of Lightning)*

Opening A.

Release thumbs. Pass the thumbs distal to the index loops and radial little finger strings and take up from the proximal side the ulnar little finger strings. Release little fingers.

Pass the thumbs distal to the radial index strings and take up the ulnar index strings.

Pass the little fingers distal to the radial index string and take up the proximal ulnar thumb strings. Release thumbs.

Pass the thumbs distal to the index strings and take up the radial little finger strings.

Take up with the thumbs the radial index strings close to the index fingers. Navaho thumbs.

Insert the middle fingers from the distal side into the triangles at the base of the thumbs and extend by turning the hands palms forwards and carefully releasing the little fingers.

*Tsuri (The Mortar)*

Pass the double string under the ankle and hold one end in each hand.

Pass the right-hand loop through the left-hand loop and draw tight. Release the strings so that one loop hangs on either side of the leg. The four strings on the leg should be parallel.

Wind the first string twice round the second string, and the third string twice round the fourth string (counting from the knee downwards) and draw up the first and third loops to their full extent.

This figure represents the wooden mortar in which mealies, &c., are pounded.

## Sikhomo (The Hoe)

Wind the string once round the toe so as to form a loop in front, and place the other end of the string on the right hand in Position I.

With the right index finger pick up the string on the front of the toe from the proximal side, and return.

Pass the left index finger through the right thumb loop and draw out the radial index string. Release the thumb.

Similarly draw the ulnar right index string through the little-finger loop, release right index and little fingers, and take hold of this loop with the right hand.

Draw the hands apart so that the string lies in a straight line between them, representing the broad base of the hoe, while the two loops meet in the centre.

## Dlambu (The Sun)

Wind the string three times round the left wrist, from the radial to the ulnar side, and begin to wind the fourth time, but pass the string round the back of the thumb to lie across the palm and pass between the ring and little fingers (as in Position I). The same string should be wound twice round the right wrist in like manner, but the third time it should pass round the back of the thumb and be placed across the palm and over the little finger (as in Position I). Draw the hands apart, but loosen the wrist loops so that they may be manipulated.

Do Opening A.

With the right hand take the middle loop on the left wrist and passing it over the distal loop and over the tips of the left fingers, run it up the centre of the figure between the hands. Now take the proximal loop on the left wrist and similarly pass it over the distal loop and the finger tips to the middle of the figure, passing it over the previous loop. Do the same with the remaining left-wrist loop—passing it over the two loops already lying in the middle of the figure.

Raise the right hand vertically above the left hand, and with a little manipulation the loops should move up the figure to mark the track of the sun as it rises in the sky.

## Tricks

*Tinyanyane (Birds).* This is the same as the trick described by Dr. A. C. Haddon (*J.R.A.I.* xxxvi, 1906, p. 142).

*Kamba (A thief).* This is identical with 'An African Hanging Trick', by W. A. Cunnington (*J.R.A.I.* xxxvi, 1906, p. 124).

# X
# TATUING, SCARIFICATION, AND TRIBAL MARKS[1]

THE Leŋge and the Tʃopi women have the story of their lives written on their own flesh. But because the written story sometimes grows dim, it has to be rewritten at intervals, until the marks are ineffaceable. And why is this done, absolutely regardless of the inconvenience and physical suffering which such operations occasion? The women themselves say that they wish to make their bodies beautiful. The Ŋgoni say: 'If you do not pierce your ear, it will resemble a mat!' The Tʃopi would ridicule any non-tatued stranger coming to their country thus: 'Oh! you do not tatu yourself, and therefore you resemble a fish!' But there seems to be a deeper reason than the merely ornamental one. A Leŋge woman once said: 'If we see any object which pleases us very much, we go home and have a picture of it tatued on the body; but if other people envy us, and want to make tatuing like ours, we do not reveal where we have seen the object, for the spirit of the thing remains with her who has had a representation of it made on the body.' This remark must apply more particularly to personal or decorative marks.

As regards the social importance of these practices, girls suffer disabilities as regards marriage if they do not undergo them. The girls who have started having the incised tatuing made gain first entrance to the initiation schools. They have already been put to the test of physical courage and endurance, and so are more likely than others to undergo the initiation tests well.

## The Operations

The patient pays for the operations by doing manual work in the fields for the doctor-woman. Sometimes four or five patients will be operated on at the same time, but if so, they are done in order of age, and not of social precedence. For instance, the chief's daughter must take her turn when it comes; which is quite a different custom from that which obtains usually, because the daughter of a chief has social privileges above other girls. The operations are performed by men or women doctors according to the sex of the patient. All Leŋge women

---

[1] The substance of this has been reproduced from *The South African Journal of Science*, xxi, 1924, pp. 573–87, by kind permission.

PLATE VIII

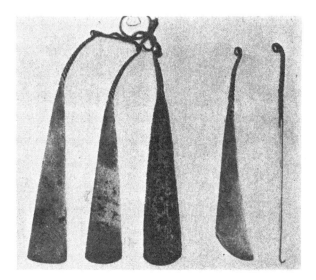

(a) TATUING INSTRUMENTS

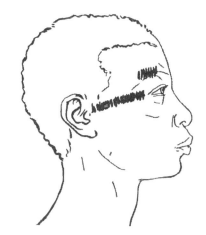

(b) FACIAL MARKING OF A LEDGE WOMAN

## TATUING, SCARIFICATION, AND TRIBAL MARKS 103

are operated on by women, but *tinyaŋga* may make cuts for injections on women patients in cases of illness.

Except in the case of ritual marks made for mourning and unfaithfulness in marriage, the conditions required of both operators and patients is that they must be in a state of ceremonial 'cleanness'. That is, they must not have incurred ceremonial misfortune (*khombo*). This is essential. Transgression of this rule on the part of the patient will cause the operator to become unclean. For instance, if a girl has been playing with a baby and nursing it, and the baby dies, that girl will have incurred ceremonial misfortune above all the other mourners. If the girl goes to a woman doctor and has her tatued incisions made, the woman, too, will incur *khombo*. If she is an expectant mother, the misfortune will extend to her unborn babe. She must procure 'medicine' from the parents of the girl, and rub it between the big toe and the second toe of her own foot, this being considered a magical spot.

The Tʃopi and the Leŋge use as instruments the native-made razors *tikari*, and a *ʃinaŋga* or small razor, with a hooked instrument like a button-hook, called an *indodo*, the two together being known as a *ʃinaŋga*.

Ears are pierced with a knife and a *ʃisuŋgunu* (awl).

The *tikari* are generally used for making the keloid scars (*titaŋga*), and the *ʃinaŋga* for the tatued incisions (*ʃitlhavelo*), the *indodo* being used to hook up the flesh so that it can be cut more easily.

Before use, the instruments are fumigated in order to cleanse them ceremonially, not for hygienic reasons. They are anointed with the sacred oil of *Trichilia emetica*. A fire is made with grass taken from the roof of the hut. The smoke is waved to and fro by means of the hand, over the instruments, and they are finally passed through the fire. This process is called 'cleansing the metal'. Grass taken from the roof of a hut has magical value.

Scars are first washed with a decoction made from the leaves of *Dodonaea viscosa* L.; and after three days with a lotion made from the leaves of *Momordica clematidea* Sond. Then a feather is dipped into the oil of *Trichilia emetica*, and the sores are anointed with it. Leaves of *Dodonaea viscosa* are then heated and pressed on the sores. This is a very painful process. Branches of *Dodonaea viscosa* are carried by girl initiates when they go to the dance which ends the initiation ceremonies. In order to attend this dance, all scars and incised tatuing will be touched up in order to make the initiates more beautiful. Every time the scars are reopened the same lotions will be used. Some women have the operation performed pretty frequently, but not when the sores are inclined to suppurate. All scars are made in the winter, for hygienic reasons, but the incised tatuing can be done at any time of the year.

The tatu-designs are blackened with colouring-matter made from the charred and pounded roots of *Royena Villosa* L., or *Randia dumetorum*; or a charred and ground maize-cob.

Measurements for the designs are made by softening and damping a strip of palm-leaf, which is then dipped into the black powder, and the designs outlined. The operator gently rubs the powder into the incision with her finger, and the powder mixes with the blood of the wound, and the permanent 'tatu' is effected. The black powder is known as *nsita*. A caustic used for the incisions is the juice of the unripe cashew-nut (*Anacardium occidentale*). This answers the purpose of an indelible ink.

The blood is carefully scraped off with the instrument, which is cleansed with the strip of palm-leaf. This strip is then buried, for it is thought that if a dog should lick the blood of the wounds the dog would die.

The patient eats very little while the *ɡitlhavelo* and *tiɫaŋga* are made on the gastric region, and her food is of a soft kind. She fears that if she eats too much the sores will be torn open (*kupanzeka*).

A patient who has had her ears pierced will not eat a split mealie, because that would make her ear split still more. Patients with open sores avoid taking salt, thinking that it may aggravate the sore.

These practices of tatuing and scarification, which seem to us so degrading, have evidently had a high ritual and social value, and have become intimately connected with all the great crises of the lives of these people.

The body markings of Leŋge women may be classed under the headings of tribal; vestigial totemistic; ritual; and personal and decorative.

*Tribal Markings*

It is possible that the tribal marks were not originally intended as such, but have become so through lapse of time, intermingling of races, and divisions of territories.

The people make a distinction between scars caused by incised tatuing, which they call *ɡitlhavelo*, and the keloid scars of all sizes, which they call *tiɫaŋga*.

I can tell a Leŋge or Tʃopi woman at a glance by noting if she has a line of tatued incisions running from the corner of each eye to the ear. In addition to this line Tʃopi women and the elder Leŋge women have two lines running from the left corner of the mouth to just below the lobe of the ear. In olden days in Tʃopiland a woman was said to resemble a fish if she lacked this mark. The younger Leŋge women do not have this mark. It is called *fiſali* (tracks of saliva), and was made at the age of puberty. A Khambana woman, whom I knew, said she had this mark because she had lived in Tʃopiland for a long time.

Depilation of eyelashes is a tribal mark. It distinguishes Leŋge and Tʃopi from the Ndau and also from some of the Thoŋga groups.

The people themselves can distinguish the tribes of Gazaland by the modes of hair-dressing of the women. When looking at the incised patterns on wooden food-bowls, they will say: 'Oh! that represents the hair-dressing of Tʃopi women of olden days!' 'Oh! and that is the hair-dressing of a young Leŋge girl', &c. These designs in the hair are made by the numberless 'partings' arranged in geometrical design.

The filing of the teeth is another tribal mark. Leŋge women do not practise this now. But the Tʃopi women often display a row of filed (upper) teeth, said to resemble crocodile's teeth. They say they do it for decorative purposes. It is quite possible that it is a relic of cannibalism.

Pierced ears are a tribal mark. The Ŋgoni made this custom of piercing the ears compulsory. Leŋge and Tʃopi women of olden days did not pierce the ears.

*Vestigial Totemistic Marks*

It is doubtful if the Leŋge ever had totems. Yet there are certain objects and creatures which are revered or shunned to an extent which makes one think that vestiges of totemism, possibly filtering in from other tribes, still exist. Leŋge women seem to have superstitions about two of these creatures, the *damarela* lizard (*Homopholis Wahlbergii*) and the *ntete*, an orthopteron which is a variety of *Schistocerca septemfasciata* Gervais. *Homopholis Wahlbergii* is quite harmless, and yet, if a Leŋge woman catches sight of one of these lizards, it fills her with terror. Mothers teach the children to beware of them. This is probably a case of tabu instruction. Hence almost all Leŋge women make a design representative of the *damarela* either on their bodies or on their bowls and gourds. The representation is supposed to act as a charm to prevent the woman from seeing the real creature. The incised tatuing of a Leŋge woman, made on the waist just below the breasts, often represents a *damarela*. This region is called *furane*. Men often have a *damarela* design incised on their ribs when they dance the men's dance known as the *aŋgalaŋga*.

A Tʃopi woman of the Muyaŋga sib who had married a Mundau told me—and she really believed what she said—that in the winter (May and June) the *damarela* makes a hole in the ground by night, and sings the *damarela* song in Ndau words. The people anxiously listen, and say: 'Oh! there is the *damarela*.' The *damarela* sings: 'To-morrow I shall cut wood when the sun rises.' But when the sun does rise, the *damarela* crosses its legs and does nothing. It waits till the night, and then repeats its cry again that it will cut wood when the sun rises, always putting off its work from day to day. Another woman of the Kosa sib (Djoŋga origin) told me that in olden days there was a saying that if a *damarela* clung to the breast of a woman, it could only be dislodged by her having sexual connexion with a *makwavu* (brother or cousin).

Even to-day, Leŋge girls are terrified, because they say that the *damarela* clings to a woman's breasts and cannot be dislodged. The modern remedy is, when a person is seized by a *damarela*, she must go to an *anyaŋga*. The *anyaŋga* impinges the *damarela* on a stick and roasts it, and afterwards hangs it up till it is quite dried. Then he heats it again, grinds it into a powder, and puts the powder into a little medicine gourd. The patient eats a little of the powder. Then the *anyaŋga* makes three injections in the breast, and rubs the powder in as a kind of inoculation against further attacks.

The variety of *Schistocerca septemfasciata* is not shunned, but very much admired, especially some peculiarity of its fore-legs. Designs in pottery and basketry are said to represent its legs.

*Ritual Marks*

The most important of the ritual marks of the women are those for mourning, adultery, bereavement by witchcraft, and initiation.

Marks made for mourning are named *tikhuvi takufeliwa*. These are made just above the breast. Charred and powdered mealie-cob is rubbed into these cuts. Mothers who have lost their children have marks made in the arm, and 'medicine' injected.

Children who have lost their mothers have cuts made on the thighs, and the caustic juice of *Anacardium occidentale* rubbed into these

PLATE IX

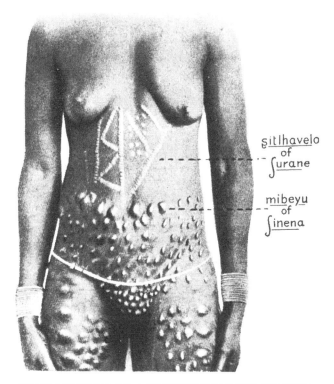

BODY MARKING OF A PORTUGUESE EAST AFRICAN
WOMAN

incisions. 'Medicine' is also rubbed into incisions made on the lower part of the cheeks of men and women who have committed adultery.

Initiation candidates have a mark made just below the division between the first and second finger of the hand, with the black colouring matter made of the charred and pounded roots of *Royena villosa* L.

People who have lost relatives by witchcraft have cuts made and ritual medicine injected in order to protect themselves against such injury in the future.

*Injections for Illnesses*

Cuts are sometimes made in cases of illness, and 'medicine' rubbed in. An incision is generally made on each side of the place where the pain occurs. The row of incisions running from the eye to the ear may be reopened in cases of bad headache, and a medicine made from roots of *Euclea* rubbed in. *Matlhaŋganiso* and *nsikiriti* are two other medicines used for injections, the former generally for sprains and bruises, and the latter for a pain in the leg.

*Personal and Decorative Marks*

These are bewildering in number and variety, and include such widely different objects as sticks for beating the Tʃopi piano, the spoor of a monkey, a pestle, a pair of scissors, a key, a watch, &c. It is often difficult to distinguish between those marks which represent objects with a possible totemistic origin and others which represent merely personal tatu objects.

We will now describe in detail some of the tatued incisions and then the keloid scars.

*Tatued Incisions*

The *ɡitlhavelo* of Leŋge women, of the *ʃurane* or waist region, consist of conventionalized designs symbolizing species of trees, grass, lizards, arrow-heads, and other objects which might possibly have a far-off totemistic significance. Representations of trees and plants are more definitely of Tʃopi than of Leŋge origin. The Leŋge prefer the *Homopholis Wahlbergii* design (stylized); or a representation of the marvellous fore-legs of *Schistocerca septemfasciata*, or possibly of the legs of the *koŋgoloti* centipede. In the photograph (Pl. IX) the tatu of the *ʃurane* is a stylized representation of the fore-legs of *Schistocerca septemfasciata*, according to one informant, but there was a doubt about it, as another woman considered the design to represent metal arrow-heads called *miseve*.

In addition to the line of cuts joining the ear to the eye, a Leŋge woman will have a line of incisions made above the right eyebrow, representing a *ſilodo*, the crook by which the branches of *Trichilia emetica* are hooked down in order that the oil-seeds may be gathered. Sometimes on the forehead there is a representation of the *ſimoŋgo*, or wand held by the women in the hand during the *aŋginya* or *masessa* dances. A cock's comb (*njere*) is also represented on the forehead of some Tſopi women. Tſopi men in olden days represented the cock's comb by a line of scars down the forehead and nose.

The Leŋge women have an important tatu made on the back, representing a *banzi* or forked pole which is placed to support the branches of *Trichilia emetica*, drooping beneath their weight of oil-seeds.

They will also sometimes have a tatu representing a wooden pestle, made just below the left breast.

A *yinzalama* or falling star representation is made near the wrist. Falling stars are held in fear and reverence.

The *muqopagwayi*, made also on the fore-arm, is supposed to be very effective when a Leŋge stretches out her hand to give her lover some snuff. He will see it and admire it very much. The word seems to be derived from *kuqupa*, to take a pinch of snuff in the fingers.

The *ɡitlhavelo* just enumerated are the most important, but there are many others.

### *The tiłaŋga (Keloid Scars)*

These are also known as *magwava* or *dzindovu*. The especially large scars of the *ſinena*, or region below the *ſurane* or waist, are known as *mibeyu*. The *mintsuŋga* or *tifuŋga* are also keloid, but rather smaller.

The *mibeyu* are said to represent sometimes the cuts or *ɡivaŋgu* made in the bark of a tree to show how many cattle or pounds have been paid to lobola a daughter of the house.

The *tifuŋga* or *miŋtsuŋga* scars derive their name from a ceremonial belt which is called *fuŋga* or *tsuŋga*, worn by married women. It is tabu ever to cut this belt. A widow must take it off, and bury it in the grass or mud near the lake when she returns from her ceremonial ablutions after her husband's death.

Tſopi women sometimes have a line or two of small scars running from the eye to underneath the chin. These are known as *mipataroŋgo*.

In olden days Tſopi women used to cover themselves almost entirely with *magwava* scars, except the palms of the hands and feet and part of the chest. The dorsal *magwava* scars sometimes represent the spots of the leopard called *ſiŋgoku*.

# XI
# PUBERTY. INITIATION

LEDGE girls are told about sexual matters at a very early age. At the age of puberty they used to be taken to the *ambutsa* or initiation school, as will be presently described. The girl's women relations would inform her of the coming event, and tell her that she would be required at the Initiation School to carry very heavy domestic utensils, and that she would have *kurwala ſitsandza* (i.e. to bear something impossible), which seems to be the euphemistic phrase for the test or operation of the ceremonies. *Σitsandza* also means a heavy log of wood.

Girls are guarded morally by their parents to a certain extent, but they are often seduced by boys, who then have to pay a fine called *maganye* to the girl's parents. The girl herself will generally give the money to her mother, because the boy will fear the father. (Cf. p. 149.)

## Puberty

*The Menses*

When a young girl reaches her first period she is told that she is now grown up. In olden days she used to sit on the ground nearly all the time.

A little rite has to be performed by her eldest brother, or, failing him, the mother of her father. The brother procures some charcoal, and chews a little. He then breathes it out on the small of the girl's back, and on the umbilicus. This is possibly a temporary separation rite.

There are certain prohibitions connected with the periods.

1. Prohibitions connected with food and food-utensils.

If the girl has been lobolaed with cattle, she must not take sour milk or go into the cattle kraal.

A woman must not brew beer or any intoxicating drink. A Leŋge girl especially must not stamp pine-apples to extract the juice for beer.

She must not make oil of *Trichilia emetica*.

She must not mash mealie grains.

She must not give men food in the wooden food-bowls.

She must not wash food-pots.

If she has been stamping ground-nuts, she must not touch them with her hands afterwards, but must use a spoon. If she touches the oily mass with her hands the man who eats it will suffer with pains in his legs so that he will not be able to walk.

2. Tabus or prohibitions connected with men relations.

A woman must not sit on a man's mat.

She must not step over the threshold of a man's hut unless she has first chewed *Juncus* root and then spat it out.

She must not touch a man or wash his clothes. If she touches a man her legs will be so painful she will not be able to walk.

As soon as the period is finished, she must smear her hut and wash herself at the lake. It is tabu for a man to step over or on blood (*kukanzihela ŋgati*).

When the girl wants to smear the hut at the end of the period, she must follow this procedure: She will mix the sand with mud from the cattle kraal and with water, and put the smearing mixture in two little heaps, one at the men's side of the hut and the other at the women's. She finishes the women's side first, leaving a little pile of mud near the threshold; then she smears the men's side, leaving another little pile on that side. Then the two little piles are joined together at the threshold, and the remaining little bit of the hut is smeared.

3. Prohibition connected with fire.

Formerly a girl was not allowed to kindle a fire. This tabu is not in force now.

The following charm to prevent childbirth is connected with the menses. If it is feared that a young girl will find a partner in the bush, and have a baby, when the menses are seen, 'medicine' is added to the clout worn, and a hole is made in the ground near the *fikukutse* tree (*Combretum Guenzii*), and the rag is buried. If the clout is not unearthed, the girl will not have a baby. But when she is properly married, the clout will be dug up and thrown away.

A very important *anyaŋga* can give a girl medicine to hasten the appearance of the menses. One of the ingredients of the medicine is a heated and pulverized tortoise-bone.

## Initiation of Girls[1]

The rites of initiation for girls, called *ambutsa* or *ambuta*, were universally practised some few years ago by the Leŋge and the Tʃopi. Girls of Thoŋga (Shangaan) origin were admitted to the rites if their

[1] Reproduced by kind permission of the Director of the Transvaal Museum, from *Annals of the Transvaal Museum*, vol. ii, part 2, 1925, with slight alterations.

PLATE X

(a) MISTRESS OF THE INITIATION CEREMONIES

(b) *NTAKULA* DRUM

families had been settled for some time in Tʃopiland. According to my informants the Toŋga of Inhambane practised the same or similar rites, but not so the Tswa. My informants state that the secret language spoken by the candidates for initiation, during the separation rites, is understood by the Toŋga of Inhambane and the Leŋge and Tʃopi.

The Leŋge have ceased to practise the rites as a public function in Σihaɫu's territory, but they are still carried on in parts of Tʃopiland.

Some Leŋge girls pay visits to Tʃopiland for the purpose. The initiation school for boys is also still in vogue in Tʃopiland. The following description applies to the girls' rites as they were carried out a few years ago.[1]

*Social Preparation for the Girls' Initiation Rites*

In the spring the chief of a certain district would issue an order that all the young girls who had attained a marriageable age should pass through the ordeal of the rites of initiation. The girls would be 'promised' (i.e. engaged for the rites) at the time of the spring digging in the fields, and would undergo a special training during the summer months, terminating in the rites and the one month's initiation school in the autumn. The rites were compulsory; only girls who were physically unfit (through illness, or because they were immature) were exempt. Girls who had reached the age, but were physically undeveloped, were given a special medicine in order to hasten the appearance of the menses. Pressure was brought to bear upon eligible girls if they refused to go to the rites, and they were caught if they tried to run away.

After the order had been issued, the father of each girl would pay a formal call on the chief and inform him that he had a daughter who was ready for the rites. He then paid an entrance fee equal in value to ten shillings. In the event of the father being too poor to pay the fee, he would do some manual work for the chief instead. If girls afterwards appeared at the rites without the fees having been paid, the fathers would be fined. An additional sum of two *quinientos* (Portuguese silver) was required for the mistress of the rites (the *nyambutsi*). The chief also presented the *nyambutsi* with a sum of about £8 in value

---

[1] The rites have been closed in some districts owing to the fact that the parents of the candidates are unwilling to pay the fees, which are one of the sources of revenue of the Chief. In one district in 1928, the rites were compulsory to this extent, that if the candidates, being Christians, refused to take part, they had to pay the fees just the same as if they had gone. It was a kind of taxation.

when all the rites were ended, and she would give her sister about £2 for helping her in the minor rites. The chief used the money accruing to him through these rites in order to lobola another wife or wives for himself.

The office of *nyambutsi* was hereditary. It was handed down from mother to eldest daughter for many generations. Everybody held the office in great respect and honour. The *nyambutsi* would begin to offer sacrifices two days before her arrival at the chief's kraal to conduct the initiation school. She paid a visit to the divination-doctor. She entreated her ancestral spirits to help her to conduct the ceremonies well, and to help the girls to 'stand the test'. She also begged for many material benefits for herself—that she might receive presents of money, fowls, and clothing.

During the time of preparation, the candidates were instructed by their mothers, who were helped by the mistress of the rites, in the social tabus and regulations affecting the womenkind in the life of the tribe. The girls were taught strange rules of deportment and of domestic knowledge and feminine hygiene. The *nyambutsi* was looked upon as the final authority in these matters. The instruction given mainly concerned the use of, and tabus connected with, sacred things in *la vie intime* of womenkind, such as (*a*) the red-ochre ointment (*tsumane*) used after childbirth and after initiation, and on other sacred occasions; (*b*) the sacred food-bowls; (*c*) the brass neck-rings used for purposes of lobola in olden days;[1] (*d*) the bark skirts used for the initiation dances; (*e*) mourning attire; (*f*) the symbolism of the patterns on bead-baskets, girdles, and other initiation ornaments; (*g*) the magical properties of brass anklets and bracelets—and many other things. The sacrificial side of religion was not taught, probably owing to the fact that no young girl may offer a sacrifice unless both her parents are dead, and she has no brother to do it for her.

Before presenting herself at the initiation school each candidate would try to obtain a badge, called 'licence medicine'. This was the pledge or token of admission, and might be obtained from the *nyambutsi* herself two or three days before the school began. The badge or licence itself was a very rare species of fungus (*Peziza* sp.) growing on the stumps of dead trees. Failing a sufficient number of these, substitutes might be used. The price of each badge was two silver *quinientos*

---

[1] These brass rings have a magical value. Water in which they are steeped is offered to spirits. A dog who happened to drink the water was thought unable to have a litter of puppies.

PLATE XI

*LIKHALU* GIRDLE WORN IN WOMEN'S INITIATION
CEREMONIES

(Badge, Pl. XIII). Each candidate must also take with her some red ochre and oil, for her anointing.

## *The Religious Preparation*

Early on the morning of the day on which the initiation rites began, the chief offered sacrifices on account of the young girls to be initiated, in order that they might all 'stand the test' (*kurwala fitsandza*—to bear the impossible). He prayed to the spirits of his ancestors and offered libations and food-offerings.

When the eventful day arrived for the candidate to set out to the Initiation School at the chief's kraal, her relations were offering sacrifices all the morning. The divination-doctor was called upon to cast his divining omens in order to tell the débutante's fortune. The ancestral spirits were invoked in order that the girl might pass successfully through the ordeal, and not be 'pierced by thorns' (*tlhaviwa hi mitwa*) by failing.

The débutante herself fasted from food that morning, not from a ritual point of view, but because she feared what was coming, and that she might fail 'to stand the test', and had no appetite in consequence.

Certain objects or symbols played an important part in the initiation rites. These were the sacred horn (Pl. XIII), the drum (Pl. XIII), the *tinyuŋgufuma* (symbols of biological significance) (Pl. XIII), and the carved figures or dolls (*mayika*), female and male (Pl. XV).

The carver of these symbols and figures belonged to the same family as the mistress of the rites. He had to make sacrifices before he began his work, for it was considered a very great work indeed, and not to be undertaken lightly. Would it not affect the lives of hundreds of young girls yet unborn? He made offerings to the ancestral spirits, of the seeds of many plants, ground-nuts, beans, Kaffir-corn. He would scoop out a little earth with his left hand, and make a hole under the sacred tree in his kraal. He would not use his right hand for scooping because with it the sacrifices must be made. He would put offerings of food in the sacred hole, and pour a little beer with his right hand, invoking the ancestral spirits as he did so. All his work of carving was done in secret in the bush near his hut. No one might see except his wife. When he had finished his work, he would give notice to the mistress of the rites, who arrived by night with a conical-shaped basket (*firundzo*) to take away the carvings, very much wrapped up so that no one might see. She would be accompanied by another woman who had been initiated.

On her arrival at the chief's kraal the great sacrifice was offered, upon which the success of all the rites depended. In fact, they could not possibly take place without it. The *nyambutsi* invited a select circle of old people (men and women) for the rite of the consecration of the sacred symbols. The priest who sacrificed in this rite was the conductor of the initiation school for boys, who belonged to the same family as the *nyambutsi*. The sacrificial victim was a kid—a young she-goat which must be black and white. Each of the old people present had offered a solemn libation of beer to the ancestral spirits, before entering the hut in which the secret rites took place. They then sat round in a circle, and the symbols enclosed in baskets were placed in the centre of the circle. Inside the *firundzo* the sacred dolls (*mayika*) reposed. Inside a *firavi* (species of basket with a cover) were small gourds containing magical medicines. Inside an *ndzava* (another kind of basket) was the little sacred drum (the *ŋkiriŋgwane*). The sacred ox-horn and the *tinyuŋgufuma* were placed in another basket.

The sacrificial victim was slain outside the hut by the conductor of the boys' school. He squeezed the blood of the kid into another basket, and then handed the body of the victim to two adjutants (men) who prepared its flesh for the sacrificial meal. While this was being done, the priest entered the hut and sprinkled all the baskets containing the sacred symbols with the blood of the victim, uttering words of blessing as he did so. The blessing of the symbols was considered to be of vital importance. After this all the sacred objects were anointed with red-ochre ointment and rubbed with *psanye* (the half-digested food found in the goat).

The flesh of the kid was then brought into the hut, and the old people, beginning with the *nyambutsi*, partook of the ceremonial meal. The fat (the word used was 'hard fat') of the victim was hung up to dry in order that it might afterwards be mixed with medicine and used in the purification rites. All that night the *nyambutsi* and her husband were beating the drum in the hut in order that all the people in the district might know that the initiation school was beginning.

## *The Initiation School*

The *nyambutsi* arrives at the chief's kraal the day before the school is opened. She brings with her the objects which are to be the vehicles of the ʃikwembu, or ancestral spirits, in the great initiation ceremonies. These are carefully wrapped up in a basket, ʃirundzo, so that none may see them. They consist of the tiny sacred drum, the carved figures, and the biological symbols. No *nyambutsi* is allowed to conduct the ceremonies without these symbols, which are handed down from mother to daughter as the most sacred treasures. If the old ones are worn out or broken she must procure some others, but one set will probably last many generations. The old Tʃopi woman who sold me the set which I possess told me that they had been carved by the grandfather of her father.[1]

When the *nyambutsi* has been duly installed in the hut appointed for her at the chief's kraal, the chief himself will beat the little drum as a signal that the mistress of the ceremonies has arrived. The sound of the drum can be heard for a considerable distance. When the chief has finished beating the drum his principal wife takes a turn at it, and after her the *nyambutsi* herself.

Thus summoned the candidates for initiation begin to appear at the chief's kraal, one after another, each accompanied by her mother, and perhaps elder sisters and aunts on both sides, or grandmothers. They will find many groups of girls with their chaperones sitting about in the kraal outside the *nyambutsi's* hut. The new clothes (strips of material bought at the Indian stores) which they have brought as presents for the *nyambutsi* are hung on the roof of the hut, which presents a gay appearance as if it were covered with flags. The fowls given are lying scattered about tied together by the legs.

The beating of the drum goes on all night. Early the next morning the girls are all mustered together. There may be any number from forty upwards. The principal wife of the chief conducts the girls to the clearing in the bush where the ordeal is to take place.

The *nyambutsi* has remained in her hut to take out the little drum and the carved figures, carefully wrapped in bark cloth. She then follows the girls to the large clearing made in the bush by the chief's wives and their attendants. If, however, there are very few girls to be initiated, the ceremony takes place in the *nyambutsi's* hut, a certain number of girls entering at one time with their chaperones.

The girls greet the *nyambutsi's* arrival by clapping their hands. She returns their greetings. The girls begin to shake with fear. The *nyambutsi* begins the initiation dance as a solo. The chaperones of the girls follow her example. It is a nude dance; and the novices begin to cry

[1] This set is now in the Transvaal Museum, Pretoria.

with fright. It is considered essential that they should cry. Even worse is to follow, for the girls themselves must take part in the dance. The dance is accompanied by songs of the *ambutsa* and the beating of the little drum, which is supposed to be now the vehicle of the *ṣikwembu*, (spirits of the ancestors of the *nyambutsi*), by reason of the sacrifices which have been offered.

After the dance has gone on for some time the ritual operation, which seems to consist of the defloration of the girls by mechanical means, the horn apparently being used in some districts, takes place. If the girls try to run away they are caught. If any candidate refuses to undergo it, she is scolded, beaten, and reviled by the relatives, and driven home again covered with abuse, so that her people may sacrifice and sacrifice until she at last can 'stand the test'. It is considered a great disgrace if she fails to do so. She may fail once or even twice, but she is brought to the test again and again until at last she has passed.

It is probable that if there are a large number of girls a certain number of them are operated upon on the first day of the school and others on ensuing days. After the operation the girls feel unwell and must rest. A sedative medicine, made from a botanical species, the leaves of which perspire, is given them. Later on, when the girls have returned from the bush, they are gathered together in the chief's kraal. Two women are told off to count the girls. These two women have cooked food (mealie-meal porridge, cassava root, &c.) in large pots for the girls. Then a general meal takes place. It is tabu for one girl to touch another while she is eating her food. The women who feed the girls will be very angry and scold them if they do. The girls must receive the food with both hands, and a lump of food is first placed in one hand and then in the other. The arms must be stretched out and folded close to the sides, and the palms of the hands held upwards. The elbows of the candidates must not touch one another, though the temptation to elbow each other at times must prove irresistible. It seems to be rather difficult to maintain order at this meal, for if one of the women turns her back, the girls sometimes quarrel and scratch each other. On her return the woman asks: 'Who has been scratching?' Then the girls hang their heads and do not reply.

After the meal, the candidates and chaperones rest till late afternoon, and dancing goes on in the evening for those who are able to take part in it. The dancing is accompanied by the *ntakula* drum. Late that evening a ceremony takes place which is intended to take away the ceremonial defilement or misfortune incurred by the opera-

PLATE XII

SACRED HORN, INITIATION BADGE, HEAD-DRESS,
BIOLOGICAL SYMBOLS, AND *ŊKIRIŊGWANE* DRUM

tion and dance. After this the girls are gathered together in a large hut which is closed. They sit in rows closely huddled together. A fire is made, the burning logs of wood are then taken away and a medicine is put on the smouldering ashes which causes a great smoke. This preparation is made from the roots of a tree named *pupuma*. The roots are taken, scraped, heated on charcoal, ground to a powder, and mixed with the fat of a goat. Then little balls are made by rubbing the mixture in the hands. It is these medicine-balls that are put on the embers.

The *nyambutsi* waves the smoke to and fro with her hands so that it reaches the faces of the candidates and they can inhale it. While she does this she prays to the ancestral spirits. Then she puts out the fire with water and gathers up the residue of the balls (known as *mula*). With this sacred mixture she draws a straight line from the tip of each candidate's chin to the tip of the breast bone.

During the month which the candidates spend in the school, dancing takes place every day. In the early morning they dance to the *ntakula* drum; then they take some food and perhaps sleep or play; and thereupon they march to the clearing in the bush to the sounds of the *ntakula*; and dance the special dance of the *ambutsa*. When they have danced for some time the mothers of the candidates say to the *nyambutsi*, 'Now let us see your *mayika*.' She replies: 'Very well, produce your money.' The money is collected in a wooden bowl. The *mayika* and the biological and natural symbols are taken from the basket in which they have been hidden, and instruction is given the candidates in the mysteries of sex and marriage. A kind of midwifery as practised by the natives is also taught at times. Each time the candidates have to pay for the privilege of seeing the *mayika*; otherwise they are not allowed to do so. The secret language is also taught during this month, together with the rules and prohibitions which the girls must observe during the period of separation which immediately follows. As regards food, all meat, especially goat's flesh, is forbidden, and so also the use of salt when cooking.

*The Symbols*

During the initiation school instruction is given on the mysteries of sex and marriage by means of the symbols, which are at once of biological and magico-religious significance. The first of these is the drum called *ŋkiriŋgwane* (see Pl. XIII). *Symbolum uteri mulieris est.* The body of the drum is carved from *muhondʒwa* or sometimes *ntʃene* wood, and like all the objects used in the initiation rites, is covered with the sacred red ochre. The membrane is made generally of ox-hide or of the skin of the *maŋgulwe* (rooibok). The herring-bone pattern on the drum represents the mode of hair-dressing of an initiated girl of olden times.[1] *Paxilli qui pellem retinent membrum virile vaginam penetrans exprimunt.* Inside the sacred drum are two small symbols called *tinyuŋgufuma*. These represent, according to the statement of the natives, the male and female principles, *in utero mulieris*. Another larger symbol also called *nyuŋgufuma*, or sometimes *pfula*,[2] is also placed in the drum. *Symbolum clitoris est* (see Pl. XIII).

At the religious ceremony of the consecration of the symbols described above the priest of the ceremonies 'writes in the air', according to my informant, i.e. makes mystic passes with the *pfula*, uttering magical formulas over the top of the *ŋkiriŋgwane* (drum). The three symbols are then placed in the drum. They are supposed to be a very great sacrificial offering on the part of the *nyambutsi*, and the candidates will kill her afterwards if she deceives them by not having fulfilled this rite. The *ŋkiriŋgwane* drum in the Transvaal Museum contains the two small *tinyuŋgufuma*, which represent the male and female principles referred to above. The *pfula*, or third *nyuŋgufuma*, had been taken out of the drum before it was brought to me, and was only obtained some months afterwards.

All three symbols have to be covered with the sacred red-ochre ointment. The mistress of the ceremonies sent word to me that the two symbols which are at present in the Transvaal Museum drum were substitutes for those which were used at the rites. Her explanation of this was that the last time that the drum was used she was unable to procure the 'children', i.e. products (stones or hard fruit) of the *maŋgwa* tree, from which the symbols are generally made or carved. Another explanation was given me by another informant, namely, that the two small symbols are generally two small red-ochred bones of a goat and that after the instruction has been given they must be taken out of the drum and buried immediately, otherwise the mistress of the rites will be killed by the candidates. The third *nyuŋgufuma* is generally a product of the *maŋgwa* tree, but it may be a *pfula* of the *makanye* plum

---

[1] The natives, when asked the meaning of the designs they carve on their food-bowls and other wooden objects, invariably say that they represent *ṣitlhavelo* incisions made on the body as tribal marks, reproduced in special methods of arranging the hair.

[2] *Pfula* is the name of the stone of the *Sclerocarya caffra* plum.

PLATE XIII

*MAYIKA* DOLLS

PLATE XIV

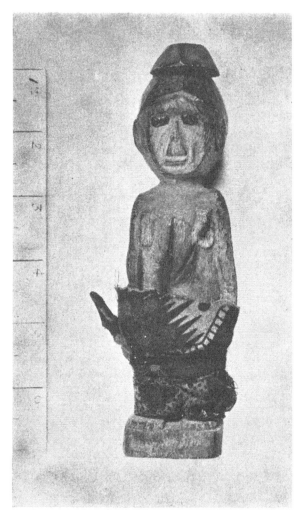

*MAYIKA* FEMALE DOLL

tree. This symbol is not a substitute but the actual one used at the rites with its covering of sacred red ochre.

The object with which the operation is performed on the girls is a horn called *tsondo* (see Pl. XIII). *Symbolum phalli est.* It does not appear to be invariably used. It is placed in another drum, the *ntakula* drum, at the time of the secret religious ceremony. It is generally carved from ox-horn, decorated with goat or rooibok skin, and filled with 'medicine', of which a sample is in the Museum. I was told that the candidates 'fear exceedingly' whenever they see the horn, and therefore it is not used for purposes of instruction, the pegs of the *ŋkiriŋgwane* being used instead. The *ntakula* drum is itself considered important. A great deal of the dancing at the initiation school takes place to the accompaniment of the *ntakula* drum.

In addition to the drum and the symbolic objects described above there are two human figures, male and female, used in the rites. They are carved from the wood called *ŋkaɬu*. The black wax which represents the hair is made by a small species of bee which deposits its wax in the ground. The male figure has his beard cut in the peculiar fashion customary amongst the Tʃopi. The black zigzag incision on the body of the female figure is called *ʃitlhavelo*. One of my informants said it was supposed to be a representation of a *damarela*, a species of lizard (the *Homopholis Wahlbergi*) regarded by the natives with superstitious fear. Representations of this lizard are made on walls, calabashes, wooden bowls, and many other things, including their own bodies. Sometimes the female figure carries on her head a tiny carved representation of one of the sacred food-bowls.

The figures are called *mayika* (see Pls. XV and XVI). They are used in explaining to the girls the physiology of sex. But their function in the rites is not confined to this. They are of high religious value as they have become the vehicles of the ancestral spirits by means of the sacrifices which have been offered.

### The Ceremonial Meal (Ndʒaŋgi)

At the end of a month the novices, accompanied by the women, pay a day's visit to the sea. While there they dance and sing *ŋgelegele* songs. They bathe and wash away the ceremonial impurity incurred by the dances and the previous rites. When they return they partake of a ceremonial or sacramental meal of goat's flesh and mealie-meal. The meat is cooked with medicine prepared from perspiring leaves. Many large fires are made. The rule is that the girls must take their own food from the cooking-pots, seizing it with their hands while it is still burning hot. The *nyambutsi* eats first. The girls must eat in silence. Some of them cry because they are afraid of the huge fires and the burning hot food. Do they not burn their hands while trying to get the hot food from the pots? If they cry their mothers beat them with sticks on the backs of their hands. If their hands are not too painful as the result of the beating they will eat. If their hands are very painful the mothers will afterwards put cooling leaves upon them. The food must be eaten very hot.

With their meal the girls must take a medicine prepared by the *nyambutsi*, the idea being that this medicine and the hot meal will in some way help the girls to become mothers. The medicine is made from leaves which the girls call *kanzi* leaves (*kukanza*—to grind). They are leaves of the *finoŋgo*, and the same leaves are used as purificatory medicine in funeral rites. The *nyambutsi* prepares the medicine by grinding the leaves with water in a wooden mortar. She then puts the mixture into an earthen pot and adds more water. She takes in her fingers a little of the mixture and squeezes the juice into each girl's mouth, and then throws away the leaves. Meanwhile she entreats the ancestral spirits that the girls may become mothers.

The *ndʒaŋgi* meal is not prepared for the girls until the women who prepare it have seen at least one specimen of a species of spider called *masasasavane* (Solifuga spider) as a good omen. One specimen of *masasasavane* is put into the medicine. After the meal is finished, each girl must seize a brand or coal from the burning fires. This is taken home and then ground to powder and the powder is rubbed into an incision made on the back of the girl's left hand just below the division between the first and second fingers. The remainder of the powdered charcoal is preserved in little gourds.

The remains of the *ndʒaŋgi* meal are taken out of the pots by the elders, rolled into little balls, put into a basket and taken home, where they are eaten as the sacred remains of the feast. This sacramental meal is the only occasion on which the *kundʒwa* (novice) may eat goat's flesh until she has been anointed with red ochre.

### *The Period of Seclusion*

After the ceremonial meal of the *ndʒaŋgi* each girl returns to her own home with her mother. The first person to greet the novice on her arrival is her handmaid, the young girl who is to act as a go-between as regards her and the outer world. A peculiar relationship exists

## PUBERTY. INITIATION

between the handmaid and her mistress. The little girl is always chosen for her *savoir faire*. She is a near relation of the novice. A girl to whom the office would belong by right, such as a younger sister, would be passed over if she were not intelligent enough. On the arrival of the novice at her own home, the handmaid comes forward silently, and greets her by rubbing her right hand with a circular motion over the left hand of the novice.

The rules the novice has to observe during her period of retirement are as follows:

1. You must not laugh. If you laugh you will be beaten.
2. You must speak only in the secret language and as little and as softly as possible.
3. Never be angry, or scold or revile any one.
4. If any one steals your beads or takes anything belonging to you, you must not try to hinder the theft nor must you reveal the identity of the thief.
5. If you see some one stealing anything else in the kraal, you must be quiet and say nothing about it.
6. If a child cries do not try to pacify it, but merely look at it.
7. If people ask you questions do not answer them.
8. If people call to you, you must only make a little wail in reply, '*weh-h-h.*'
9. Never eat in other people's presence, but alone in your own hut.
10. If any visitor to the kraal greets you, you must make a circular motion with your right hand over the palm of your left hand but say nothing.
11. You must be very careful not to give a big *ambita* (water or cooking-pot) to your handmaid or any other small child to carry, but only one suitable to the size of the child.
12. Never carry your own water-pot on your head if you go out to draw water. It is strongly tabu to do so. You must carry it under your arm.
13. When you return with the pot full of water then you must carry it on your head.
14. You must carry your little bead basket in a special way. It must hang on your wrist by the handle with your fingers spread out in the shape of a fan over the side of the basket.
15. The *nsimbu* (a little wreath of rags or leaves to support a pot) you put on your head in order to carry your pot must be of the very smallest size necessary to carry the pot.

16. If fowls come to peck at your food you must not drive them away.

17. When you eat you must do so slowly without appetite (as if it were a bore).

From these rules it is clearly seen that the girl must act and be as different as possible from her ordinary state of life.

The night of her return from the *ndʒaŋgi* meal the man arrives who is to be her husband for one night only. He is generally her *fiancé* if she has been taken by lobolo, but failing her *fiancé* the man must be her brother-in-law (sister's husband). He presents her with nice new strips of print for a garment; she must give her old garment to the oldest woman in the kraal. He has also brought with him a pig, which he gives to the elder women of the kraal.

The next morning early, the girl will first wash the bridegroom as an act of ceremonial purification. She herself will go to the lake.[1] While she has gone to the lake the man must sweep the entire ground of the kraal. This also is looked upon as another little act of ceremonial purification. It pleases the mother of the girl and she thinks it very nice of him. He will invite his brother to help him sweep. When the sweeping is finished, the pig which he brought the day before is killed. The girl must not see the man again after her ceremonial washing. She eats her portion of pork in the hut with the door closed. A leg of pork is taken to her by the brother of her husband of one night. The rest of the pork is given to the girl's father and mother who keep it in their hut, and dole out portions of it as they like to their remaining relatives.

The girl now remains hidden for nearly two months, during which time she has to keep the rules referred to above. During this period of separation she remains in her hut a great deal. When she emerges into the kraal she must be careful not to be seen by any stranger. If she sees any one coming she must hide herself quickly. For six days she never leaves her own kraal, but after that she may go to draw water at the lake, always accompanied by the handmaiden. She must go during the middle of the day, or at a time when she is not likely to meet other women engaged on the same business. Some time during this period the keloid scars of the pelvic region are made.

The two months are passed in seclusion excepting towards the end of the time when the novice attends dances at the chief's kraal, but in this case she is preceded by the handmaiden, who goes in front to warn her if any one is coming, in which case she hastily hides herself in the bush.

As soon as the man who has taken away the ceremonial defilement

[1] This corresponds to the ceremonial ablution of the usual marriage ceremonies.

incurred by the operation and dance has gone away, the mother and elder sisters or other near relatives begin to prepare the girl's toilet. Her mother first prepares a mixture of red ochre and *mafurreira* oil, and the body of the girl is anointed all over with this mixture. Her hair is arranged in numberless little short curls anointed with red-ochre clay. Her hair was previously prepared for this by being rubbed all over with ashes, while she was still at the initiation school. When asked why the hair was dressed with ashes, the reason given in reply was that it made the hairs stiff enough to receive the application of red ochre with advantage. The red ochre has a religious significance. It is supposed to please the ancestral spirits. It is used after initiation and childbirth, and also in mourning ceremonies, but in the last case it is prepared with water and not fat. The *tsumane* (red ochre) is sacred to women, and men wear red-ochred rings when they consider themselves possessed by ancestral spirits.

The children are taught to procure mud containing red ochre from the lake. It is then patted between the hands like putty, and spread out in dabs to dry in the sun. When it is dry it is put in a fire and wood is placed above it. It is tabu for a married woman, who is living with her husband, to put *tsumane* in the fire. Her mother-in-law does it. They think that if a married woman does it the red ochre will lose its colour and acquire the colour of ashes. If, however, the husband is absent, working at Johannesburg or elsewhere, the married woman may put *tsumane* in the fire. If a child puts *tsumane* in its mouth, attracted by its colour, that child is supposed not to be able to bear children when it grows up. If a woman visits another woman who has just had a baby, and touches her pot of red-ochre ointment, she is supposed to have sinned with the husband of the woman with the baby.

The mistress of the initiation ceremonies teaches the candidates that they must be anointed with red ochre because it is a sacred adjunct of the rites. She also teaches them that they must anoint themselves and their child with the sacred mixture after childbirth. The red ochre has probably also hygienic value. It is also used as a depilatory.

When the girl has been anointed all over with the red mixture, her mother and admiring female relatives look at her and say, '*A yo tsu*', an expression called by M. Junod 'a sacramental expression'. *Tsu* seems to express the red colour (*psuka* means red). The dancing skirt of the girl is made from the Tʃopi bark (the *mphama* tree)[1] by her female

[1] Referred to by M. Junod, *The Life of a South African Tribe*, vol. ii, p. 78, footnote 2. This tree is probably *Ficus utilis*.

relatives. The Tʃopi are clever at preparing this useful material. These skirts resemble in shape those worn by the ancient Egyptian men. They seem to consist of two triangles. Red-ochre ointment is rubbed all over the skirts which are ornamented with white beads (Pl. XIV).

Beautiful bead ornaments are prepared—bracelets, anklets, girdles, and head-dresses. The colours are black and white with touches of blue here and there. There is a definite order in the putting-on of the ornaments. The upper-arm bracelets must be put on first; then the head-ornament (Pl. V), which is known as *ʃikhuti*, and which is made of plaited vegetable fibre covered with red ochre. Then the heavy girdle of beads is donned, and then the wrist bracelets and the anklets in succession. The girl is also presented with a necklet and vanity bag for personal use (Pl. V).

During the third month the chief will invite the *nyambutsi* again for the great cult dance which is to end the ceremonies. She arrives at the chief's kraal and all the novices (*tikundʒwa*) are invited. The girls remain in the chief's kraal all night and dance the *aŋginya* and play. In the early morning they take some food uncceremonially and all go out into the bush.

Then begins the great dance, the *tʃuruvula*, which ends the ceremonies. It is the same dance as that of the 'test' day. The dancers all stand in a circle, in a certain pose which they have been taught. They dance to the *ŋkiriŋgwane* drum, which is placed near a huge fire in order to make it resound better. When asked if this fire was in any way considered sacred, my informant replied that it was simply for the sake of the acoustics of the drum, so that the sound may be heard a long way off. The *nyambutsi's* sister beats the drum; it is also her office to kindle the fire. The dancers are nude with the exception of the ornaments, of which a full complement is worn, and their bodies are covered with red ochre.

The *nyambutsi* is begged to bring out the sacred dolls (*mayika*). This she consents to do if they join in making her a present of money. The initiates clap their hands and dance round the dolls. Some climb the trees in order to be able to see them. They all cry: '*hitlaŋgela ŋwina, ɡiɬaŋgi ɡakuɬauleka, hikusa misasekile ŋgopfu.*' 'We greet you, elect children (babes), because you are beautiful.' They present the 'elect babes' with little wooden bowls full of fresh-water fish which they have caught in the lake. The mother of the babes, the *nyambutsi*, eats the fish afterwards.

At the end of the dance the *nyambutsi* wraps her treasures up care-

PLATE XV

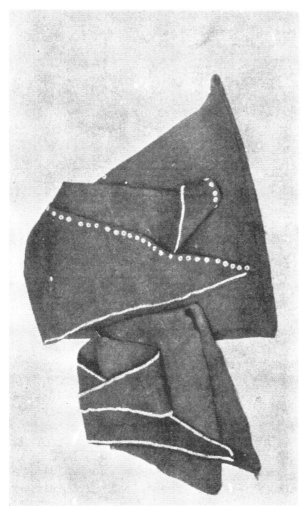

SKIRTS OF BARK CLOTH

PLATE XVI

BEADWORK (INITIATION ORNAMENTS)
Necklet, upper-arm bracelets, girdle. Vanity bags. Bead bracelets worn on forearms. Bead anklets.

fully and takes them away. The initiates go home and their mothers take off their ornaments, which will be hidden in a box or basket.

*Aggregation Rites*

Early the next morning the initiate's mother will cut her hair. The girl is now *tſiŋgiwa*. Very great importance is attached to this act. Meanwhile her father has bought a red cloth for a head-dress, known as *ſiyandani*. He presents it to his daughter, and she herself must tie it on her head. This is a strict rule. There is also a special way of tying on the head-dress, which has to be strictly observed. It is folded, passed round the back of the head, and brought to the front and tied; the two ends are then passed back again in parallel lines, over the top of the head to the back, and tucked in. 'It is very much tabu,' said my informant, 'to omit to cut the hair and tie on the *ſiyandani*, because now the initiate has finished the misfortune (*a hetile khombo*)'. She has now attained the status of an adult member of the community.

The initiate is afterwards known by the *ſiyandani*. She will wear it till it is quite torn and worn out, but will leave it off when her hair has grown again. After they are *tſiŋgiwa*, the candidates will wear their old clothes again, for everything is finished, and they will go to other districts and take part in the *tſuruvula* dance of other novices. The initiated girls must never reveal anything about the ceremonies to the uninitiated girls. It is a very great tabu. 'The initiation rites are the greatest of all rites,' said my informant. When going to the *tſuruvula* dance the girls wear the bark dancing skirts, although they are taken off while dancing, and put on again when going home. The bead ornaments are carried in the vanity bags (Pl. V). Later on the skirts may be given to the handmaiden for her approaching initiation, but the beads are hidden away as sacred treasures.

*The Secret Language*

This language is taught by the *nyambutsi* to the pupils as part of the instruction they receive in the initiation school. It is forbidden to use any other language during the period of separation which follows. A fine is exacted by the *nyambutsi* for each breach of this rule. It is said that the chief reaps a harvest from these fines. One may wonder how the *nyambutsi* comes to know about the offences, but probably there are always people willing to be tale-bearers, at least my informant seemed to think so.

The elder members of the community all understand and can speak the secret language. The little ones 'hear it but do not understand'. The Toŋga of Inhambane are said to use the same language in their initiation ceremonies. My informant appeared to think that the ceremonies originated with the Nyambana or Koka (people of Inhambane).

The chief characteristics of the secret language are as follows:

1. Some words of the ordinary language, Leŋge, are used, for example, the cardinal numbers and most adjectives.

2. Descriptive words are substituted for the ordinary names of certain objects, e.g. a house must not be referred to as a house or a dwelling-place, but may be designated as a 'hiding-place' or a 'stalking-place'.

4. Whole series of objects are grouped together under one general name, which may be used for any of them instead of its proper name; for example, the word *gikalana*, plural *dzikalana*, is such a general term for sky, sun, moon, stars, thunder, lightning, birds, beasts, fishes, spirits, ghosts, and gods. Clouds and rain, however, are known as *dzitsomekela*, and wind is called *dzikupetela*.

The following words are very commonly used in the secret language:

| English. | Secret language. | Leŋge. | Tʃopi. | Ɛaŋgana. |
|---|---|---|---|---|
| food-bowl | gi-gyelo | mbiya | mbiya | ŋgelo |
| to eat | gu ndaula | gu gya | ŋgu dya | ku dla |
| to drink | gu sela | gu seya | ŋgu seya | ku ŋwa |
| mealies | timbele | mafake | mafake | ʃifake |
| water | dziselo | mati | mati | mati |
| hoe | ʃikheti | nsuka | nsuka | ʃikhomo |
| earthen pot | ʃi-reŋgele | ŋgadi | ŋkadi | mbita |
| wooden spoon | noŋga | muku | ŋko | ŋkombe |
| baby (child) | mvelekwana | mwanana | nwanana | ŋwana |
| mortar | tiŋgadi | tudi | ditudi | tʃuri |
| to pound (grind) | gu bhimela | gu kanda | ŋgu sindza | ku kanza |
| winnowing basket | livatsi | gi-seyu | gi-selo | ʃitelo |
| conical-shaped basket | gi-gelo | gi-hundu | gi-rundu | ʃirundzo |
| wooden trough | ndoŋga | gi-govolo | ʃi-gowola | ʃigovolo |
| house | ʃi-baramu | nyumba | nyumba | yindlu |
| to dig | gu phamutela | gu dima | ŋgu dima | ku rima |
| to sleep | gu dzivama | gu eteya | ŋgu ruama | ku etlela |
| to go | gu kandetela | gu tʃuwa | ŋgu tsula | ku famba |
| Kaffir-corn | dimbele | mafake | mafake | mavele |
| loin-cloth | dzigama | mveno | mbene | ŋguvo |

| English. | Secret language. | Leŋge. | Tfopi. | Ɀaŋgana. |
|---|---|---|---|---|
| domestic beasts | ɀifuyo | dʒipoŋgo | dʒipoŋgo | ɀifuyo |
| lake | gova | gova | gova | ntfombe |
| calabash | gi-bembe | gi-guve | fi-gove | fikutso |
| hand-basket | gi-pakatso | gi-raŋgwana | fi-raŋgwana | findzavana |

The otherwise obsolete words *haku* and *maku* for 'your father' and 'your mother' are also used.

The prefix *gi* is interchangeable with *ki*, among the Leŋge.

It would appear that the rites vary a little in different districts, and on different occasions. This is not to be wondered at, considering the mixed nature of the population. Variations in the rites will be seen in the following descriptions:

*The Initiation of P.*

An elderly woman of the Muyaŋga sib, gave me this account of her initiation which must have taken place about thirty years ago.

P. and her companions who were to be initiated sat on the ground surrounded by a large circle of women. The *nyambutsi* produced the *nyafirukurukwe*. This mysterious object was described by P. as the head of a dead man, cut off at the neck, and evidently mummified by continuous applications of oil and red ochre. This skull, according to P., was impaled on an arm-bone of the same man—also very much oiled and ochred—and rested in a carved wooden vessel resembling a small wooden mortar. A triangular piece of goat-skin to serve as a drum-membrane was skewered to the top of the skull of which a piece seemed to have been cut off. A drum-stick or *khoŋgo* consisted of a similar arm-bone of the same man. I suggested to P. that she might be mistaken, and that the *nyafirukurukwe* was probably the little sacred drum (*ŋkiriŋgwane*) which is in use at the rites at the present time. But P. said that she was perfectly certain it was a man's head; and when I still pretended to doubt it, telling her that it all happened so long ago, and that being a young and frightened girl she might easily be mistaken, she became more emphatically certain than ever, and so I left the matter, and she went on with her story.

The *nyambutsi* took the *nyafirukurukwe* and placed it on the head of the initiation candidate, and then at her knees, as she sat on the ground. The candidate herself then had to lift the 'skull' to her head. The conductress made passes with her fingers over the face of the novice, starting with a line drawn from the top of the head to the chin underneath, and then across from one cheek to another under the eyes.

Then the drum stick was placed in P.'s hand, and she was told to tap very gently but very decidedly upon the membrane, saying:

> (Tap! Tap!) 'If I tell even my husband,
> May I be bitten by a snake (Tap!)
> May I be stung by wasps (Tap!)
> My name is so-and-so (Tap!)'

Here she gave the new name she had chosen. Then she was told that she must cry; that she must imagine that her father and mother were dead, and anything else that would cause her to weep. The *nyambutsi* made passes over her face, saying anxiously 'Oh! cry! my child!' (i.e. to bring forth tears). This is one of the great tests of the initiation *ambutsa* rites, as to whether or not the novice can shed tears. Sometimes snuff is passed under the eyes of the hapless maiden who is tearless, to produce the desired effect. It is a very great disgrace if the initiate cannot produce a tear. She is scratched and slapped, and dragged away finally by an angry and disappointed mother, to be brought again another day, after more sacrifices to the ancestral spirits, to see if she can 'stand the test'.

P. apparently did manage to squeeze out a few tears, and the *nyabutsi* wiped them away with her thumb, passing it from the eye down the cheek, away from the sides of the nose.

The *nyaſirukurukwe* was passed to each novice in turn, and she had to take the same vow not to reveal anything about the rites afterwards.

The candidates were then told to imitate the *nyambutsi* and remove their clothing. She then showed them how to perform a small operation which P. called 'piercing' or 'puncturing' (*kuboſa*). I was informed by another woman that the horn was used for this purpose if the candidate failed to perform the operation with her fingers, and that the *nyambutsi* 'will dance with the horn'[1] if the candidate is in disgrace by failing.

After this, the initiates had to sit in perfect silence, with head bent,

---

[1] Sr̃. Don A. A. Pereira Cabral, in his work *Raças, Usos e Costumes dos Indígenas da Provincia de Moçambique* mentions the fact that the conductress dances 'with a piece of wood' (evidently for the same purpose). Sr̃. Pereira Cabral also states that after this dance the initiate has to submit to the operation of the distension of the labia, known to ethnographers as the Hottentot apron (*op. cit.*, p. 43). I have not known of this custom among modern Leŋge, who make pubic scars, but M. Junod mentions it as occurring sometimes among the Roŋga.

Sr̃. Pereira Cabral does not refer to any specific tribe. The MaKua and the BaToŋga also have initiation rites for women. The *nkiriŋgwane* drum mentioned in the description of the rites has the same name in KiKua (language of the MaKua).

PUBERTY. INITIATION

and their hands spread out over their knees, their limbs in a stiff and rigid attitude. If any food were given them afterwards they must take it in the palms of the hands, raising the palms to the mouth without bending a limb. If it were necessary to speak, it had to be done in a faint and die-away sort of voice. (My informant, being an admirable mimic, was able to reproduce exactly the voice and gestures which she and others had used at the ceremonies.) The carved wooden images of a man and woman were then brought out, the *nyambutsi* saying: '*mi na mona*[1] *ʃigweni mayika waŋgu*' ('You will see in my basket my *mayika*' —name given to the images). The *nyambutsi* was tossing up her money keli children playing a game called *maŋgadi* (*kubayela maŋgadi*).[2] (Cf. Games, p. 92).

The novice P. being then in a state of *khombo* had to spend two days in this depressed state when she had returned home, being dead to the world as it were. On the third night came the man who was to take away the *khombo*. He had to light a (ceremonial) fire in the hut. She had to lay aside her old clothing, contaminated by the rites. In the dead of night her mother slipped into the hut, and took away the old clothes (*masetsa*). It was the boy's duty to provide new clothes for his fiancée. He had also on arrival presented a pig to the girl's people. In the early morning P. had to wash her fiancé ceremonially. After two days he went away, and she did not see him again till after the *tʃuruvula* dance. During the interval she wore her red-ochred garments and beads, and was considered a *kundʒwa* or débutante.

P. informed me, after this description of what had happened to her at the initiation rites, that there was something inside the *nyaʃirukurukwane*, which was the heart of the victim. She was either told this or supposed it to be so. There were also some other things, but her description of these was so vague and confused that I failed to understand it. She mentioned definitely the wooden pegs, and some little carved objects.

My own idea about the symbols is that a drum and carved objects have in modern times replaced what in olden days may really have been a skull and parts of the victim's body. But I may be mistaken about this.

[1] This looks like a Sechuana word.
[2] I was very much interested to read in Smith and Dale's book, *The Ila-speaking Peoples of Northern Rhodesia*, of the game which the initiate plays in the *mulao* with broken pieces of pottery, only in the case of the *nyambutsi*, she uses her coins instead of the potsherds.

P. told me that the victim was slain by the *nyambutsi* herself, and that there was one victim in every *nyambutsi's* family. But, from what she said, I gained the impression that the same head, in a mummified condition, might be handed down from mother to daughter for generations, and that it was kept carefully in a large basket with the *mayika*.

If what P. told me was true, the skull was probably the relic of a human sacrifice to promote fertility. I asked her also to tell me about the *ŋkiriŋgwane* drum, and she said it was the same as the *nyaſiru-kurukwe*, but she declared: 'It is not a drum, but the head of a man'. P. also said there was a little drum to the accompaniment of which the candidates danced after initiation. This was probably the *ntakula*.

P. remembered these words of the secret language which she was taught to use during the rites and the period of her seclusion:

| English. | Secret language. | Tſopi. | Thoŋga. (Ɀaŋgana) |
|---|---|---|---|
| to eat | gu ndaula | ŋgu dya | ku gya |
| to sleep | gu falala or pfuma | ŋgu ruama or eteya | ku etlela |
| mortar | tiŋgadi | ditudi | tſuri |
| hand-basket | ſipakato | ravi | ndzava |
| winnowing basket | livata | giselo | fiłelo |
| pestle | ndoŋga | mupsi | musi |
| fire | mudzika | ndiyo | ndzilo |
| hut | ſikotamu (lintel) | yindlu | nyumba |
| children | timvelekwana | vanana | vana |
| water | dziselo | mati | mati |
| in the fields | tsuraruni | matembweni | masiŋwini |

## The Initiation of M.

The following was the account given me by M., who is possibly ten to fifteen years younger than P., and therefore her initiation took place at a much later period. It was a private one. M. was lobolaed to a man in Johannesburg, and, on his return, she was taken to be initiated before the actual marriage took place. M. said that her mother and elder sister accompanied her. They told her that she was going *kurwala ſitsandza*, and that when she was told *kurwala*, she must weep. She said she did not want to go, and they said it was not proper that she should refuse. They started at about the time of *mpindeliso* (2. to 2.30 p.m.) and arrived at about 5.30 at Maviyeni. Nyamphekani, the *nyambutsi*, came to meet them without greeting. She conducted them in silence to the bush near her house, where there was a big fire which had been lighted by the women relatives of the *nyambutsi* who were present, together with some women relations of M.'s promised husband and her own mother and sister. These women sitting in a circle round the fire began to chant:

*Utaſiwona haweſe ſikuŋgumari*[1]
Thou shalt thyself the mystery see.

Then the old woman went into the hut and brought out a basket in which was the *ſitande* (Tʃopi for *ſitsanda*) and placed it in front of the candidate. M. thought the object was a stone, but she was (and is) very nervous, and was far too frightened to take notice of details. She noticed, however, that when it was placed in front of her it was covered over with a very white cloth, but this was taken off. The old woman then beat the stone (or whatever it was) with a stick, saying: '*Gho! rwala!*' (Imperative.) And all the others continued singing: 'Thou shalt thyself the mystery see', clapping their hands. The old woman repeated beating the object again: '*Gho! rwala!*' The candidate sat on the ground and was slow in obeying the order. She did not begin to cry till the *nyambutsi* had repeated the command several times, the others exhorting her: 'You must shed tears'. The singing was weak while the candidate delayed 'to shed tears', but when they began to flow, then the singing became loud and joyful. The old woman said: 'Screw up your courage, my child' (lit. harden yourself.) Then the circle began to dance one by one, accompanied by clapping of hands. The initiate also had to take off her clothes and dance. The old woman had beaten the drum (or whatever it was) ten times, then she beat again twice, saying that one stroke was for the red ochre (*tsumane*) and one for the oil with which it was mixed. She then squeezed *kanzi* medicine (to help a woman to conceive) on her mouth, and then anointed her with oil and red ochre. The initiate's mother finished the process at home. When the *nyambutsi* had finished anointing M., she said: 'What is your name?' M. replied: 'I am *Ŋgumaŋgatate*' (i.e. in father's power). She informed me that she did not want to be taken by her husband, but her new name showed that she was going to resign herself to her father's will about the marriage.

I asked her if she could remember what the 'stone' was like which served as a drum, and she pointed to a Miller lamp which was on the table by me and said the shape was something like that, i.e. with a bowl

---

[1] Mystery (*ſikuŋgumari*). This word is only used in this connexion.

and a stem. So in that case it may have been the small mortar described by P., and the 'stone' may possibly have been the skull.[1]

After having given the name, all the women made that shrill noise known as *kuluŋgela* (trilling); then M. and her mother returned home in the morning. She had only one day of silence afterwards, and she remained four months without going to the *tfuruvula* dance.

*Initiation Dances*

On July 11th, 1928, a party of young girls were dancing in the early morning at the kraal of the *ŋganakana* or petty chief of *Σidandani*. They were young initiation candidates. The dances over, they went out into the fields to gather *ŋkaka*, *Momordica clematidea*. Their hair was dressed with red ochre, and they wore little loin-cloths. When M. and I reached the chief's kraal we were shown a hut which had been given the candidates to sleep in. We arrived too late to see the dances, but we saw the children in the fields gathering *ŋkaka*.

On another hut in the kraal there were strange designs, some of which had reference to the women's initiation rites. The front wall of the hut was covered with a black wash (made from the charred roots and stems of ground-nut plants). This black wash was covered with white spots. 'Those are meant to be the spots of the leopard', said M. On this spotted background was a design in white representing the *fivenyula* skirts of initiation candidates, and below that a kind of swastika, and above all a bird with a long neck. To the right of the swastika was another *fivenyula* in red, and a red bird.

Every now and again as we passed along the roads we would see a fully fledged débutante or initiation candidate, her hair and body flame-red with ochre. Sometimes we saw one, and sometimes two, of these women with other groups of women on the road. July may be described as the 'height of the season' for these débutantes. M. was always excited when she caught sight of them. 'Oh! look! there are *tikundʒwa*', said she.

We arrived at Bukeni (Zandamela) late in the afternoon of July 13th. After the evening meal we heard a tinkling sound in the bush about a mile away. There was singing accompanied by clapping of hands and drumming. I asked what was going on, and was told that it was a *matiŋgari* or *fimbutabutana* (little *ambutsa*), a practice of women's initiation rites in the bush. The night was dark. I announced my

[1] Cf. also the objects of the *mbusi* described by the Rev. P. Éd. Labrecque in 'Le Mariage chez les BaBemba', *Africa*, iv, 1931, pp. 209–21.

PLATE XVII

DESIGNS ON WALLS OF HUTS

intention of going to see the dances. M. said it was only a children's practice, being evidently disinclined to go. We were both tired, and I was tempted not to go. To go wandering about the bush on a dark night in a place which I had only seen that day for the first time did not seem very attractive. However, we braced ourselves and set out, accompanied by a boy with a storm-lantern. We were told that no men or boys were allowed to see the dances or go anywhere near, so we left our boy in a kraal about a hundred yards away from the place whence the sounds proceeded. Fortunately we met a woman just coming away from the dances, and we asked her to show us the way there. We stumbled over some rough ground in the darkness, and at last came to the clearing in the bush where the women were gathered together. They were astonished to see a white woman, as well they might be, for they keep these performances strictly secret. M. explained politely that I had heard about the dances and would like to see them. After a little murmuring and a little debating, they agreed to our staying, and some of them glanced at me with real interest.

This is what we saw: Around a fire of crackling logs and branches, the fuel of which was being constantly renewed by one of the party, there was a circle of thirty women or so. There were some elderly women with red-ochred hair, some young married women with babies, some big girls, and twelve or thirteen girl initiation candidates, I should think about thirteen or fourteen years old. Their hair was dressed with red ochre, and they had little loin-cloths of dark blue print. The circle was arranged thus:

|  |  |
|---|---|
| Little girls (Initiation candidates) | Women drummers |
|  | Young women and girls. |
| Young women. | Elderly women. |

The little girls clapped their hands continually to accompany the dancing. They watched the dancers in order to be able to dance themselves later. They all called out '*Woh!*' with an especially loud clap, when a dance was finished. The first dancer was evidently a conductress. She was tall and graceful, and her movements were slow. She stepped out into the circle, with a drum-stick as a baton. An old paraffin-tin was being used as a drum, as they lacked one. Occasionally the dancer admonished the little ones by lightly touching them with her baton, like a school-dominie, and saying: '*Woh!*' They all chimed in: '*Woh!*' While she was dancing she sang a little song, spreading out her hands like the Arabian dancer in 'Kismet'. In the midst of the song she would pause for two or three bars in each verse, and then end up with a haunting little refrain in five notes. The slow motion of her limbs and hands was very graceful. 'Come! Youths! all of you, and see sloth', sang she.

The second dancer was a mourner. She had the white band of mourning tied round her head.

'My husband who loved me
Semende who loved me
Now he has left me
He has died of phthisis.'

The third was also a graceful dancer. She imitated the movements of a dove and sang:

*Gho! Gho! Gho! Gho! Gho! Gho! Tuva!*
*Gho! Gho! Tuva!*

(The 'Gho!' was supposed to represent the cooing of the dove. A dove is evidently an initiation candidate.)

*Whee!* (She fell down)
*Woh!* (She rose)

This was to imitate a dove when it comes to the ground. The children meanwhile clapped hands and sang:

(Chorus) *Whee!*
(Chorus) *Woh!*

and followed her in the dove song.[1] The fourth dancer sang in the Gi-Toŋga language of Inhambane. The fifth dancer did not dance well, and was called off the arena.

Then as it was getting late we came away. It is difficult to describe the impression that this scene would give to an onlooker. It was like an act in a children's pantomime, or a mimic comic opera, the musical accompaniment being the songs and the hand clapping, and the very much emphasized *Whee*'s and *Woh*'s. The leader moved her baton up and down like a conductor at a concert, occasionally touching the ground with it, or the knees of one of the children.

---

[1] A man in olden days, when his wife was dead, remained in his hut and played a kind of instrument resembling a Shangaan harp, called *quqa*, singing at the same time the 'dove' song. 'It is the song of the dove', *iŋwamandere wagugu*. Just as a dove flies about collecting all the food it wants, so did his wife collect food for him. The Ndau have also a pretty 'dove' song.

## PUBERTY. INITIATION

The dances did not strike one as being vulgarly done. I came to the conclusion that this was because they were not performed for amusement, but as a very serious part of the training of the young girls; and the training had to be carried out in an eurhythmical way to make it attractive; hence the expression of it in the dances, which evidently take the place of Swedish exercises practised by more civilized races. The distinguishing characteristic movement of all the *ambutsa* dances, is the bewilderingly rapid movement of the breasts and ribs, which is evidently intended to strengthen the chest.

When the elder girls had finished dancing, the little ones would try. All the dancers wore waist-cloths, and most were as fully dressed as usual.

On the morning of July 14th we attended the *timbila* (marimba) dances at the kraal of Małatini (chief of Zandamela). Just before the dances began we heard the *ambutsa* drums in a neighbouring kraal. Some of the candidates came on afterwards to watch the men dancers at the chief's kraal.

On the afternoon of July 15th, we came about four o'clock into the kraal of another well-known Tſopi chief. The sound of a desultory drumming could be heard. We had tea with the chief, and discovered that the drumming proceeded from a kraal where the *ambutsa* rites were being carried on. M., the Tſopi woman who accompanied me, and I set out down the hill towards the kraal. We heard a chorus of about a hundred voices, saying: '*Heh! Heh! Heh! Heh!*' continuously, as if urging some one to perform some act. When we reached the kraal we found a very large crowd of women watching some initiation candidates whose bodies were ablaze with red ochre, under a big tree. At first, no one seemed to pay any attention to our arrival; and then suddenly an old woman caught sight of us, and begged us to come away. Of course we did as she requested at once. She accompanied us, saying that she would explain presently. When she learnt who we were, she calmed down, and asked for a small present of money. I gave her a shilling, with which she seemed satisfied, and was quite interested to hear that I knew quite well the mistress of the rites in another district. I was told afterwards that it is believed that death will befall any one who sees part of the ceremonies without going through the rites or taking an active part in them. I had time to notice that there was a drum in the circle, and that the red-ochred candidates were sitting on the ground, while one or two women in ordinary clothes were beginning to dance. One of them, when she caught sight of me, began the special *ambutsa* dance. She may have thought that as I was a stranger, I should guess what the rites were if I saw that. M. and I returned to the chief's house, and the old women went back to their archaic rites. The chief's brother said the old woman should have permitted us to see the rites.

One of our Christian women in the vicinity gave us hospitality for the night, and nearly all night long we heard the sound of the *ambutsa* drums in one direction; and in another, the *mandiki* drums of the Ndau spirits, at some spiritualistic seance.

Women have to observe certain rules in connexion with the boys' initiation rites. If a woman carries food to her husband or son at the boys' initiation school, she has to cry aloud '*makati*' ( = females), as she deposits the food, and return without being seen. If a boy is at the *yitinyapapyato* (initiation school), and his mother happens to be heating the food which she is going to take to him, she must not walk over, or pass over, one of the logs which feed the fire, for fear lest her boy should die at the school. If the woman is seen and caught when she brings the food, she runs the risk of a death penalty.

# XII

# MARRIAGE, RELATION BETWEEN THE SEXES

## Marriage

### The Media of Akulobola

TƩOPI bark cloth was used of old in Gazaland as a medium of *akulobola*. Sacks of mealies were also used, the sacks being made of the same bark cloth. Then white beads called *tſifula* came into vogue. These may have been brought into the country by Arab traders or early Portuguese settlers. These beads were worn in the initiation ceremonies. The beads would be exchanged for goats, which were used for *akulobola*. Sheep seem to have been in the country from very early times, and were sometimes used. Bees-wax,[1] and the tails of wildebeest were bartered for goats. After goats, or perhaps before them, hoes came into fashion, and then bright blue beads of Dutch origin, now worn round medicine-men's ankles as ornaments. Then pieces of print were requisitioned; and lastly oxen, in conjunction with metal rings, *tibhetu*, *titlatla*, and *masindza*. When used for *akulobola*, the *masindza* were tied up in a bundle, and the father of the girl sought in marriage would use them to lobola another wife for himself or for one of his sons.

Thirty goats, thirty pieces of cloth, thirty hoes was the usual price paid, or £20–30 at the present day. The heads of cattle seem to have varied in number. Metal rings seem to have been introduced by people of Zulu origin. The Ŋgoni had a ritual dance in marriage ceremonies in which the mother of the bridegroom held aloft a metal ring called *libhetu* (pl. *tibhetu*), and bemoaned the loss of the cattle which her son had paid for *akulobola*. These *tibhetu* rings were thus used in conjunction with cattle only—at first, at any rate. The Ŋgoni also used large metal rings called *titlatla*. Enterprising store-keepers soon produced trade-copies of these old solid brass rings, but one can distinguish at a glance those made for trade in iron, partly by the smoothness of the surface, and occasionally by a trade-mark. The original rings show signs of the native anvil, and are very heavy. The mother of the bride, if the latter were of Ŋgoni or Ndau origin, used to wear a little spoon

[1] Bees-wax was made by the natives. A large mass of the honeycomb was taken, the honey pressed out, and the wax melted, and then the lump was buried in the earth till the next day.

made of a monkey's bone in her hair, at the time of the *akulobola* negotiations. This was supposed to 'sanctify' the match, as monkeys' bones were sacred to the Ŋgoni and to the Ndau of the *Va ka Simaŋgu* sib.

A Leŋge woman once illustrated for me the dance of a Ŋgoni bridegroom. Taking the big ring in his hand, he danced up to the bride, saying: '*Hifamba livaleni, hifamba livaleni*' (i.e. 'We go to the pasture-land, we go to the pasture-land'—evidently referring to the cattle). He placed the ring at her feet, and a coin in the midst of the ring. All media of *akulobola*, such as rings, &c., were returned to the owners in case of dissolution of marriage or the breaking-off of marriage negotiations.

The number of pounds paid for lobolo[1] are often marked as notches on the trunk of a tree, or on a stick. As in olden days messages were sometimes sent by sticks, so a stick could be sent to a distance, notifying the number of pounds paid for lobolo, by the number of cuts on the stick.

### Charm for procuring a Husband or a Wife

If a girl wants a husband, and fears she will not find one, she goes first to the *anyaŋga* of the divining-bones, who advises her to go to a *nyamusoro*[2] (either man or woman). The *nyamusoro*, after a preliminary sacrifice to his (or her) ancestral spirits, orders the girl to procure a black cock. She puts the cock round her neck, clasping it by the wings in front, and under her arms by the legs. The *nyamusoro* kills the cock by cutting its neck while it is still on the girl's neck, and the blood flows freely. The dripping blood is mixed by the *nyamusoro* with medicine and oil of *Trichilia emetica*. The girl rubs herself with the mixture all over. While she does this, the fowl is cooked and eaten by the *nyamusoro* and the girl's friends, but she herself must not eat any. It is prohibited. She will never get a husband if she breaks this rule. Then she must pick up all the particles which have fallen after the rubbing, and hide them in the bush. Other people must not see those particles. She will not get a husband if they do.

The same love-charm is used by a boy who wants a wife, but in his case a hen is sought for instead of a black cock.

### Akulobola, a Leŋge Woman's Account

The following account was given me by a Leŋge woman:

When he begins to lobola he begins by catching (finding). He asks her father

---

[1] *Lobolo* is the actual sum paid in *akulobola*.   [2] See p. 199.

saying, 'You, father of the girl, I want her.' And then, if there are many girls, their father will call them, telling them: 'He wants you, that man, he wants to take you.' Then the girls say: 'We do not know who it is he is wanting to take.' He, their father, says to the man: 'O! they say this, you must choose for yourself, her whom you want. He says: 'O! I want that big girl.' The father says: 'O! all right! if she will want you, if she will love you.' He will call the girl, he will ask her, 'Do you want him?' She says: 'I want him.' The father says, 'Take your stick, and put it in the hut.'

The would-be bridegroom has arrived carrying a stick. The father asks the girl if she has placed the stick in the hut. She replies that she has sent her younger sister to do so. The father announces his intention of going into the girls' hut to question the young man. The first question, of course, is, how much money can the young man pay for *akulobola*. If the sum named is agreed upon, the father says: 'Very well, they will take a mat, and spread it for you.' The bridegroom spends the night there and sleeps with the girl he has chosen. She must not become pregnant. In the morning the girl goes to the lake to fetch water to wash the bridegroom ceremonially. He agrees to this if she loves him; if not, she is not allowed to wash him. Also if the girl does not spend the night with the young man, the ceremonial ablutions are not performed. Then the girl goes to the lake to wash herself. This also is a ceremonial act. Then the man tells the father he is going home. The father asks what day he will return, and he replies that he will come back in four days' time. The mother of the girl begins to brew beer. This keeps her busy till the youth comes back on the third day. The bridegroom arrives with his best man (*figela*), a boy who carries his mat. 'I have come', says the youth, 'and my father will arrive to-morrow with the pounds.' This is a signal for the beer to be strained. It is put in pots and covered over. That night the bridegroom spends with the girl again, and the washing rite takes place in the morning. The bridegroom's father and his friends arrive in the evening, and they show them a hut for their habitation.

The next day but one the *akulobola* is begun. The father of the girl has not yet seen the pounds. It is rarely that the whole sum, £25 or £30 is paid at once. Generally, the bridegroom's father produces a sum to start with, say £10 or £12. If the girl's father is not satisfied with the sum paid down, negotiations are broken off, and the party goes home again.

If the pounds are many they will catch a hen and give it to the father of the bridegroom saying: 'Take your wife.' They will give him his food and his beer.

They take another pound, they buy wine; they take another, they buy a goat or a pig, saying: 'We give you (the father of the bridegroom) your food.' They cook the pig, they put a fore-quarter in the hut of the mother of the girl, they place it there. It is her limb. *Mamane* will eat it when they have gone to their home. The father of the girl will seek three other girls; the bridegroom and the bride and the other three will go home in the afternoon. When they want to go, they will call the girl, and her mother and grandmother and aunt will tell her "You must work well and nicely. You must go to the lake in the morning, return, take out the ashes from the hut of the mother of the bridegroom; you will learn to give water to the father of the bridegroom and his mother; you will learn to pluck out the superfluous hairs of the bridegroom; you will learn to pluck his eyelashes; you will learn to shave his hair; you will learn to take water and procure sand, and smear there in the kraal of the mother of the bridegroom. You will learn to draw water, and give it to the grandparent of the bridegroom and his brother, they will wash with it. When you have done this, you will learn to cook *vuputso* (light beer).'

*A Bridesmaid's Story*

The bridegroom and bride, accompanied by the 'best man' and the bridesmaids, then go to the bridegroom's home.

The following account was given me by a Leŋge girl of a wedding at which she was a bridesmaid.

She and three other bridesmaids (*sigela*) accompanied the bride to the bridegroom's home. On arrival the girls sat outside the hut which had been prepared for them, and when invited to enter, refused to do so. (This is etiquette.) The invitations to enter were pressing, but were only accepted after the bridesmaids had been bribed to do so, with a Portuguese coin worth about sixpence or a shilling, or a headkerchief or a piece of print. When they entered the hut, mats were spread for them, but they refused to sit down until another small gift of money was produced 'to buy them'. Then food was brought; at first they refused to eat it; but on the presentation of other small gifts they made a hearty meal.

For the rest of that day and the whole of the next day the bridal party remained in seclusion in the hut allotted to them. If the bridesmaids wished to leave the kraal they had to crawl on their knees to the entrance, though they could stand upright when they reached the bush outside. If they fetched wood to put on the fire they had to put it down very gently, and not throw it down as usual. If they stamped ground-nuts in a mortar they had to stand very upright, and not bend their necks, as they usually do. The next morning very early they got up and swept the kraal. Then they fetched water and sand and smeared all the huts in the kraal. After that they poured water into all the washing-pots of the bridegroom's relations. Into each pot they put a small coin equal to about 6*d*., so that when the owners of the basins came to wash themselves, they saw a small silver coin glittering at the bottom of the pot. But this gift must afterwards be returned, for after the ablutions had been performed, the recipients would in their turn put small coins into the pots of the bride and her maids, who would look purposely and find them there.

Another informant tells me that the bride and bridegroom sleep together in the bridal hut; and the best man and the bridesmaids also sleep in the same hut, during the first visit of the bride to her new home; the best man on one side of the hut and the bridesmaids on another.

*A Young Bride's Duties*

A young bride is subject to much criticism and testing at first. Some mothers-in-law will lay traps by putting a monkey-nut or two on the ground in different places in the hut, and then when the daughter-in-law has swept the floor, will count the nuts to see that not one is missing.

The young bride's duties are roughly as follows: she will begin the day by sweeping out the ashes from the sleeping-hut, and afterwards from the cooking-hut. Then she goes to the lake and washes herself and draws water. Returning, she pours some water into a clay bowl, and offers it to her mother-in-law, kneeling in front of her. Next she proceeds to make her husband's toilet, if he is at home. She procures a razor (*likari*), kneels in front of her husband, and shaves him. Then she washes him and rubs him with oil from her cosmetic gourd. This done, she prepares her husband's light beer (*vuputso*). Sometimes she will make her husband's toilet at cock-crow, and then go to the lake afterwards. Her home duties done for the time being, she goes to the fields to dig or sow, or cut down wood, or to seek for green vegetables. She returns about midday and rests a little and takes some food. In the early afternoon she may go again to the lake for water, returning in time to begin the many preparations for cooking the evening meal.

*The Bride revisits her old Home*

After a few days at her new home, the bride says to the bridegroom: 'I want to go home.' He replies: 'Very well, I will buy some garments.' He has four pieces of print (which he has probably bought beforehand). He gives one piece to his wife, and one each to the three maidens who accompany her. Then he procures a goat, and kills it for them—the bridesmaids and his wife. They have a feast before starting to go back, but will reserve the head and a fore-quarter and the skin of the animal to carry home with them. This first visit of the bride to her old home is very important. Very frequent references are made to it in the folklore, as will be seen. Just before they start, the new wife eats the liver of the goat by herself. The bridegroom goes to his father saying: 'I want to accompany Mevasi (or whatever his wife's name may be) to her home. Can you let me have one pound?' The father produces the money. The bridegroom ties up the head and fore-shoulder of the goat in the skin, and the party starts off.

On arrival at the bride's old home, they take the skin, the head, and the fore-quarter of the goat, and place them in the hut of the bride's father, but the bridegroom remains just inside the kraal by the entrance. The bride's father sends a little girl to take the bridegroom's stick and place it in the hut allotted to him. The father and the little girl then come to greet the bridegroom, and after that, the father retires to his own hut, and has no further intercourse with his son-in-law that day. This rule of silence is broken the next day, when the bride's father will talk to the bridegroom. Then the three bridesmaids will go to their own homes.

Very early in the morning the bride's mother will give her some water to wash her husband. Then the bride goes herself to the lake to wash. The father of the girl will go to the bridegroom and say: 'you must inform me of the health of your people at home.'

He tells him: 'We are well at home.' Then when he has finished, the bridegroom takes the pound, he gives it to the father of the girl, saying: 'With this pound I accompany your child to you,' because when he, the bridegroom, stabbed the goat there at his home, he was thinking that, 'This goat which I am killing to give to the girls is a return for that which they killed for me when I lobola-ed with pounds, because if I do not kill this, they will subtract the cost of the other if the girl refuses to be taken by me.' Then he goes home with his wife, and remains there. The pounds they will bury in the ground there in the hut.

*The Rite of the Goat and the Log*

This goat is called the *lisiva*. One informant told me that the pound accompanies the *lisiva* goat, in order 'to stop up the gap made by the death wounds of the goat'. *Kusiva* = to fill the place of, or stop up a gap. The same word is used for a 'feather', but my informants did not see any connexion at all between the *lisiva* goat and a feather. The

Leŋge girl who gave me the description of the time which she spent at the bridegroom's home as a bridesmaid, said that the *lisiva* goat was killed on the day in which the coins were found in the pots, and that on the succeeding day the bride returned to her own home, accompanied by the bridegroom carrying parts of the *lisiva* goat. They remained two days at the bride's home and then returned to the bridegroom's home, after fixing a day for the *mabuyisatʃani* rite. After two days, the bride, her mother, and women relations and bridesmaids cut faggots of wood and returned with them to the bridegroom's home. They piled the faggots up, cutting living wood, and made a *tʃiŋgu* or wood-pile just inside the entrance to the kraal. They took a log cut from a living tree, and anointed it with oil and red ochre, which they had brought from the bride's home. This log was called *mabuyisatʃani*. It was a sign that the lobolo had been paid and the marriage consummated. After the anointing of the log, some old women danced, and made the accompaniment by trilling. The bride's mother also anointed the bridegroom's mother with oil and red ochre.

After the anointing of the *mabuyisatʃani* log, it is usual for the bridegroom's father to suggest to his son that a gift of a pig to the bride's mother would be acceptable on her part. She accepts it as a ceremonial gift, and will cut it carefully by the ribs twice, saying: 'It is the *titʃo* (kidneys) of my son-in-law.' 'This is a sign that the bride's body belongs to her husband', said my informant. The bride's mother then cuts a fore-quarter and gives it to her daughter.

About a couple of months after the anointing of the log, the bride's relations send a message to the effect that the wood must be dry. They arrive bringing pots of beer with them, and the log is burnt, amid general rejoicings, by old people of the status of grandparents, the parents themselves not being permitted to burn it.

*Problems of Akulobola*

Some little time after the bride has been settled in her new home, the parents invite her and her husband to come on a little visit to them. This was related to me as follows:

> After this they will call the bridegroom and the girl saying: 'Tell us, perhaps our girl looks after your work well?' He says: 'She is a good girl, she does our work nicely', because she respects her husband indeed. After that, the father calls the girl (after three months) saying: 'Shall I eat (spend) the pounds? I want to spend the pounds. Are you all right there?'

By this means the father assures himself that he will not have to return the *akulobola* money, as his daughter is happy in her married life. The father uses the money to procure a wife for his son, unless there is something urgent for which the money is needed. If the bride comes to her old home one day and says she is unhappy, she must return to her husband's home for a week, and after that they call her back to her father's home. This is managed somewhat in this way:

She goes to her husband and says, deceiving him: 'There is a sacrifice to be offered at home.' He replies: 'In that case I ought to go with you.' She says: Oh! no! I will go first and see what is happening, and then I will send a messenger to fetch you.' He asks: 'When will you be back?' She replies: 'Oh! I shall only stay a day or two.' She goes, but does not come back. He waits for about a month, and then gets impatient, and goes to see what is happening. On arrival he says to the father of the girl: 'I want my wife.' The father replies: 'You must not take away my girl any more. She is not happy with you.' The husband exclaims: 'Why did you not tell me this? She deceived me saying that there was a sacrifice to be offered at home.' The father replies: 'You go home and bring your father back with you.' The husband hastens to go back, because he sees there is something very wrong. He tells his father: 'My wife deceived me. There was no sacrifice. I want you to return with me.' They go. When they arrive, the father of the girl returns the *akulobola* money. The husband is angry. He says: 'I don't want the money, I want my wife. If she will not come with me, you can keep the money and the girl, too.'

He does not really mean this, for he would do everything possible to get the money back in the event of his wife not returning to him.

The father remarks to his daughter: 'This will be a pretty serious business for me if you do not go back. I shall get into trouble with the Chief, and be heavily fined.' So the girl has to return to her husband after all.

If, on the other hand, the bridegroom does not like his wife, he tells her bluntly that he does not want her, and that she must go home to her father. When she reaches home she tells her father that her husband does not want her, and has driven her away. The father asks: 'What did you do to upset him?' She replies: 'I did not do anything. He will tell you.' When the husband 'sees time' (i.e. in his own good time) he will come to see his father-in-law. The father of the girl calls a little girl as before: 'Go and take his stick, and put it in the hut.' The child shyly approaches and asks for the stick. The man says: 'I have no time. I will hold my stick myself.' The little girl will go to her father saying, 'He does not wish it.' The father says: 'If he refuses to give you his stick, ask him to come to me.' The husband saunters up to the father, who says:

'Tell me about your affairs at home. Are all well?' The man replies: 'They

are all well. But I am pressed for time. I want you to give me my money.'
The father asks: 'What has my child done to you?' The man says: 'I do not understand what you are saying, I want you to give me my money to-day.'

*Father*: I haven't the money now. I have eaten it. You said you wanted my daughter, and so I ate the money.

*Husband*: You must give me my money to-day.

*Father*: Really, I haven't it.

*Husband*: I must have my money to-day, or I shall punish you.

*Father*: If you punish me, it does not matter, because it is you who wish to leave my daughter.

*Husband*: Your daughter must be taken by someone else, and you must return the money to me.

During this time the all-important stick has been retained by the husband. He takes it up and goes away, muttering threats. In about three weeks' time he returns.

*Husband*: Haven't you got my money yet?

*Father*: I have not yet got it.

*Husband*: I shall tell the police-boys of the chief to-morrow.

The next day the police arrive, and tell the father he must go with the girl and her mother to the chief's kraal *laha muteki aŋga maŋgala kona* (where the bridegroom had brought a lawsuit).

On arrival the husband accuses the father-in-law of having 'eaten his money'. The father defends himself:

'I have not eaten his pounds. He took my daughter by *akulobola*, and now he says he does not want her, and drives her away.' The chief asks: 'Have you driven the girl away?'

Then follows a long parley, the upshot of which is, that the chief decides that the girl is to return to her own home, but when she is again taken in *akulobola*, the father must return to the first husband the money paid by the second suitor to lobola the girl.

*Sacrifice made by Bride's Father*

The following is a short account of the sacrifice performed by the father of the girl when the bridegroom takes the bride to his home for the first time, i.e. when the *akulobola* arrangements have been satisfactorily negotiated.

When the bridegroom wants to go away with the bride, the girl's father performs a sacrifice. First, the mother takes water and washes a *fihiso* (clay-bowl used for mashing) and a *mbita* (pot). She then calls the girl's father, saying: 'I have finished the work which you sent me to do.' The father goes into his hut to fetch a *gombe* (carved wooden goblet). He will search for a fowl's feather and a few mealies. He takes the water which has been left in the bowl and the pot, and pours it into the goblet. He then goes to the *nṭapfu* tree, and makes a small hole under the tree. He puts the mealies in the hole, then he takes the feather and places it among the mealies. Now the goblet is filled with the water in which the scrapings of the bowl and the pot have been soaked. The father drinks a little of this pseudo-beer, then he utters the forceful syllable '*Psu!*' and pours the remains over the mealies. He invokes the ancestral spirits: 'You, father, grandparents and (paternal) aunts, help me by aiding my little girl to go away well.'

If the father is rich, he will offer a fowl instead of a feather, but the fowl must not be killed, unless the spirit of an ancestor is angry, when the fowl is sacrificed in order to appease the spirit. The rinsing water is used in the sacrifice just described instead of the beer which was formerly in the pot, and the mealie-meal which was in the bowl.

*Order of Rites*

There appear to be the following stages in the marriage ceremonies:
1. The visit to select a wife. Preliminary nuptials.
   The role of the stick. Bridegroom returns home.
   Preparation for feast at girl's home.
2. The return of the bridegroom and his friends. The *akulobola*.
   Presents of beer and first *lisiva* goat and *mugwazu* pig to bridegroom's party.
3. Bridegroom's party returns home with the pig. Bridegroom stays for two nights, and then
4. The bride and bridesmaids go to bridegroom's home.
   Given presents. Fetch water and smear huts. Put money in pots.
5. Bride returns home accompanied by the bridegroom.
   The *lisiva* goat. A day is fixed for the log rite.
6. The log rite. Feasting. Ceremonial gift of pig.

It will be seen that on both sides, that of the bride's family and that of the bridegroom's, two animals have a role to fulfil. The father of the girl gives a *lisiva* goat followed by a *mugwazu* pig; and the bridegroom returns a *lisiva* goat and another pig.

When I asked about the *ŋquto* beast which I have heard is used in some tribes as a payment for the virginity of the girl, I was told that 'only the Ŋgoni do that—the people of this country, they do not know that custom'. Also as regards the *ubuluŋga* beast of good luck which a woman takes from her own home to link her up with it, I was told that 'some people take a goat, but there are very few who do it at the present day'. The practice is known as *kuquva* (a word of evident Zulu origin).

*Other Marriage Customs*

If the woman dies soon after marriage, e.g. in childbirth, her sister or brother's daughter used to be taken in her place, but a small additional sum of *akulobola* money was paid, perhaps £5. If the woman dies at her husband's home, i.e. not separated from him, he cannot claim any of the *akulobola* money.

If a father has two children, a boy and a girl, he may perhaps use the *akulobola* money which he receives for his girl to procure another wife for himself, trusting that he may have another daughter in time, whose money he may use to lobola a wife for his son. The first wife of a man is called his *iŋkosikazi*. If one is inquiring after the health of a man's wife, it is more polite to call her *iŋkosikazi* than *nsati* (wife). The second wife is called *ntandakazi* and the third *muloŋgwana*. But if there is no third wife the second wife is called *muloŋgwana*. The second wife serves the first by cutting wood, mudding the hut, and drawing water. If the first wife has her brother's daughter living with her as the third wife of her husband, this niece will rank before the second wife, even when she has been taken later in *akulobola*. A wife whose lobolo money has been paid will rank before one whose *akulobola* has not been paid in full.

A chief will have, in addition to his chief wives, others scattered about in the district over which he rules, and he is responsible for their hut-tax. He sometimes takes two sisters of one family.

'*Ukumbile*' ('You are old') is said by a man who puts away his first wife for that reason.

The penalty for adultery is a sum equal to £5. If a man has seduced one of the wives of the chief, he must pay £10 fine.

People of the same surname (unless only very distantly related) may not marry. First cousins may not marry. First cousins once removed may marry, but they must kill a goat (*kudlaya vuloŋgo*). In polygamy, generally, when a second wife is taken, the first leaves the 'big hut' and lives some little distance away. But if she has a boy-child she will remain in the kraal. These rules are practised by modern Leŋge. Sometimes the husband takes his wife's sister, and sometimes he will take his wife's brother's child. The father of the first wife will use her *akulobola* oxen, or pounds, while her brother will use those of the second wife, also those of his sister, or of his own daughter. But he must take a wife while his father and mother are yet alive.

*A Remedy for Jealousy*

Jealousy is a very common failing among the Leŋge, especially among women who are the wives of a polygamist. A jealous woman will sometimes prepare a medicine called *fikotsolo*, which will 'take the heart out of' her husband, and put him in her power. While he is away diverting himself with another woman, the jealous wife will find a kind of spider called *firwalahunye*, which builds its nest in a twig. She returns home with it and hides it. She finds leaves of *ŋkaka* (*Momordica clematidea*) and cooks them with ground monkey-nuts and the spider. Then when the spider is cooked, she takes it out, grinds it, and mixes it with a little of the other food. It is then put back into the pot, and all the mixture is stirred up together, and served in her husband's food-bowl. She then carefully washes the pot. When her husband comes home, hungry, she gives him this choice dish. She thinks it will put him in her power. He will be afraid to beat her, and will 'fear her exceedingly'. It may be that the omens have revealed the fact that his wife is preparing 'medicine', in which case he will refuse to take it, because warned by the doctor of the omens.

*Christian Marriages*

Christian marriages are now becoming almost universal among the Christians of Gazaland, although many of the heathen still keep up the old rites. In any case, in addition to the blessing of the Church on the marriage, the *akulobola* system is still adhered to, and this seems the safest plan at present.

I heard the following three little songs at a modern wedding:

1. My pretty flower!
I lack pounds to take it!
I will stand by Janetta (i.e. be true to her)
Now I will say good-bye to her, saying
Adieu! I shall return!
We shall see each other.
Come! You will see it! Come!

2. (This is an attempt at English.)
Puwa! Puwa! Puwa!
Little feature-boys
Why don't you sleep?
There is no demon
In dark, is night.

Which being readjusted meant:
>  Poor little fisher-boys,
>  Why don't you sleep?
>  There is no demon in darkest night.

(What the allusion is here, it would be hard to say.)

3.
>  The day has arrived
>  The Chief's day
>  We, the *Va ka Masiye*
>  Do not fear anything.
>  Greetings! Greetings!
>  You of the wedding!
>  We salute you
>  In the name of Abraham (i.e. the school-teacher)
>  And of your teachers
>  Greetings! All of you!
>  Yes! Greetings!
>  Greetings! All of you!
>  In the name of Abraham.

### The Relation between the Sexes

Dr. Malinowski in one of his lectures states that 'parenthood determines marriage, and marriage determines sexual life. Thus, sociologically speaking, good sexual morality is morality which leads to a stable marriage and to an efficient parenthood. Parenthood, including the education of the maturing young, as well as the cares of the immature infant, is therefore an essential condition of the whole process of sex.'

How far the Leŋge code of morals conforms to this principle may perhaps be seen in the following notes on pagan and Christian conduct in this respect.

The old tribal system seems to have consisted in—

1. Early marriages after initiation at puberty, preceded by a certain amount of licence (within limits) before marriage.
2. Polygyny as a recognized state, but polyandry not practised.
3. The existence of the levirate and sororate.
4. The existence of forms of ceremonial and public licence, as practised in fertility rites and in purification rites after death.

*Early Marriages and Prenuptial Unchastity*

Small children of both sexes are allowed to play together, and young people flirt together. I have often heard it said that every Tʃopi boy before marriage has a girl, who must not become a mother. Generally speaking, a girl is not looked down on if she calls out to a boy or speaks to him, or walks about with him alone, but families vary very much in this respect, and there is a good deal of clandestine intercourse in the bush. After initiation the sexes are separated much more rigidly. It may be that the early marriages so much encouraged are partly to prevent unmarried girls from becoming mothers. On the other hand, if a marriage is consummated before a girl is physically fit, it is considered a disgrace and a misfortune, and believed to bring illness and even death upon that girl. A Christian girl whose lobolo money had been paid, and who was also expecting to receive the blessing of the Church on her marriage, asked that the latter ceremony might be delayed until she was 'old enough for marriage'. 'I am a child yet', she said. On another occasion I heard a sad wailing one night in the distance, and when I asked the reason I was told that it was a funeral lamentation for a young girl who had been married before she was fit, and had become ill and died in consequence.

Having already had a child illegitimately is a great handicap to a girl's marriage either to the father of the child or to some one else. It does occasionally happen that the child's father will proceed to pay lobolo when he can (or failing that, a heavy fine to the father of the girl), in which case the child will belong to him. If he refuses to pay an indemnity, the child will belong to the mother's family. Among the Leŋge are many cases of girls with babies, who live in their own homes, having never been properly married. But as children are a source of wealth, this does not seem to be looked upon as a very great calamity, although all parents naturally prefer their daughters to be married by *akulobola*.

When once a marriage has taken place, the women on the whole are very faithful to their husbands, even though separated from them for considerable periods, especially if the husbands continue to show affection and care for them and the children by sending home clothes and money to pay the hut-tax. In the event of a woman having a child by another man when her husband is away, either he will cast her off, and the man must pay lobolo to the injured husband, or the husband will forgive his wife, and the illegitimate child will belong to him.

Lobolo money is able to settle, and failure to pay it is liable to cause, very many complications. To try to do without it at this transition stage would be disastrous.

The men on the whole are not so faithful as their wives. It is a common thing for a man to take another woman to look after him when he is working away from home. There is quite a recognized class of women in the urban locations who do this work. Tʃopi women who have escaped over the Portuguese border into the Transvaal have become prostitutes. These women have now been repatriated.

*Polygyny*

The pagan Leŋge are polygynous when they can afford to be so. This is due partly no doubt to the proportion of women over men, but also to the fact that a plurality of wives is not only a sign of prosperity but an actual cause of it, owing to the amount of field-work that a woman can do, and to the fact that children are a source of wealth. That is the way the Leŋge look at the matter, although biologists would probably tell us that polygyny leads to sterility. The preponderance of women over men is partly caused by the fact that many men die earlier than the women owing to miners' phthisis and other diseases which they have contracted in industrial centres. These diseases may also partly account for the high infant mortality, which is at least 50 per cent.

*Levirate and Sororate Systems*

The levirate system is sometimes carried to excess. A widow, P., brought up her two children alone, as her late husband had no relative to inherit her, so far as was known. Very many years (at least twenty-five) after the death of the husband, a very distant relative of his turned up, and claimed the lobolo money of P.'s daughters, and P. as his own wife. P. took the case to the chief who decided in favour of the man, and against P. This is one case of several I have known.

The examples of the sororate which I have seen have always been those of a man's marrying his deceased wife's younger sister. Although permitted by tribal custom, it is rare to find a man marrying his wife's sister when the first wife is still alive.

*Purification Rites*

The idea of sexual intercourse as a purification rite after death (as in the case of a widow) seems to be that contact with life can restore the equilibrium disturbed by death. This idea doubtless accounts for the licence permitted in some funeral rites (cf. p. 165).

The fertility rites described in Chapter XV, pp. 192–5, in which the chief takes part are doubtless for the strengthening and cohesion of the tribal life.

Two facts strike one forcibly when considering the Leŋge pagan system of relations between the sexes, the first is, that education for marriage, as for example in the initiation rites, was considered vital, and the second is that the system provided that there should be no single or unappropriated woman.

Christian education has raised the standard of morality among the Leŋge, and the many monogamous marriages are showing that these people are quite as capable as Europeans of leading faithful married lives.

## XIII

## DEATH

*Sickness and Death*

DISEASES are generally attributed to the action of magic, practised either by the man's enemies or a sorcerer (*muloyi*). If an accident happens to a man in Johannesburg in the mines, many Leŋge believe that his enemies began to kill him at home before he started. This is often the cause of the bad language used at funeral ceremonies, when the relations of the dead man will revile the supposed murderer and heap obscene epithets upon him. But if a sorcerer is suspected usually nothing is done, though when the memory of the Ŋgoni invasions was still fresh in the minds of the people and he happened to be one of the Ŋgoni, he would have been killed. It is believed that his shade (*ndzuti*) can come by night and cut the finger-nails and toes of a corpse, mix them with 'medicine' and put them in a tiny bag of python skin (*nteve*) which is worn on the neck to protect a murderer from the consequences of his act. Blood is sprinkled on the floor of the hut where any one lies dead to prevent the sorcerer from entering.

When a man dies, his wife and elder daughter will bury him. His sons will help if present, if he has not died of consumption or phthisis. If a woman dies, her husband and eldest daughter will bury her. A daughter will be buried by her father and mother.

*Death in Infancy*

All infants born dead, or who die under the age of a few months, are given a pot burial. The baby is covered with a piece of rag, and sprinkled with the sand of the hut or spot which has been polluted by the blood of childbirth; it is then wrapped up in the loin-cloth which was used by the mother as a covering at the time of childbirth, and placed in a pot.

As stated before, when a woman is about to bear a child she wears a loin-cloth only. When she goes to the lake to wash at the time of the first smearing of the hut, she will wash this garment, and if it is torn she will place it carefully in the grass in a cool place in the shade. It will remain in the bush till it rots away. The garment must not become hot in the sun; if it does, the baby will become feverish. If the garment is not torn, the mother will wash it and use it until it is worn out, and then it will be placed in the shady bush. If, however, the baby dies, it will be wrapped in this garment and placed in a pot, the *ɟeku lambita*, which is to have a hole pierced in it. The mother's old loin-cloth has suffered *khombo* because it has been associated with the birth. The baby's grandmother or father's sister will wrap the child up in the garment, and the baby's grandmother (father's mother) will carry the pot to the lake where it is to be buried. If the child has lived for some little time, say a few weeks, the grandmother and mother will both go to the lake to bury the child, one carrying the pot. This has to be carried in the hands and not on the head, as pots usually are. It is placed in black mud on which *Charophyta* and *Utricularia* grow. A stick made of *limaŋgwa*, a very hard wood, has been brought from home with the burial-pot, and perhaps carried under the arm of one of the bearers. A hole is made in the mud (*ku pendla lidaka*) and the pot first placed upside down in the mud, and then covered with it. Then the hard stick is taken by the grandmother, or, failing her, the mother, and she knocks the pot hard to make a hole. Then she withdraws the stick gently and hides it. The mourners then return home, but must not look behind them. It is especially tabu for the woman who has pierced the pot to look behind; if she does so she will be ill. If the rite of piercing the pot has not been performed, the mother will fail to bear another child.

The grandmother and mother will wash themselves all over, as a rite of purification, after the burial of the baby. Before the end of a month, the rite of the hoe and bulbs of *desa* is performed (see p. 79).

If the baby dies at an age when it is old enough to sit up, the usual purification rite of rubbing the hands with fowl's liver will be used. But this will not be done if the infant is very small.

If twins are stillborn they may be placed in one pot, but some people use a separate pot for each child.

Older babies who have been presented to the moon, their parents having been reunited, are buried when they die in a hole in the ground in their kraal with all their rags. The *nsiŋgu* which has been used to carry the child on the mother's back is spread out in the bush, and a rent is made in it. The mother believes that if this is not done she will not be able to have another child.

### *The Uvisi or Nyavuviswane Rite*

This rite is performed after a miscarriage, and also after the death of a baby a few weeks old which is not yet able to sit up. About a month after the first menses, the day before the first reunion with her husband, she will prepare a 'medicine' with which they must sleep. The idea seems to be that a 'medicine' which has been in contact with life is used to cleanse defilement from death. The woman will procure the leaves of a kind of jessamine called *uvisi* or *uvisini*, which has large, scented, starry-white flowers. She will hide these leaves in a little bit of her garment, because it is prohibited to put them in a hand-basket. The garment has been in contact with the mother. The leaves are stamped in a mortar, and water is added. Half of this decoction is put in a wooden bowl. Mealie-meal porridge is cooked in the other half. The woman and her husband 'sleep with' the solid 'medicine', while the liquid half is reserved in the other bowl. The next morning the woman will go to her own father's kraal, and place the two bowls in the bush near the kraal. Then she invites all the members of the kraal, men, women, children, and babies to come out into the bush. The bowl of water is given to the men first; each takes a tiny sip, and also a little scrap of the porridge from the second bowl. The men rub a little of the medicine on their ankles, and the women rub some on the stomach and back. Tiny babies are fed by having a little squeezed into their mouths. If the woman has lost twins, she must give the *vuswa* or porridge medicine with crossed hands. She will eat a very little herself first from one hand, raising it to her mouth, and then from the other in the same way, then she will cross her hands to give it to the people. When only one child of twins has died, she stretches out both hands with a little of the *vuswa* in each.

She will go to all the kraals where there are relations of hers, even if they live a few miles away, in order to *kukukuŋghela*, as this action is called. When relations of hers return from Johannesburg she has to perform the rite for them. It is a purification after childbirth, and is supposed to take away the *khombo* or misfortune. If she feeds other women after child-death, and has not yet performed the rite, her next child will suffer from black stools (*ſantima ſamandlamabe*). If one of twins (*mahała*) dies, and is old enough to be buried in the kraal, and not in a pot at the lake, the *nsiŋgu*, which has been used for carrying the child who is alive, is used to cover the child who is dead. A rent is made in it, or the mother will not have another child. Conversely, the *nsiŋgu* of the child which is dead will be used to carry the child who is living.

## Burial of Adults

A man's old clothes are generally burnt in the bush, and he is covered with a blanket. His mats are also burnt or buried. New clothes, if they are ceremonially defiled by having been worn during the illness, are buried with him. If they have been put away and he has not worn them for some time, they will probably also be buried, in order that the relations may be spared the pain of seeing things which belonged to their friend. If a man is killed by an assegai, and part remains in his flesh, it must be taken out before the man is buried, or else 'we shall be all killed by the Ŋgoni'. Brass anklets and shining beads must not be buried. 'These things shine because they are metal, we shall all die if we bury them.'

The rings are sometimes hidden in a little hole beneath a tree (*Sclerocarya caffra* or *Trichilia emetica*) in the bush. Then if there is a young girl who is going to the initiation ceremonies some time after the death, a doctor is summoned to bless the rings so that she can wear them. A colleague of mine met a girl wearing one of these ornaments who had been told by the *anyaŋga* that she would surely die if she ever took it off. Shining beads are hidden in a 'cool' part of the bush to rot away. If any one finds these beads which belonged to the dead, and makes off with them, that person will die too. Money is not buried usually, because if there is 'lightning in the sky, the money will go away and be lost'. If money is buried for the sake of saving it, it is put in a large snail shell, and the opening stopped up with a bit of potsherd.

All the belongings of a man who has died are called *fivenze*. His property will belong to his eldest brother, or, failing a brother, to the man's son; failing a son, to the man's sister.

The body is tied three times with strips of *minala* palm leaf. First they bind the hips, then the waist, and then the neck. When the body is buried, these strips are taken off. The corpse must not be bound, else how could the spirit come out? The arms remain crossed and the legs bent, as the attendants 'folded' the limbs at death. The head faces the west, because it must see the night, because the night is the home of the dead. A cloth covers the eyes. Food-offerings are placed above the grave, monkey-nuts, Kaffir-corn, mealies, earth-peas, snuff. Also the torn white garment and an old axe or assegai, if it is a man; an old basket and a food-bowl if a woman.

The *guŋguri* is the deepest part of the grave. It is filled with sand until it reaches the level of the little chamber excavated at the side, the *yindlu*, the 'house of the dead'. Then the belongings of the person who has died are placed in the sand, and the grave is filled up.

An *anjiti* (checked or striped red and white print) is placed on the grave of a person who had a Ndau spirit, and a white cloth for a person who had a Ŋgoni spirit. White cloth (print or calico, &c.) is placed in any case on a grave in order that the body may be 'cool'.

On return from the burial the mourners will wash themselves, the face, hands, and legs, with a decoction made from the leaves of *Heeria abyssinicum* Schweinf.

On the first or second day after a death and burial, a purification rite called *kutota fibindzi* takes place. This rite is also called *kupaŋgula* or *guhorowa* (Leŋge). If it is a man who has died, the fowl's liver (raw) is given to the widow first. She will take it and rub it over her hands and face. Then all the mourners follow her example. After which they all smoke through a reed a smoking mixture in a potsherd placed on the fire, the mixture consisting of fowl's droppings and some other 'medicine'. This rite is called *kudzaha tinyele*.

The next cleansing medicine is made from the *manone* plant (not yet identified) in this way: the roots are scraped with a knife, spread on a mat to dry, and then ground to powder and put in a little gourd and kept till wanted for use. Then some water is put in a potsherd which is placed on the fire. Young monkey-nuts are ground and put in a wooden bowl, and water poured on them. This is then placed in the hot potsherd, and when it begins to sizzle the *manone* powder is added. Every one dips the four fingers of each hand into the mixture and then licks the fingers; then the fingers are dipped again into the potsherd, and then placed upon both ankles and both knees, then in the potsherd again; then the arms are crossed, and the fingers wet with the medicine are placed on the opposite shoulder; then the arms are crossed again behind, and a line drawn with the anointed fingers from the shoulder to the waist, using each hand, one after the other, so that the whole body is purified. Then the hands are again placed in the mixture, and drawn down over the face. Thus the whole body is anointed. They say this is *kulondzovota khombo*.

I was told by a woman of the Muyaŋga sib of a very curious little rite which took place about the third day after death in olden days. The *anyaŋga* mixed together in a bowl earth-peas and mealie-meal cooked in fowl soup and *Pennisetum*. Each mourner had to kneel and take a little in the mouth and place it aside, swallowing a very little. One by one approached the bowl and performed this ritual act. The morsel placed aside was an offering to the person who had just died.

*The Σisimbu Rite*

This may take place any day during the first week of mourning. An important *anyaŋga* is called in who kills a fowl which is to be 'the great offering of the misfortune' (*khombo*). Sometimes the head man kills the fowl or fowls and the doctor sprinkles all the people with the blood. As the blood drips on the ground, the *anyaŋga* beseeches his own dead father: '*Wena, Bava, ndzipfune akuva ndzibasisa avanhu akhombo, vatshama kwatsi, avavagwi, ndziṣeka muri ṣinene*', 'You, Father, help me to purify the people from misfortune, that they live nicely, and do not fall ill, and to prepare the medicine well.' The fowls will then be cooked, and a special soot (*nsita*) medicine added by the *anyaŋga* to the soup. Then Kaffir-corn will be cooked and added to the soup, and all in the kraal must eat a little. The scrapings of the pot are rolled into little balls, dried, wrapped up in maize leaves, and hung up in a tree. These little balls are reserved for relations who are not able to be present, perhaps some are working in Johannesburg. Now, if the deceased person has not died of miners' phthisis, a mysterious little bag called a *fisimbu* is added to the fowl-soup. It is made of the fibres of the young branches of the bark-cloth tree. These fibres are made into thread and netted. The *anyaŋga* has arrived with his little skin-bag, made from the skin of a small animal called *figeŋge* or *figwinya*. In the bag are little 'medicine' gourds, the *fisimbu*, and the *gonha*, a small horn filled with medicine made of honey and some other secret ingredient, which is supposed to be a great restorative if a man is dying.

The *fisimbu* is filled with half-digested food from the entrails of a goat, and a bundle of little sticks and roots of plants, some ground, some not. The *anyaŋga* takes the fowl out of the soup and puts it aside for the moment. The dripping *fisimbu* is taken out of the soup; but before beginning to asperge the people the *anyaŋga* entreats his ancestral spirits thus:

'You, So and so, So and so, help me in this work which I am doing in this kraal, that all the people there may be cleansed. Even if enemies come, they may do nothing, that they may not be maimed when they have done nothing. Therefore, you, Father, and you, Grandparents of mine, help me to strengthen this kraal, to be a strong fortification, so that he who wants to do wrong, cannot enter in this kraal. I know that where you work, the owner of the kraal has set up his sweetheart or picked up money [i.e. is well provided for], and that all the people of the kraal are well.'

The *anyaŋga* takes the *fisimbu*, and lets the hot liquid drip into his left hand, then he sips from first one hand and then the other (*kukweva*). He asperges himself on the legs, the chest, and the back of the neck. He inhales the steam from the *fisimbu*, and then sprinkles his face. He goes to the chief mourner (the husband, if it is the wife who has died) and gives him hot water *kuhisa mandla* (to make the hands hot and to wash the hands). Then the chief mourner must sip the soup from his palms, just as the *anyaŋga* did, the latter having dipped the *fisimbu* into the soup a second time. The *anyaŋga* asperges the chief mourner on his legs and body, then on his shoulders at the back; then the mourner must inhale the steam, and his face is sprinkled. After that he is told to smell the *fisimbu* again, and the *anyaŋga* gives him a final aspersion and goes on to the next mourner.

All the men are sprinkled first and then all the women. When the *anyaŋga* has finished, he prepares a special medicine from the contents of the entrails of the fowl and gives it to the chief mourner who eats it. After this he tells them that the *khombo* is finished.

A few days after the death, to finish the immediate period of mourning, and to feed the relatives who come from afar, probably on the completion of the *fisimbu* rite, an animal or animals belonging to the dead man must be sacrificed. Blood must be spilt because these domestic beasts follow their master and go with him. If a woman dies, her husband must not kill the animal, but his brother must do it. The brother (not the next in age, but the succeeding one) will also kill the beasts, if his elder brother has died.

For instance, if the eldest brother, the head of the kraal, were to die, the next brother by his brother's death has now become the eldest of the family, and must entertain the mourners who arrive on that day, so the third brother will kill the goat.

This brother, who has killed the goat, will give the skin of it to his elder brother, who will cut it up in small pieces to make wrist-bands. All in the kraal will wear these wrist-bands till they rot away, and pieces will be saved for relatives who have not yet arrived. It appears that the goat is the sacrificial animal, and the pig is killed for food. A wrist-band of this nature is called a *ligoto* (pl. *tigoto*). When both parents are dead, straps of the goatskin, rubbed with *psanye* by the *anyaŋga*, are worn over the shoulders.

The sacrificial goat has to be divided according to definite rules. In a specified family Josiah, the eldest brother, will have the head and brains, the lower jaw, and a leg. Elina, his wife, being the wife of the chief mourner, will have a leg. Josefa, the second brother, who has killed the goat, will have a fore-quarter and the meat on the top of the head near the horns.

The horns are sometimes placed on the roof of the hut. (This is a sign that people may see and say: 'Oh! that man eats meat at all times!')

The wife of Josefa will also have a fore-quarter. Zephaniah and Absalom, younger brothers, will have the shins and trotters (*mancina*). Saria, wife of Zephaniah, will have a fore-leg. Simone and Jonathane, Josiah's sons, will also have a little bit of the fore-legs, near the ankles. The widow of the dead man will have the breast and ribs. It is to be noted that the wife of the eldest brother, Elina, is of more importance than the widows of the dead man. Zephaniah's wife, Saria, will eat in one spot with the two lesser widows of the dead man. They will have part of the back or ribs. The chief widow will sit with the wives of the two elder brothers. They will eat a leg (hind-quarter) together. Josefa, who killed the goat, will also cook it, and bring it to Josiah, who will divide it and tell Josefa to carry to each his portion. All the meat (with the blood) will be cooked in one huge pot, and then served up in a very large wooden bowl. The cooked blood is known as *uvenze*. The soup is also divided among them and served out with a large wooden spoon. Sometimes a stick carved at the end, called *manya*, is used to impale the meat. It is made of the hard *limaŋgwa* wood.

The children of the dead man will be sitting in another place with the children of the brothers. Even the youngest babies will have a little bit of the meat rubbed inside their lips. Boys will be separated from girls; they will sit in different groups. Everybody throws down a little meat on the ground before eating, in memory of the dead person. Beer is also poured for him.

The spirit of the dead man is supposed to be near protecting his family when the goat is eaten, which is done to please him.

*Groups at Funeral Feasts*

Groups at a funeral feast if the deceased is a man:

1. The brothers
2. The sons } of dead man.
3. Sons of brothers
4. Eldest brother's wife. Chief widow. Second brother's wife.
5. Third brother's wife and remaining widows of dead man (if he has had more than one wife).
6. Daughters.

Groups if woman dies:

1. Her husband and his brothers (grown up).
2. Father of dead woman and fathers of wives of husband's brothers.

3. Younger brothers (unmarried) of husband.
4. Sons of husband's brothers.
5. Dead woman's mother-in-law, own mother, and mothers of other wives of husband.
6. Wives of husband's elder brothers.
7. Wives of husband's younger brothers.
8. Wives of husband's brothers' wives' brothers.
9. Daughters.

The hut of death.<br>(Woman dead).

Fire for cooking goat.    Fire for cooking ordinary food.

| *Men mourners.* | | *Women mourners.* | |
|---|---|---|---|
| Husband's younger brothers. | Her own son and sons of husband's brothers. | Father's sister (of dead woman) and wives of husband's brothers. | Own mother. Mothers-in-law of herself and husband's brothers. |
| Fire for warming themselves. | | | |
| Husband and husband's elder brothers. | Father of deceased woman and fathers of husband's brothers' wives. | Daughters. | Wives of husband's brothers' wives' brothers. |
| Visitors. | | Visitors. | |

This is the general plan of arrangement, but it may not be always universally followed. It will be seen that the grouping is more or less that of age sets. If the chief wife of the eldest brother dies, then the second brother will kill the goat in her honour, unless there are other younger brothers, when the second brother will keep company with the bereaved man. (If a woman's husband's father is alive, she and her brothers-in-law, the *valamu*, can use familiar language to one another, *kutsoma*, in their lifetime, but if the father-in-law is dead, and her husband has become the head of the kraal, they can no longer be on familiar terms.)

Division of the goat:
- Husband's elder brothers . . The neck and back of neck.
- Own husband . . . Tongue.
- Husband's younger brothers . Head.
- Husband's brothers' sons . . Shins and part of ribs.
- (Portions for women as before.)

The head of each group will have a food-bowl from which the others will be served.

When the women are served, the wives of the elder brothers are served first, then the daughters of the dead woman, then the wives of the younger brothers, and then the group of the in-laws, the youngest *mukoŋwana* having to eat up the meat, in the last group.

*Ritual Acts*

Cohabitation is prohibited during the whole week of mourning. The second week after the death, the mourners will get tired of sitting, mourning, and doing nothing, and will want to go to their work in the fields. They will say to the youngest brother that he must have ritual connexion with his wife (*kutʃelela* or *kuhapa*). In the morning when the wife of the youngest brother comes out of her hut, she will wash her hands first, and then sprinkle all the mourners with cold water. This ritual act has purified the family a little. Much still remains to be done. The other brothers may now have intercourse with their wives. Of course there is an *anyaŋga* for this *kutʃelela* rite. He brings a very important medicine called *tʃiŋgu* (cohabitation) medicine. Hence the rite is also called sometimes the *kutʃiŋga* rite. After the ritual act of cohabitation, each of the people concerned will take a little of the 'medicine'. If the *anyaŋga* has intercourse with his wife while the medicine remains in the kraal, he will die.

There seem to be some variations of this rite in the different sibs. The modern tendency is to perform the *tʃiŋgu* rite quite soon, a few days after the death, even before the rite of the ceremonial aspersion with the *fisimbu*. In one case in 1928 on the third day after the death of a petty chief, Maswenda Masiye, the headman of the kraal, the nearest relation of the dead man, after ceremonial union with his wife, poured water at the threshold of the hut, and all in the kraal had to tread over the water. This was one of the purification rites. An elaborate *tʃiŋgu* rite in connexion with the death of the same chief took place the following year.

If it is a woman who has died, her husband must have intercourse with his second or third wife. This rite is called *kutʃiŋga kufa ka* ŋkati kulogwe. It generally takes place about the third week after the death. However, the parents of the second wife object to this, as a matter of form. The second wife will incur ceremonial defilement by the very act which purifies the rest of the family. Hence the man will have to pay a fine to the parents, and give new clothes to the wife in order to pay her for agreeing to the act of *kutſiŋga*.

The *tſiŋgu* rite is not universally practised now in Leŋgeland. In order to save expense, often the same *anyaŋga* will perform both the fumigation and aspersion rites.

*The Chief's Death Rites*

In olden days the death of the chief was kept secret. He was buried secretly at night, and the people were told that he was on a visit, and then suddenly they would hear gunshots, or if it were in the days when guns were unknown, they would hear a great wailing, and they would soon know what had happened.

When a chief is buried (fully dressed) his wooden head-rest, spoons, bowls, and clothes (generally) are buried with him, but his staff becomes the property of his successor. A small palisade is built round the grave of a chief, and it is covered with clothes. A sacrifice is offered to him and to the spirits of his forefathers. If a child of the chief afterwards passes his father's grave, going from one place to another, he will always place an offering, generally mealies, upon it.

The Ŋgoni are said to have had a very curious custom on the death of a chief. At first, no one was told about the death. The body was washed, and afterwards put into a bag of ox-skin, and the dead chief was put in a standing position against the wall in his ox-skin bag. Meanwhile a fire was made in the hut, and the flesh of the ox and of other oxen was roasted over it. The mourners, especially the wives of the chief, partook of a ceremonial meal. The wives remained in the hut for three months. After that an official announcement was made to the people that the chief was dead.

On November 9th, 1928, M., the eldest son of Maswenda Masiye (petty chief of one of Σihaɫu's districts), died of phthisis. He had been acting as chief for his father, who was very old. The people were forbidden to work in the fields for a week. If a woman were seen with a hoe, it was taken away from her. Just a month later, his father, the old chief, died, and again the people were prohibited from working in the fields for a week as a mark of respect for the chief. Hence they lost a fortnight's digging at the most important season of the year, when they ought to be sowing maize and ground-nuts. (A widow will wait a fortnight or a month before resuming her work in the fields after her husband's death.) On November 10th I was informed that preparations for the mourning (for the son) were being made. The women were beginning to make the *minala* mourning ornaments. The rite of the fowl's liver and smoking the *tinyele* took place early in the morning of the same day. I was told that a sacrifice to the dead man could not take place until the lamentations (*firilo*) had been made; that is, they will wait till some one in the kraal is ill, and then it will be revealed to the headman in a dream that the dead person is causing the illness, because he desires a sacrifice, or wants to be lamented. The spirit will sleep under a tree in the bush until it has revealed its will in a dream or by causing a member of the family to be ill. Then the headman and his wife will pay a visit to the *anyaŋga*, who will find out from the omens what day will be suitable for the celebration of the *firilo*, or great lamentation, generally called the day of *masari*. This may be six months after the death, or even longer. It varies very much in different clans. The Leŋge are inclined to hasten the event, but it is usual to delay it till after the monkey-nut harvest, for they must have time for proper preparation, and the maize is not dry enough to make beer.

The *firilo* is a very important event, but much more so nowadays among the Tʃopi than the Leŋge. Relations come bringing sacrificial animals from all parts of the country. Quantities of beer are brewed. Offerings are made at the *gandzelo* of every possible kind of seed. Dancing and funeral lamentations take place. All drink and eat in honour of the deceased, to whom offerings of all kinds are made, each person putting a tiny scrap of meat on the ground for the *ʃikwembu* or pouring a little beer on the ground. When a chief died in olden days among the Tʃopi and Leŋge, and a son of his was going to succeed him (it is generally the brother who succeeds), the son would have ritual connexion with his wife, and then he would go out to the fields with some helpers and cut slits in the bark of all trees whose fruits were used as food. This act was supposed to help to take away the ceremonial misfortune. At eventide, when he returned, his own fire was put out, the *anyaŋga* putting another in its place. Then the fires of all the people in the neighbouring kraals were put out, and the *anyaŋga* put new fires in their place.

*Purification of the Country after the Death of a Chief*

An important rite which took place in May 1929 was called *kutʃiŋga tiko*, and was a purification rite after the death of Maswenda Masiye (who died soon after his eldest son) in order that the country might be cleansed. Maswenda's successor (a second son) invited two *tinyaŋga*, Mabumu Σileŋge, of his own tribe, and an important *anyaŋga* of the Ndau tribe, to help him to carry out the rite. On the night of April 28th–29th, the chief's adjutants were sent all over the district of Masiyeni to extinguish the fires with water blessed by the Ndau *anyaŋga*, and mixed with *nsita* medicine. These old fires were supposed to belong to the old chief, although he had been dead some months. The adjutants carried the water in a gourd, and when it was exhausted they poured fresh water on some of the *nsita*, which was carried in another gourd. The district was divided between three and four of these adjutants. A man named Fakubi Mbwaŋge (connected by marriage with the Masiye sib, and living at Masiyeni) and a helper performed the rite of extinguishing the fires in the immediate neighbourhood of our Mission.

I was unable to discover all the ingredients of the *nsita* medicine, but charred and pulverized roots and leaves of plants were among them. Cohabitation was prohibited on the night of extinguishing the fires, but enjoined on the following nights, when a certain amount of licence among young people was permitted. The chief and his wife had ritual intercourse.

Early at dawn on the morning following the extinguishing of the fires, the Ndau *anyaŋga* lighted a large sacred fire in the chief's kraal by means of friction of fire-sticks. Mabumu Σileŋge helped him to kindle the sparks produced into a blaze. I saw the remains of the fire before noon. All that day the chief's subjects were arriving with small presents, receiving in return a faggot from the sacred fire to rekindle the new fires in their kraals. Apparently it did not much matter if the faggot were extinguished on the way, so long as it had formed part of the new fire, for I saw one woman carrying away a faggot on which not one spark remained, only ashes at the tip. The new fires were supposed to belong to the new chief.

At sundown on the afternoon of April 29th, after the kindling of the new fires, the chief's *tinduna* (headmen) went to peg out the land over which he had jurisdiction. Sixteen stakes in all were used. This work was done by two headmen, each with one assistant. Each *induna* was responsible for driving eight stakes into the ground at regular intervals, thus marking the boundaries. Some words such as these were used: 'Let this stake stop the way of any one coming from another district, here, with malice in his heart.'

## DEATH

*Widowhood*

Food is not taken by a widow until her husband is buried, neither does she sleep the first night after the death. If a man dies in the night, his widow will go outside, light a fire, and shut the door of the hut in which the man has died. No one but the relations in the kraal must approach the hut until the man is buried. If there are ground-nuts or mealies in the hut, these will be piled up in a field-basket and then thrown out to the fowls.

The husband's brother, if he lives near, will come to watch with the wife who is bereaved. This is called *kulaŋgulela kufa* or *kutʃuʃa kufa*.

If she has formerly sinned with this brother, and he arrives and sees the corpse while it is still unbound, and there is a fire in the hut, he will call out to the widow to extinguish the fire, for if he sees the corpse while the fire is still alight he would die. The widow's hair is all cut off[1] the day following the death by the dead husband's mother. This does not seem to be an invariable rule, as we shall presently see when considering the case of the ritual cleansing of a widow who is too old to marry again.

On the same day that the hair is cut, the rite of anointing with the fowl's liver, and of smoking the *maʃimba* of the fowl, takes place, to be followed by the rite of the broken egg.

The widow will remain two days in her hut in seclusion. On one of these days the *vanyini* (mother, husband's mother, or father's sister) will raise her up in their arms singing funeral songs, and she climbs herself to the top of the hut, and pulls out a little grass from the roof with her hands. The women spread out the grass on the ground outside the kraal, and cover the widow entirely with a white cloth. She sits on the grass thus wrapped up. Sometimes the women throw ashes over her. Then the grass is lighted with a burning brand which they have brought with them. They take off the widow's clothes and light a wisp or two of grass between her legs (it is not very hot, mostly smoke). They take away the grass and put in an egg, and she clasps it with her legs in order to retain it, and breaks it by squashing it. The shell is thrown away, and the broken yoke runs down in a stream and is rubbed into the legs. The widow has then to step over the fire once forwards and once backwards. Then they mix water and red ochre (*tsumane*) and anoint (*tota*) her. It is essential in mourning rites that the red

---

[1] A mother mourning for a daughter will leave a strip of hair (*lidodo*) running from the forehead to the back of the head.

# DEATH

ochre should be mixed with water, not oil. This is one of the early rites of taking away the *khombo* (ceremonial misfortune or defilement).

The widow generally cuts off her bead girdle (*fuŋgu*),[1] on the occasion of her first washing herself after the death. And here it must be noted that all washing of the body is more or less of a ceremonial character. It is not a mere cleansing of the body; it is almost sacramental in that it is a type of cleansing from the moral defilement of illness, death, and loss. In fact it is an aggregation rite, bringing the person who performs the ablutions once more into the common life. We have noticed frequently that when people are ill they will not wash themselves until they are well again or on the high road to recovery—even if cleanliness would have helped in the first place. The exception to this is the washing with plant decoctions to reduce fever.

The widow's mourning ornaments (*minala*) are made of *minala* palm, and consist of necklets, deep anklets or gaiters, and gauntlets. Those worn on legs and arms are plaited, the ends joined to form a cylinder and drawn tight by lacing after being put on. Ten or twelve strips of *minala* palm are knotted loosely round the neck. These ornaments are put on generally on the third day after the death for near relations, such as a husband or child. It takes about a day to plait them. The goatskin wristlets or shoulder-straps are generally first worn on the day of the killing of the goat.

On the day of the adjudication of the inheritance, which in the case of a young widow will be in the third month after death, the relations of the late husband (not of the wife) will assemble together. 'To-day you must all come, in order that we may speak of matters connected with the dead.' The elder brothers of the dead man will remain in the hut; some of the other members of the family will go outside. The sister of the deceased man will say to the widow, 'You must now choose whom you will have among the brothers of your late husband.' The sister then indicates the eldest brother, and if the widow does not want him, she is permitted to say so, stating that she prefers a younger brother. A bad custom is sometimes practised by a younger brother.

---

[1] Most women wear a bead girdle (*fuŋgu*) of black and white beads. They wear it on their marriage, as a sign that they are marriageable. Widows will hide this *fuŋgu* or *likhalu* in the mud and grass. It is tabu ever to cut the *fuŋgu* until the husband is dead. If the wearer becomes too fat for it, she must unstring it without cutting it. The thread is made of pine-apple-leaf fibre. The white beads are a sign of ceremonial cleanliness, because if a woman has a husband, she is clean. The black beads are on the 'touch wood' principle in order to ward off misfortune, lest she be *too* happy and fortunate.

He may seduce the wife while the husband is still alive but ill, thinking he may not recover, and that the widow will belong to him. It must be admitted that the widow generally chooses a younger brother in preference to an elder one. Sometimes a sort of pretence is kept up among the brothers. One will say: 'Oh! that woman is a bad woman! I don't think I want her. She killed our brother.' Then there will be a discussion, but in the end one consents to take her. If not, she has to take a man 'in the bush', and goes from bad to worse. When the widow has consented to take one of the brothers, he makes her a present of new clothing and mats. They have a ritual connexion. After that he goes home, and she may remain four months in her old home before going to her new husband's home. Sometimes he leaves his other wife, or wives, and comes to pay her a visit. Failing an own brother to the deceased man, she will belong to his parallel cousin.

Then there comes the case of the ritual cleansing, after the death of her husband, of an old widow who will not be able to find another husband.

After the *tʃelela* rite described previously, when the brothers begin *kutʃiŋga kufa*, the eldest son of the deceased man will have ritual connexion with his wife in the hut. He will then take bits of the garment which he wore when purified, and will make *mula* medicine of them. This medicine is dipped into a pot of water, together with a piece of charcoal. Then he takes a leafy branch of *Trichilia*, and sprinkles the widow and all the other mourners with it. Then his wife sprinkles the others in the same way. When the aspersion is finished, the eldest son and his wife and the widow will go to the ash-heap with a bit of broken gourd (*ʃikambazi*), a razor, some *mbowa* (fruit of *Momordica clematidea*), and a piece of live charcoal sizzling in a little water in the gourd. The water extinguishes the charcoal, but is warmed by it. The eldest son then cuts his wife's hair and puts it in the broken gourd. She in return cuts her husband's hair and also places the snippets in the gourd. Then the eldest son cuts the hair of his mother the widow, and his wife follows his example. She rubs the old widow's forehead with a bit of the *mbowa*, taking care not to touch the forehead with her fingers, and then cuts the hair above the forehead with the native razor, placing the hair in the gourd. The eldest son then puts his foot on the broken piece of gourd (*ʃitʃapa*). His wife rests her foot lightly on her husband's foot. The widow puts her foot on her eldest son's wife's foot, and her second son rests his foot on the widow's. Then the eldest daughter of the dead man rests her foot on that of her brother, the second son, and her younger sisters follow her according to their age. The dead man's brother places his foot on that of the youngest daughter of the house. Then simultaneously they all press on the foot of the eldest son, and he crushes the gourd there in the ash-heap.

*Widowers*

A widower is also purified by taking a wife of the bush. He will probably remain a month or so after this temporary union, and then marry again by means of *akulobola*. As signs of mourning, he will shave and put a white rag round his head, and wear goatskin shoulder-straps and a wristlet.

When I asked why 'mourning' is worn, the reply was 'because people of old did it'.

*Widowhood and Akulobola*

The man who inherits his brother's widow will pay a small additional sum of money as *akulobola*, perhaps £2. The ritual act performed in the bush with another man perhaps takes place two months after the death of the husband. At the end of three months the widow will be taken quietly by the husband's brother without ceremony. Failing a brother-in-law she will belong to the parallel cousin of her late husband, or to her husband's sister's son. If the man who inherits her is too young to marry her, he has the right to take her *akulobola* money if she marries some one not belonging to her husband's family, and this *akulobola* should be a sum equal to that paid by the husband when she was first married. If no one takes the widow she must remain and work for her mother-in-law. However, she is considered the child of the old couple, and she will cook food, and serve the other members of the family. I know of such a case where the widow is a Christian girl, and therefore could not be taken by her brother-in-law, who had two wives already.

In the case of heathen women, and if the parents-in-law are old, and there seems no chance for the woman to be married again by *akulobola*, she is advised to have an illegitimate child (without *akulobola*) in order that the child may grow up and help her parents-in-law. Sometimes she returns to the man who took away the *khombo* in the bush, but her children by the first husband belong to the parents-in-law.

I know of the case of a woman who, when her husband died, was taken by his brother. He soon tired of her and wanted, in lieu of a debt which he had, to give her to another man who was no relation of hers. The woman had character enough to object strongly to being bartered in this fashion, especially as she was a Christian and the man in question was a heathen with two or three wives already. But the native chief decided the case against her, and so she lived in daily terror of visits of the police to her kraal, to take her off by force.

Eventually, after some time, a sum of money was produced, part of her original *akulobola* money, enough to satisfy the claim of the man. The difficulty was that her father had spent her *akulobola* in procuring a wife for one of his sons, so there was considerable difficulty in raising this sum of money, especially as her family was already heavily in debt.

If the widow marries into another family by the usual way of *akulobola*, she has to perform this rite on the third month after the death of the first husband: A little circle is made with mats set up on end, two for the man, two for the woman. There is a fire inside the mats, with a pot of medicine. This the couple, beginning to perspire, have to stir with sticks. The *anyaŋga* comes and covers them over with blankets, and he tells them that, when night comes, they are to unite in the widow's hut. Then when the cocks crow, they must carry the pot of medicine, one clutching each side of it, and throw it out into the bush.

Sometimes people will move to another spot as the result of death in the kraal. On arrival in the new kraal a little offering of maize will be made to the dead person. The maize will be thrown on the ground under the tree which is to be the sacrificial spot. 'Bless me, because I have moved from that kraal. If I have reached home, give me life.'

When some one dies, and it is desirable that his widow should not leave the kraal, they will give her medicine of *vuriva* (ground and cooked roots of a species of *Commiphora*) which is supposed to cause forgetfulness. This medicine is also used for children who are being weaned.

A curious little square flat rattle called a *fikitsi* is sometimes used to summon mourners. A widow will shake the rattle, dancing. It is made of *tibelele* grass stems bound together with vegetable fibre of barkcloth tree and *minala* palm. The seeds are *Abrus precatorius*, little red lucky-beans, generally. It is said that this rattle may only be used on occasions of mourning.

### Abnormal Burials

Suicides have a special burial, the head being inserted in a hole in the side of the grave-hole.

Men killed in battle are buried like suicides, if they are buried at all, which depends upon whether they have a relation to do it for them or not.

The body of a woman dying in childbirth is cut open in order to extract the child, which must not be buried with the woman, as before stated; if this custom is not observed, all the woman's relations will die.

A leper is buried in the hut which he inhabited. If the leper has a wife, she must come out of the hut. The walls are then taken away, and the roof falls down over the grave. It is burnt generally.

Sometimes a woman who is the sole survivor will bury her husband in their hut and then abandon it. If a woman who has many children dies, a hole must be cut in the wall, and the woman taken out that way, if the children sleep in the hut. It is tabu to take the body out by the door in that case.

*Chronology of Funeral Rites*

The chronological order of the funeral rites seems to vary very much, but the main order seems to be as follows:

    1st day: Burial. Purification by washing with *Heeria abyssinicum*.
    2nd day: Fowl-liver rite. *Manone* washing.
    3rd day: Fumigation. Sometimes *tſiŋgu* rite.
    4th day: *Σisimbu* rite.
    5th day: Slain beast.
   Interval.
   *Σirilo* after six months.
   Repeated at end of a year.

# XIV
# DANCES

'WHEN primitive man comes in close contact with the mysterious forces that rule his life, and when any important event is taking place in the community, he feels the need to renew the bonds of communal solidity, and it is in the dance that he is best able to do so. The total effect of the dance is to merge the individual will for the time being in that of the group, and so produce harmony and a common will. The dance is a powerful form of ceremonial which has as its function the strengthening of the tie between the group and the individual. The dance is essentially religious in origin.'

These words, which so tersely sum up the attitude of primitive mankind towards dancing and the dance, are specifically true of the Leŋge and the Tʃopi. In their dances can be read the idiom of the soul, for dancing is their favourite form of self-expression. The initiation rites of the women, by which they are 'born' into the full life of the community, are sometimes referred to as *kukina* or *kuʃina*, the dancing.

Dancing forms an important element in marriage rites, harvest gatherings, funeral ceremonies, and spiritualistic seances. The social life of the Leŋge may be termed operatic, for they like everything to be done to the accompaniment of music and dancing. Tiny tots, hardly able to toddle, can be seen heaving their little shoulders and stamping their little bare feet, clutching dramatically a little rag of a garment, in just the same way as a lady dancer on a more civilized stage would manipulate her dancing skirt.

At the sound of the drum a little boy will immediately begin to stamp his feet rhythmically.

It must also be noted that the congregation on Sunday afternoons at evensong at Masiyeni, in the heart of Leŋgeland, is often a poor one, when at the harvest festival season the annual dancing contests are taking place in the chiefs' kraals. These dances are held in honour of the spirits whose favourable influences are supposed to have produced a good harvest.

These dances, undoubtedly of very old origin, which figure so prominently in the folk-lore of Gazaland, take place in the winter, after the ground-nuts have been harvested. These contests are called *nzumba, ndzau,* or *luwela,* and take place in the kraal of each petty chief or *ŋganakana,* who consults his ancestral spirits beforehand to find out if the dances will be successful. The finals are held in the kraal of the chief who rules all the *tiŋganakana* and may last a fortnight or three weeks, the contingents from the various districts competing in these.[1] On the last day the award (metaphorical) is given to the sib which has displayed the greatest prowess. The act of contesting is called *kupikisana fivaŋgu.* In the year 1930, at the kraal of Σihaɫu Ɖwamusi, the people of Kondʒweni were adjudged to be the best dancers for the year.

I watched the contests during some of the week-days, and could quite applaud the decision. The chief Σihaɫu took an axe and cut a gash in the tree-trunk in his kraal saying: 'Your reward is this, people of Kondʒweni!' ('*fivaŋgu faŋwina ilefi, vaka Kondʒweni*'). Then the Kondʒweni people danced with rejoicing, to thank for the reward of victory, and they went away singing: '*Wandʒodo! Wandʒodo!*' 'Victory! Victory!'

## Some Dancing Contests

It may perhaps be worth while to give a short description of some of these dancing contests which I saw in 1927-8.

On passing one day by the chief's kraal at Ɖkumini (one of the Leŋge sibs), I saw this dancing contest (*nzumba* or *luwela*) in full swing. I passed by gaily dressed crowds of Leŋge, young men and maidens, old women and children, standing, talking, sitting, in woodland ways, or wending their ways to the sports—time four o'clock in the afternoon. Girls were puffing the little musical instrument made with a *Strychnos* shell (*figoriha* or *figoriyu*) in order to summon their companions to dance the *masessa.*[2] Sounds of the *mbalapala* trumpet intermingled with the trilling made by the old women between their teeth (*kuluŋgela*) came from the kraal. As I passed by, the *filembe* dance was beginning. Some said it was the *dibi* dance, but one of the women said it could not be the *dibi* dance, as the men are accustomed to wear lions' skins while dancing the *dibi,* whereas these wore skirts of wild cat and buck sewn together.

In the *filembe* the dancers brandished rods and staves (*nduku* and *mutfiso*), and many feathers were stuck in their hair. Some of the girls

[1] Cf. my paper in *Bantu Studies,* ii, 1926, pp. 265-7.
[2] *Masessa* = to dance with the loins—is a favourite dance for all women, married or single, at the annual contests.

climbed a tree in order to see better. The dancers, standing in a semi-circle, did a good deal of foot-work in the way of stamping, going down on one knee and stamping with the foot of the other leg. The dance was accompanied by the clapping of hands by the women, who sang a refrain, to which the men replied in singing. I did not catch the words. At this dance I saw the largest Shangaan harp (*ʃitende*) I have ever seen. The bow must have been about eight feet long, and the gourd which acted as a sounding-box was a very large one. It was carried by a tall youth, but was taller than he.

The *ʃilembe* is said to be allied to the *mutʃoŋgolo*.

One evening in June 1927, when preliminary practices were being carried on in the kraals for the annual contests, I saw in a kraal in Mahumaneni the *ʃitʃobe* dance of the women. This was supposed to be a Tʃopi dance originally, but had been learnt by the Leŋge from their Tʃopi neighbours. This dance was accompanied by two drums, a large drum resembling the *ntakula*, but much larger, and the *ʃidekela* drum. The large drum was first placed for some little time near a fire for the sake of the skin membrane, to make it sound better when beaten. It was then moved near the *ʃidekela* drum, which was hung on the forked branch of a tree. A Tʃopi piano (*timbila* = *marimba*) was brought out, and the musicians began to tune up. The girls formed a procession in single file to the place near the drums where they were going to dance. Boys banged the drums and the piano with great energy, and each girl in turn took the floor (which was the sandy ground of the kraal). The dancers moved their ribs up and down like a concertina.

Some dogs gambolling in the kraal actually began to dance when they heard the music of the accompaniment, and some goats looked as though they were quite used to it all, and would very much like to dance, too, if they had not been tethered to a pole.

On July 25th, 1928, I witnessed part of one of these dancing contests in the kraal of the chief of Nteteni. It is to be noted that some of the local contests take place after the finals which have already taken place in the kraal of the premier chief. Notably this year this happened at Masiyeni and Nteteni, though both these sibs had already taken part in the finals at Nyamfuŋwini.

I was in a kraal at Nteteni one morning when a long line of women, girls, and children came through in single file. They were on their way to dance the *masessa* at the kraal of the *ŋganakana* of Nteteni, Maphamu Ntete. Some young girls were piping the *ʃigoriha*, some had whistles, and all carried batons of white wood decorated with black rings.

We followed the procession until it came to the chief's kraal, and there we found another dance going on which had nothing to do with the contest (*nzumba*). A circle of women were sitting round clapping their hands in accompaniment to a soloist dancer, an elderly woman with red-ochred hair who was dancing the spiritualistic dance of the *Ndau ṣikwembu*; but this was stopped when the other band of women arrived on the scene, and lined themselves up under the trees and began to dance. The leader stood in front of the row of women, who held up their batons as if in salute. Then she exhorted them, pointing with her baton like a musical conductress, and they gave her a hearty greeting. They all then planted their batons in the sand, leaning on them with the right hand. Rising again, they all clapped their hands, and one or two gave forth the peculiar *kuluŋgela* trilling. Two dancers stepped out into the arena, brandishing their batons, which they held aloft. They had pinned their long loin-cloths together so that they looked as if they were wearing knickers, and they wore other loose pieces of print tied round them in the usual way. The first movement was a kick-and-stamp dance. There were high kicks and resounding stamps. Sometimes two women danced alone, sometimes two others came to meet them. One young girl who trilled, and two small children, also danced a little at the side of the main performers. I was surprised to see the dancing of one little mite, hardly more than a baby, who had evidently been trained to take part in the dance. She carried a baton and occasionally turned to the main line of dancers and shook it at them like some old world dominie. She imitated perfectly the dancing of the elders. Another child, a little older, also danced well. It was evidently a dance of mothers and children.

The second movement in the *masessa* was a dance in which, first, the three children fell on the ground resting on the right arm, and moved their back limbs up and down; then three of the women did the same exercise, stamping with one foot at the same time. The musical accompaniment was the clapping of hands by the long line of women singing songs of which the *leit motif* seemed to be:

1. *Eza Dumayi, seda.*
2. *Tʃuka se!*
3. *Jimi! makwāā.*

When I asked the meaning of the songs, they said they did not know.

On several days in July 1928, while the dancing contests were being held, I visited Σihaɫu's kraal in order to watch the dancing, which was to last for a fortnight.

The first day I arrived I saw a very large *ʃikulu* drum being heated by a fire in the kraal by some men. Five boys then rolled it over till they reached the spot under the tree where it was to be placed. It was then raised a little from the ground and bound to a stout pole driven into the ground. To the left of the *ʃikulu* drum was another stout forked pole on which a *tluriso* drum (rather smaller than the *ʃikulu*) was tied, and to the left of that again was a *ʃidekela* drum, also on a two-forked pole or stake. A basket of drumsticks was hung on a fork of the pole which supported the *ʃidekela*. Then going still farther to the left were two Tʃopi pianos, of the kind known as *vamalandzani*, also supported on stakes, a stake on each side of each piano. The young men who were to beat the drums and play the Tʃopi pianos stood each behind his own instrument. A group of spectators, not very many (because it was a dull day), watched from opposite, the wives of the chief and other court habituées sitting in circles, and going on with their work of peeling manioc and preparing food for the evening.

After several réveillés (for the dancers appeared to be rather coy and unwilling to appear), a band of ten boys came dancing and prancing slowly from the hut which they had been using as a cloak-room in which to don their finery. They were going to dance the *aŋgalaŋga*. They first faced the music, keeping time with their feet and then, dancing all the time, they arranged themselves as if they were going to have a tug-of-war in two lines, five on this side, five on that. They wore feathers in their hair and *mafowane* rattles on their legs, and highly coloured handkerchiefs round their heads, knotted in front. Over their loin-cloths were worn grass girdles. Most wore *mafowane* rattles on one leg, and something like a horse's tail on the other. Wriggling and jumping movements are the characteristic of the *aŋgalaŋga*, especially the girdles are twirled round rapidly. The two front dancers bowed to each other occasionally. They were lined up before dancing so that the taller dancers stood in the centre. After the dance they wriggled back again to the hut, and another contingent, the Kondʒweni dancers, came out, very high stepping as they advanced. These were older than the first lot and more elaborately dressed, and although they danced better the dance was the same.

Another afternoon during the same contest, when I arrived in the chief's kraal, the dancing was in full swing. There must have been at least 1,000 people there, probably many more, for they were standing

PLATE XVIII

*AŊGALAŊGA* DANCE

in serried ranks some feet deep all round the kraal in a huge oval. Some of the girls had climbed a big tree as usual, in the centre. Even some Indians from stores in Vila de João Belo were looking on. The chief and his *tinduna* were sitting together watching the dancing. It was a very motley crowd, and a very orderly one. No one seemed to get into anybody else's way, and everybody had a good view, for the taller people withdrew themselves to the back row, and the front row were able to sit on the ground. Quite certainly I was the only person of European race present, and I was received very politely and a chair was brought from a hut for me and placed in the front row, likewise a mat for my native woman companion. The *aŋgalaŋga* dance, which I had already seen, was going on; but there was a variation in it, for one or two of the chief performers gave a mimic performance of all the other known dances, both those of men and women. Even the distinctive dance of the women's initiation rites was imitated. I should think it was a clever imitation of the other dances, for the congregation applauded and seemed much amused. During the performance of the *aŋgalaŋga*, occasionally one or two of the elder women would run out into the circle and encourage the dancers by trilling, and once a quite small boy danced out of the circle, right up to the chief, danced a *pas de seul* in front of him, evidently to salute him and win his applause, and returned. In a savage kind of way the scene was a brilliant one; the sunshine, the crowds of gaily dressed and good-natured onlookers; the girls looking on from the trees; the orchestra of huge drums and Tʃopi pianos; the extremely graceful dancing; the brilliant splashes of colour of the women's orange, blue, and red prints, with long fringes and head-kerchiefs, and the red-ochred hair of several women, made a memorable scene, and one not often witnessed.

On two other occasions when I saw the *aŋgalaŋga*, once at Ntʃoŋgweni (Chongoene) and once in Tʃopiland, the dancers were wearing wild beast skins, with a girdle of tails of the civet and genet cats, apparently. The favourite dance in 1928 was undoubtedly the *aŋgalaŋga* for the men, and the *masessa*, *ʃitʃobe* and *aŋginya* for the women. The *ʃitʃobe* dancers followed the *aŋgalaŋga* in the dance at Σihaɫu's. They wore grass and palm petticoats over their usual *tiŋguvo* and carried their batons in their hands with a *ʃigoriba* stuck on the top. The *aŋginya* dance I did not see. It is said to resemble the *masessa*.

## The Timbila Dance

I was fortunate enough to witness the great *timbila* dance at the kraal of Maɫatini, the chief of Zandamela, in the height of the dancing season in 1928. The time was early in the morning, and from a neighbouring kraal could be heard the drum of the women's *ambúʹtsa* dance. There were nineteen Tʃopi pianos of various kinds and sizes, two of which were much larger than a grand piano. They were named respectively *ʃikulu, ʃinzumani, bindagari, ʃilandzani,* and *dholi.* The dancers, who were all men, wore leggings and armlets of beasts' skins, with long hair, mostly of oxen and goats. Some wore skin-aprons, and three had brightly coloured dyed ostrich plumes, and one or two a head-dress (*ʃiŋgundu*), decorated at one side with a coloured wool rosette from Johannesburg; one had two horns as a head-dress; one carried a black ostrich feather slung over his arm with red wool. One had a rattle made of an old tin of metal polish into which a handle was stuck. The master-of-the-ceremonies walked up and down with an imposing looking staff with a knob. All the dancers carried staves or assegais and shields. They moved their assegais over the top of their shields, as in battle, to the right and to the left as they sang. Such a stirring war-song! Two men danced in front of the instruments, one impersonating a woman, while the rank and file of dancers were lined up behind. An old woman or two trilled most shrilly to incite the warriors. Crowds of men, women, and children witnessed the *timbila* dance. A few weeks later I saw the dance repeated in a neighbouring kraal. On this occasion, while the women were watching, some children danced out to the warriors, performed a *pas de seul* and danced back again.

*Other Dances*

*The ʃiŋgombelo.* The origin of this dance is lost in the mists of antiquity. It is a moonlight-night dance for young people of both sexes.

*A ʃiŋgombelo Melody*

'It was ordained by people of old that it should be danced at night only,' said my informant. The Tʃopi, the Thoŋga, and Ndau all dance it. A large circle of dancers is formed in some clearing in the bush, or in a large kraal. It begins about eight o'clock and goes on until midnight or after. One performer will dance out into the ring, choose somebody who will come out and dance too, then the first performer retires, and the second chooses some one else and so on. Meanwhile, the other dancers clap their hands (kutʃayela) and sing topical songs. All the news of the neighbourhood can be heard in this way. Engagements are announced, petty jealousies revealed, and sometimes the dancers hear surprising news about themselves, and what the world is thinking of them generally; but they hear it with music and rhythm.

One dancer sings a solo, and the others take up the refrain:

*Yeh! Yeh! a hi bati*
*Ndziku yavuya Ŋkambeni nuna wamina*
*Dlala ṣakuvuya*

(*Dlala* is an obsolete word for *kutlaŋgela*, 'to rejoice'. *Ŋkambeni* = general term for region occupied by white people.) *Yeh! Yeh! a hi bati!* (obsolete word for *kukina* or *kutʃina*, 'to dance'.)

My husband is returning from white man's land.
Rejoice! Let us dance!

The following resembles:

Peter Piper picked a peck of peppercorns
Ne'er a peck of peppercorns did Peter Piper pick.

*Ɛiŋgombelo ʃa makone, ʃa na hola mali!*
*Siku ʃana ʃamakone ʃi na hola mali!*

The *ʃiŋgombelo* of this year, it will receive money!
What day of the year shall it receive money?

(*Makone* = 'this year' in Leŋge.)

And again:

*Yeh! eh! eh! ʃiŋgombelo! ho tʃava Nyamandi*
*Eh! Eh! Eh!*
*Hi lava ʃiŋgombelo, aṣakona ha tʃava Nyamandi*
*Yeh! eh!* We fear *Nyamandi!*
We want the *ʃiŋgombelo*, but we fear Nyamandi!

(Nyamandi was a chief of the Zulus of olden days.)

*Dzakka! Dzakka! Dzakka! Dzakka! Dza! ha dlus!*
(Onomatopoeic for the sound of stamping in dancing.)

In the olden days the *ʃiŋgombelo* was played according to the method of dropping the handkerchief, each dancer choosing his or her beloved, but now it is done on the method of Sir Roger de Coverley, so that all get a turn in order. To the favourite tune given above are sung some such words as these:

*Ndza muvona nikukwela ʃitimela*
*Ya kwela ʃitimela Masiye*
*Ayo ndzi leleza* (*ku leleta* = 'to command').

All are quiet while one sings:

   *Ndza muvona*, &c. . . . *ſitimela Masiye*.

Then all the others join in the refrain:

   *Yeh! Yeh!*

(See *ſiŋgombelo* melody.)

> I see him going on board the steamer,
>  He climbs on board the steamer, does Masiye,
>   He commands me.

A tiny song to finish up the *ſiŋgombelo*:

> *Pau lo! Pau wa matube! Hiku hu!*
> *Hiku watumbe! Hi yetlela kwihi?*
> 
> (*Matube* is a white kind of manioc. *Kutumba* is to roast it by heaping up hot sand on it.)

This is sung in somewhat the same way as

> Hot cross buns!
> Hot cross buns! One a penny, two a penny, hot cross buns!

and may be translated as follows:

> Manioc bread! Manioc bread!
> Bread of manioc! All piping hot! Where shall we sleep?

The *Mutſoŋgolo* is the boys' version of the *timbila* (men's dance). It is also accompanied by the *tſiŋgu* drum,[1] which resembles a mortar.

The *ſigayisana* is also a boys' dance.

The *ſindzundindzaku* is a Tſopi dance. The women sit down on the ground, place their legs together, and wriggle backwards moving their shoulders. 'The men run away because the women have taken off their clothes', said my informant. In the *ſirwala*, with the accompaniment of the *aŋginya* drum, the women take off their clothes and put them on their head while they dance. The men run away. These dances must be unusual. I only heard of them from one informant. They are zoomimetic.

*Mourning Dances*

Some years ago, when I was present at some mourning ceremonies, I saw a dance called the *kumueleketa* = 'in order to accompany him' dance. The women formed a circle and two men in the centre of the

---

[1] The *tſiŋgu* and the *ſidekela* and the *ſikulu* are the same species of drum (apparently not used by the Ndau), resembling a mortar pierced below. The *ntakula* and the *ŋkiriŋgwane* drums resemble each other. The *ntakula* also resembles the *aŋginya*.

circle danced out through an opening in the ring, singing: '*Ya halatiwa ŋgati ya wena*', 'Thy blood is shed'. These words I took to refer to the victim, a goat which had been sacrificed to please the spirit of the person who was being mourned. The goat had been eaten ceremonially by the mourners.

On the same occasion a woman dancer executed a *pas de seul* in the circle of women, one or two old women making the shrill trilling called *kuluŋgela* which is supposed to please the ancestral spirits. The name of this dance was *mutaŋgala*.

I was told of a very old dance called *Gi-tʃa*, which has been dropped. The men danced it while the women clapped hands. The men made passes with rods over their heads.

*The ʃigandu* is a boy's dance. The boys donned *mabedzi* (skins) of *tihleŋgane* (small mammals). They made a ring and the *tʃiŋgu* drum accompanied the dancing.

*The Masessa* = to dance with the loins (see pp. 174–5). The origin of the name is not known. All women, married or single, take part in this. It is one of the favourite dances of the annual *nʒumba* or dancing-contests. The Tʃopi and Thoŋga dancers wear garments with long fringes. The women accompany this dance by clapping hands. Small reeds (*titekane*) are worn on the forehead and bosom.

## XV
# RELIGION, MAGIC, AND SORCERY
## I. RELIGION AND MAGIC

[NOTE. The Leŋge, like so many other tribes, have a genius for religion, exhibited sometimes in debased forms, such as demonology, but attaining its highest expression in ancestor worship. The spirits of ancestors in the direct male line are all-important, and their service and propitiation are the main concern of every religious mind. There is no belief in the existence of a Supreme Spirit, but, like the Thoŋga, the Leŋge refer vaguely to a power named *Tilo* or Heaven, which, however, does not seem to exercise much influence upon their lives. They believe, like some other South African tribes, that the first man and the first woman 'came out of a reed', and they will, if asked, show the kind of reed, apparently some species of bamboo. The common idea of origin connected with a reed suggests the possibility of a common origin for these tribes in Upper Egypt in prehistoric times. In the following pages I have tried to trace the outline of the old religion of the Leŋge. Pagan soil can 'suffer a change into something rich and strange' when the seeds of Christianity are planted in it, as the lives of many Leŋge bear witness.]

RELIGION among the pagan Leŋge revolves round the *tinyaŋga*, augurs or divination doctors, with their *titolo*, omens, or divination objects. These are the real priests of the people and their decrees are usually strictly obeyed. These are the different kinds of *tinyaŋga*.

(1) *Anyaŋga ya fikwaŋganza*, augur of trial by ordeal.
(2) *Anyaŋga ya titolo*, augur of divining omens. These are always men.
(3) *Anyaŋga* of the ancestral spirits[1] (*ṣikwembu ṣa maloŋga*), death rites, and plant medicines. These are usually men, but plant lore is often known by women who have picked up their husband's trade.
(4) *Anyaŋga ya ṣikwembu ṣa Vandau, ni ya kufemba ni ya mifukwa*, augur of Vandau spirits, of 'smelling out' and of *mifukwa* spirits, or demons. These, if women, are called *vanyamusoro*.

[1] An ancestral spirit, like that of one's own father, is a *fikwémbu*, with a marked emphasis on the second syllable, whereas the Ndau and Ðgoni spirits are referred to as *ṣikwembu* (no special emphasis), just as we should make a difference in intonation when we speak of 'The Great Being', in contradistinction to the word 'beings' in some such phrase as 'those little beings over there'.

(5) *Anyaŋga ya ɀikwembu ɀa Vaŋgunu*, augur of Ŋgoni spirits. These may be of either sex.

(1) *The ſikwaŋganza*

The *ſikwaŋganza* who superintends the trial by ordeal is the most important of the *tinyaŋga*. His role is that of a magistrate[1] as well as a diviner. His five methods of divination are (*a*) the *mondzo*, (*b*) the *ſipondwana*, (*c*) the *muɫaɫe* or *ſiteve*, (*d*) the *ſigwavuɫula*, and (*e*) the *bakata*.

(*a*) A Leŋge resorts to the *mondzo* ordeal to satisfy his honour. The augur prepares a very unpleasant, and intoxicating, as well as poisonous potion, called the *mondzo*. The person who takes it without harm is innocent. The guilty person falls down senseless or intoxicated. If he is delirious as he falls, that is supposed to be a proof of guilt. The mixture may be given in a liquid form in a small gourd, or in a solid form, mixed with cooked greens. One may ask the reason why one person can take this without harm, and another be poisoned thereby. The *anyaŋga* can answer this question (though if he did so perhaps his office would be ended). The reason is that after having heard all the facts of the case he gives either a very small quantity of the *mondzo* or a comparatively harmless mixture to the person whom he supposes to be innocent. One of my informants told me that the liquid in one little gourd will be water, and in another little gourd will be the poisonous mixture. I have no doubt that she was right, for she lived for a long time with a sister who was married to an *anyaŋga*, and learnt many of their little tricks.

A woman once came to our Mission starving, and an idiot. She had been accused by her relations of bewitching people, and had been given the *mondzo*, and had fallen down senseless. They left her where she fell to recover and to starve. She had a big open sore on her arm. She stayed with us till the sore was nearly healed. She seemed to be becoming more rational, and then one day she went away secretly and we never heard of her again. It was supposed that she feared her relatives had found out where she was, and were coming after her.

A girl who was about to have an illegitimate baby accused a certain boy of being the father of the child. The boy indignantly denied the accusation, and the girl was equally persistent in accusing him. This went on for months. At last the boy's father, who was a heathen,

[1] For this reason the natives have named a certain European magistrate *Σikwaŋganza*.

decided that the case must be referred to the arbitration of the *mondzo*. The boy, who had been baptized, refused. The case was never cleared up. The baby died.

A bundle of new clothes was stolen from a hut in which a number of persons had been sleeping. As it was impossible to prove the thief, some heathen tried to have recourse to the *mondzo* to settle the case.

It is a law of our country, a man when he lies persistently, and another does not know, they are very troubled, until they go to the chiefs. Also when they have arrived at the chiefs, the chiefs ask them: 'You, do you know what is being said by that man?' He [who is asked] denies, saying: 'I do not know.' Also the chiefs ask others: 'Did you see him stealing?' That man who is sure says: 'I saw him.' And the chiefs say: 'All right. It is our law here that you must settle the dispute with a fine.' Indeed [the accused] one says: 'I will bring forth my child [daughter] and give you if indeed I have stolen from you.' And he, the other, says: 'And I, I will give you another child, if you have not stolen from me.' Indeed they both go off with two policemen again. They arrive at the *tinyaŋga*. They tell them this matter. They begin to make them drink the *mondzo*. If one falls the police will come, they will capture all of them, they will return with them to the chief. They will tell the chief, saying: 'That one has fallen.' Indeed the chief tells him, 'Go and take your child and give it to him, while we, the chiefs, see him with our eyes (i.e. while we see that you do it').

(*b*) *The ſipondwana.* I have never had an opportunity of seeing this, but it was described to me as a kind of small buck's horn filled with medicine, and placed in a little gourd with a handle (*ſindzekwana*). The *anyaŋga* addresses the horn saying: 'Such-and-such a thing has happened. Perhaps so-and-so had something to do with this, and we suppose that he, or she, did such-and-such a thing.' If the horn is perfectly still in the bowl, the person is innocent, but if it begins to move, it confirms the person's guilt.

(*c*) The *muɫaɫe* or *ſiteve*, a tiny reed mat, fastened, like a flag, to a little pole, is also used as a means of divination. If a sick person consults the *muɫaɫe*, it is said to shut when the person is going to die. Also if the *anyaŋga* waves the flag to find out if a person is guilty or not, it will shut if the person is guilty.

(*d*) *The ſigwavuɫula.* This was described to me as a kind of pointed rod or stick fitting into a reed, from which it projects. A guilty person will fail to pull out the stick from the reed. Another informant told me that the pointed rod was made of the *ſitsalala* tree wood, and the outer receptacle was of carved *ŋkwakwa* (*Strychnos*) wood. I was informed by a Tʃopi woman that there is a little hole in the outer receptacle, and that if the *anyaŋga* presses on this with his thumb, the suction is such that the *ʃigwavutɫula* cannot be pulled out by the person whom the *anyaŋga* deems guilty.

(*e*) *The hakata*. It was the Ndau who taught the Leŋge this method of divination, which is rarely used. The *hakata*, which are sometimes pierced seed-pods, are used as omens, in cases where Ndau spirits are concerned. Divination omens of any kind seem to be termed *hakata* by the Ndau.

(2) *The Tiɫolo*

The method of divination with the *tiɫolo* or divining omens is as follows: The *anyaŋga* spreads out a mat. He takes a little *Juncus* root, and chews it and spits it out, saying, '*Psu!*' He beats himself on the back of his neck and on his chest. Then he takes his little bag and throws his bones on the mat. First, he finds out from his own *ʃikwembu* if he will be well himself. The answer being in the affirmative, he proceeds to find out the fortunes of the client according to the various positions in which the omens fall.

This method of divination has been thoroughly described by M. Junod.[1] I can just add a few remarks about some sets which I have myself seen. One day, on walking from one village to another, we passed through a kraal in the golden noon, and saw an *anyaŋga* with his bones spread out on a mat. Two men clients were sitting by listening eagerly to what he had to tell them. His rod with which he pointed lay beside him on the mat. It had a large copper ring inserted as a handle. Among the usual assortment of bones bound round with thin wire there were some curious and rare-looking sea-shells. Besides the bones and shells there was a tiny metal artifact, which the *anyaŋga* called a 'hoe'. It had probably been beaten out from an ordinary hoe. It was in shape like an elongated triangle, with incised lines, which were not the same on both sides. It was about two inches in length. The *anyaŋga* very kindly explained some of the positions of the bones. I should have liked to have bought the little hoe, but he would not sell it.

On another occasion, at a place in Tʃopiland, I saw a set which contained a curious semi-transparent glassy stone, of very irregular shape and surface, about one and a half inches long, of a very faint yellow

---

[1] *Life of a South African Tribe*, vol. ii (2nd ed.), pp. 541–72.

tinge (possibly a quartz crystal). I offered to buy it, but the *anyaŋga*, quite politely, but firmly, said that he could not sell it under any circumstances. He said that it had come from Johannesburg. There was something strange about that stone, though it is difficult to define what it was. It might possibly be a rain stone. I reflected that there must be many a curious object hidden in witch-doctors' skin-bags in the heart of Tʃopiland.

Ten shillings is the fee for divination, but you may have your fortune told by the bones for a shilling or a fowl. As regards the signification of the bones it is evident that it differs a little in different parts of the country and under different conditions. In a set from Dkumbeni the following significations were given me:

| *Titolo.* | *Signification.* |
| --- | --- |
| Buck, male | A man who deceives many women. |
| „ female | A woman who has committed adultery. |
| „ astragalus | A very bad woman. |
| Antelope(?) *mhala* | A woman who has had a stillborn child. If the bones reveal that this woman has caused the death of another child, by giving it food, before giving it 'medicine', she will be fined £2, which is given to the father of the dead child. |
| Ram (large) | Chief or headman. |
| Sheep | Wife of the chief or illness of a woman or girl. |
| Goat | An illness bone. Skin of goat must be sacrificed. |
| „ female, young | A young girl, *ŋombegyana*. If she is going to have an illegitimate child the bones reveal the father. |
| „ female, old | To find out cases of adultery; also cause of parent's illness. |
| Kid or lamb | Cases of delayed birth. |
| Pig, old | Spirit (*ʃikwembu*) of a parent. |
| „ young | Generally a child's spirit. |
| „ wild | Signifies that offerings must be given to the *ʃikwembu* when a child is sick. |

If these occur near the big *Cypraea* shell, this signifies that the *ʃikwembu* are sleeping.

| Turtle | Illness of man, woman, or child, according to the size of the bones. |

PLATE XIX

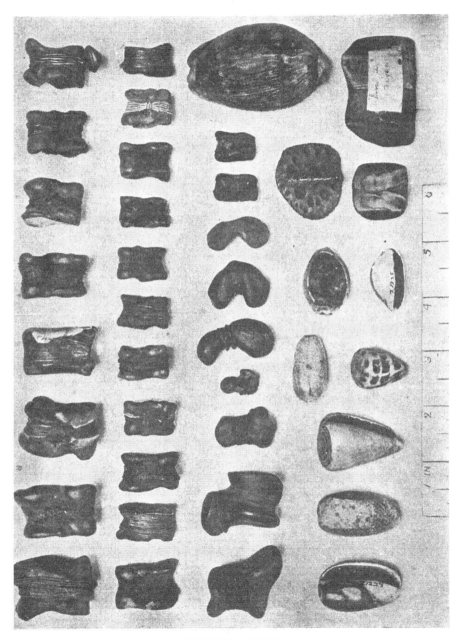

DIVINING OMENS

| *Titolo.* | *Signification.* |
|---|---|
| Tortoise, breast bone | A woman. |
| „ lower chin bone | A woman in a case of delayed childbirth. |
| Monkey | Sometimes the diviner's wife, sometimes a gadabout person who cannot settle down with one spouse. |
| *Cypraea* shell, spotted | An ancestral spirit. |
| *Tfakaho* shell | A widow in a case of ceremonial purification (*kulała khombo*), i.e. the woman has taken another husband. |
| *Σivimbiri* and *vimbi* shells | Young girls. These occur in cases of sorcery. |
| *Σirwalandzundza* | Some one who does not want to take medicine, and hides it. |
| Plum kernels of *Sclerocarya caffra* (*makanye*) | Signify that sacrifices must be offered by the father when the child is sick. |
| Astragalus of goat | An important *anyaŋga* works with this bone. He cuts a boy's[1] tongue with the native razor (*likari*) and injects some medicine into the cut. The bone is put upon the boy's wrist on a metal bangle. The *anyaŋga* prays to his ancestral spirits before performing this rite. It is supposed to be a very powerful charm against the sorcerers. |

One afternoon when at Mahumaneni, I saw an *anyaŋga* casting his bones time after time, the whole afternoon, in order to obtain new combinations of them. He must have done this at least thirty times. It was in order to find out what combinations of circumstances had made his youngest child, about two or three years old, ill. The next morning, early, I heard piercing shrieks coming from the other side of the kraal, and looking out of the door of my hut I saw the ailing child being held up naked in the open air by its mother, while its father, the *anyaŋga*, was spraying it vigorously with a brush of leafy twigs, dipped into a large wooden bowl of medicine. I suppose the shrieks were caused by the fact that the child had spent the night in a hot hut, wrapped up and close to the fire, and naturally objected to being brought out into the cold air of an early winter morning to be sprayed with an icy decoction. I was told that the spraying was to reduce the temperature of the child, but I have no doubt at all that it was also to ward off the evil influences of sorcerers. I heard afterwards that the child had recovered.

[1] A boy in the omens is called *murisane* or *fikunana*.

(3) *The Şikwembu or Spirits*

Şikwembu to be propitiated by the *tinaŋga* are of three kinds:

(A) The *maloŋga* (slaves)[1]. These are the ancestral spirits of the immediate relations of the Leŋge *şikwembu*.

(B) Vandau *şikwembu* and (C) Vaŋgunu (Ŋgoni) *şikwembu*.

There are also three other kinds of spirits whose occurrence is accidental rather than universal—that is to say, they do not form an integral part of the religious cult of the Leŋge. These are:

(D) *Tindzundzu* or water spirits.

(E) *Mifukwa mademona* or demons (sometimes ghosts).

(F) *Şitukutwane* (messenger spirits).

(A) *The Maloŋga or Ancestral Şikwembu*

The most important of these are the father, the father's sister, and the grandfather (of the same surname).

The father and father's father are really the only ancestors who count, the great-grandfather being just mentioned sometimes. The mother and mother's brother are also mentioned casually, as it were, because they belong to a different line—the mother being more important than the mother's brother, because she is counted as one with the father.

A man cannot sacrifice directly to his relations on his mother's side, but he may include the names of the chief ones when making a direct sacrifice to his father and mother. Thus Jacob, the eldest son of Jeremiah, cannot sacrifice to his mother's brother David in the kraal at the altar (*gandzelo*), but he can do so outside the kraal, just to make a little offering. Jacob cannot sacrifice to his mother if his father is alive; the father himself will do it. A wife may sacrifice to her dead husband, but not if her husband's father is alive to do it for her. Her son may, of course, sacrifice to his father if he is old enough. A sister may sacrifice to her brother, but she must do it in his kraal, not hers, if she is married.

If a boy or girl dies unmarried, the *şikwembu* of this young person has no power to make a living relative ill. Boys may not offer a sacrifice if unmarried, unless all their relations are dead. A young girl may only offer a sacrifice if the whole of her family who are older than herself are dead. If both her parents are dead, and she has no elder brother or sister, then she may sacrifice to the parents. The women of a family

---

[1] Possibly called 'slaves' because of the Zulu conquests previously described.

can never offer a sacrifice if they have brothers to do it for them, unless it is a woman who is sacrificing to her husband.

The Leŋge do not distinguish between good and bad ancestral spirits, beyond the fact that they would not offer a sacrifice to a person who committed suicide.

## *The Primitive Altar*

In the case of the *maloŋga*, the sacrifice (*mhamba*) will be offered at the *gandzelo* (the primitive altar) under the sacred tree in the kraal, if the spirit to whom the sacrifice is being offered is that of the father (with the mother), grandparent, or father's sister.

If the propitiatory offering is to a relative like a mother's brother, or some one not in the same (paternal) line of descent, the sacrifice will be offered at a *figodo fakufa* (tree-stump of death) outside the kraal.

A man will return to offer sacrifices at the tree near which his father or mother died, even if it be dead (in which case it is called a *fikunzulu*).

The point is that sacrifices cannot be offered within the kraal, at the *gandzelo* under the sacred tree, for any one not in the direct male line.

A father may make an offering to his dead daughter in his own kraal if she was grown up and married, because she was of the same line of descent as he. Her husband, the widower, could also sacrifice to her in his kraal.

After death an ancestral spirit will remain in the bush, 'the *ɡikwembu* are sleeping',[1] until such time as it shall desire a sacrifice. Then it will return to the kraal and make some one ill. A *fikwembu* is, of course, never driven away. It would kill the person who attempted to do so. If a snake is seen which is supposed to be the embodiment of the spirit, then the people will be glad. When the required sacrifice has been performed, then the spirit will dwell afterwards at the altar made for it under the tree. Spirits like to dwell near the trees because their altar is there. A tree under which there is a *gandzelo* is never cut down. Spirits seem to have power to haunt the bush, although their altar is under a tree in the old kraal, for sacrifices may be offered in the bush or on the path.

In passing through a kraal one often sees a rag with a fringe tied round a tree. Underneath the tree is a little pot containing beer of some kind, placed in a little depression scooped in the sandy soil. Trees in the kraal to which these rags are tied are *ŋkanye* (*Sclerocarya caffra*); or *ukulu* (*Trichilia emetica*); or *nlapfu* (a tree with a curious knobbed

[1] See p. 186.

bark). A rag tied round a tree is a substitute for clothes given to an ancestral spirit.

If any big sacrifice is being offered, little handfuls of beans, mealies, Kaffir-corn, monkey-nuts, or any produce of the fields in the way of seeds are put at the *gandzelo*. Also the sacrificer will take a sip of beer from the chalice (*gombe*), and spit it out, uttering the magical syllable '*Psu!*' This is for the *fikwembu*. The people will be very careful not to tread on these offerings. The fowls may eat them, or they are allowed to rot away.

If a person visits the place where a father or mother died, he will take some mealies as an offering. A man will also offer snuff.

*Sacrifice and its Conditions*

On the occasion of very important sacrifices a whole week of continence is observed.

The key-note of the worship of the ancestral spirits is certainly propitiation.

*The Sacrificial Animal*

The divination *anyaŋga* decides by the throwing of the bones which animal is to be offered for sacrifice. If the omens refuse a male animal, then a female will be chosen. Failing the father in a family, the father's sister will go to the *anyaŋga* for this purpose, if the sons are not grown up. If a man goes to one diviner, and his sister goes to another, the verdict of the two diviners must agree, if not, then the sister must go to her brother's *anyaŋga* again. If, however, a man goes to the *anyaŋga* and the decree of the omens is that a female animal must be killed, then the man will have to pay a second visit accompanied by his sister.

The *anyaŋga* who comes to purify a kraal will perform a sacrifice on his own behalf to his own ancestor in order that he may be helped to do the work of purification, but in cases of direct sacrifice it is the headman of the kraal who will perform it; first the father, failing the father, the elder brother, failing the elder brother, the one next to him. If the sacrifice is not acceptable to the spirit, some one in the kraal will be ill. If all goes smoothly then the sacrifice is acceptable; and why not? Of course the spirits desire sacrifices. They have probably revealed their desire for such in a dream to the owner of the kraal or one of his relations.

A kid with a black and white skin is a favourite animal for a sacrifice. One is often seen tied to a tree for the purpose.

When food is eaten as a sacrificial offering, nothing must be left of it. If an animal is killed, three small pieces of meat mixed with a little bit of skin are put at the *gandzelo* for the *fikwembu*. Everything else is eaten but the bladder, the *psanye*, and bones. The teeth and skull are hung up in a tree or put on the roof of a hut. The bones are sometimes burnt. The eyes and brains are eaten by some. (Others fear that if they do this, white hairs will put in an appearance too quickly.) Any remains which may be left on the ground after a mourning lamentation (*firilo*) are swept up and put on the ash-heap. The gall-bladder (*anyoŋgwa*) is worn by a *nyamusoro*, also by a bride and bridegroom and best man at the time of an *akulobola*. Small strips of the skin are tied round medicine-gourds (*tinoŋgovane*) in order that the *fikwembu* may know about it. A strip of the skin (*voya*) of an ox or ram is tied round the neck of a big pot 'to strengthen the pot'.

If fowls are sacrificed the Leŋge kill them at the *figonzo* (back of head). The Ŋgoni stab their sacred animals with a spear.

When a kid is sacrificed, sometimes the bones are taken and heated in the hearth-ring, and added to roots of *Desmodium dregianum* (?) and the fat of the kid to make *muri wa baselo*, the great *baselo* medicine. The bones and ashes are hidden in the bush among the deep grasses so that no dog can get hold of them. The *baselo* is a great medicine for people who are dying. It is given them as a 'blessing' medicine. Torches are made of it and burnt in honour of a possessing spirit.

The sacrificial goat is not always killed. Sometimes one is dedicated and then let loose in the manner of a scapegoat, as described here.

Also the heathen, with regard to their spirits, some are with very troublesome spirits, they constantly make them ill every day, and they begin to go to the divining bones, the *tinyaŋga* tell them, saying: 'Go and search for a goat and sacrifice with it, saying the name of a grandparent who is dead, that the sufferer may be well.' Indeed they look for a goat. They come with it outside to their altar. They sacrifice it, mentioning the names of all their dead relatives, saying: 'Here is the goat, I give it to you, that you may cease to be angry with me, I confess to you, give me life that I may be like other people here on the earth.' Indeed he finishes, he starts off and begins to put aside the goat that it may not be killed by any one, because if they kill it, they must find another to fill its place to please the spirits, that they give him life.

In the case of mourning ceremonies, each person throws away a tiny bit of meat on the ground for the *fikwembu*. If both parents are dead, the right hand and the left hand will be used simultaneously, the right hand for the father, the left hand for the mother; right hand if father only is dead, left hand if mother only is dead. As regards the division of the animal, the men usually have the head and legs. A *hahane* will have a leg, too. The daughter-in-law has ribs or a fore-leg. The sacrificer shares the liver with his *hahane*. The *anyaŋga* will have liver also, or a leg, if he is present. The head and the feet go to the *vakokwane* usually. The kidneys (*titʃo*) will be given to the son-in-law, and the hoofs to boys.

The ritual of sacrifice is as follows for sick people:

Every one spits[1] when they sacrifice. If they wish to sacrifice a goat, they cut a little of the skin of the goat, chew it and spit it out, saying: 'You, so-and-so, it is a goat which I am giving you. When I am well, I will kill for you the goat which I am giving you.' Also when they wish to offer beer, they sip it and spit it out, saying: 'You, so-and-so, it is beer which I am giving you when I am well' (i.e. it is an earnest of the gift to follow).

Or if a water-sacrifice is offered:

This is the dividing stream! let me conquer my enemies that they fear me (This is an introduction to be followed by a torrent of words).

Another prayer of a sick person is as follows:

*Psu!* Why, father, do you trouble me, you father, and grandfather, we wish to sleep *ti! ti! ti! ti!* (*ti* = sound of coolness expressive of health.)

Let us alone, father, that we may be well, we your poor children! Gently! father, gently! let us alone, father, that we may be well! Don't you see your child, &c., &c.

An entreaty for the increase of live stock:

You, Σimiti (name of father) and you, Ɖgenzi (name of grandfather) and you, Davane (name of father's sister) and your relations, give me health, that you fight for me against those who kill me. I give you my fruits and your animals and your fowl. Help me indeed, that I sleep well, every day.

### Ancestral Spirits and Agricultural Rites

Sacrifices are made to the ancestral spirits before sowing. In June it will be *vuputso la mahila* (Kaffir-corn beer). 'Greeting (i.e. the sun is up!) Help us to sow good fruits!'

*Sacrificial Rites.*[2] The digging in August and September is preceded by sacrifices offered to the ancestral spirits. The headman of a kraal will one day invite many women to congregate in order to dig a large

---

[1] The Ndau do not spit when sacrificing, but clap their hands. Leŋge ancestral spirits may not be greeted by hand-clapping, but by having dried palm fronds waved in their honour.

[2] The substance of the following notes has been reproduced from my paper in *Bantu Studies*, ii, 1925, pp. 193-7.

field. They meet at sunrise. Before they begin to dig the owner of the land addresses the women: 'Give me some mealies that I may offer a sacrifice.'

He uses the mealies scraped off the cob. He takes some maize in his right hand for his father, and some in his left hand for his mother, if he has lost both parents. If neither of his parents is dead, he cannot offer a sacrifice, not even to his grandparents or other ancestors, but one of the diggers who has lost one or both parents will sacrifice (*kupała*) instead.

Failing mealies, Kaffir-corn can be used in this rite, but if neither is accessible, handfuls of earth may be used as a substitute. The grain is thrown on the ground by the headman as he utters a little invocation, such as: 'You, my Father and my Mother, give me of all kinds of the fruits of the earth.' When he has finished, the diggers who have lost one or both parents will sacrifice in the same way in order that their friends' fields may be blessed with fruitful increase.

*The Kahola Rite.* About the end of November or beginning of December a very important religious rite takes place. The people take baskets of seeds of various kinds to the chief, who invites the great *anyaŋga* to come to his village. The chief gives the *anyaŋga* a basket of seeds. The *anyaŋga* sacrifices to his ancestral spirits, and rubs the seeds all over with a kind of soot made from the charred and pounded roots of sacred plants and trees.[1] The name of this important medicine is *kahola*. Two of the chief's helpers carry other basketfuls. In the dead of night the *anyaŋga*, carrying a basketful of seeds, goes out to the fields accompanied by two of the chief's men carrying more baskets, who show him the various gardens belonging to the chief's people. The *anyaŋga* scrapes a hole in each garden, and places a few seeds of various kinds in it, mealies, ground-nuts, beans, earth-peas, &c. He does not use any form of invocation while placing the seeds in the hole.

*The Day of Muzilo.* Next day at daybreak the *anyaŋga* returns from his rounds and goes back to the chief's kraal. He procures two large bags made of rooiebuck (*maŋgulwe*) skin. He commands the helpers to go and fill the bags with leaves of all kinds of trees and plants. They fill the bags and return about midday. Two large mats are spread on the ground and the leaves are first heaped up on the mats and then cut up into small pieces by the helpers, while the *anyaŋga* and another assistant seek for wood to make a fire. An enormous fire is soon kindled

---

[1] I was told that the Va ka Nyahule, one of the Leŋge sibs, derives its *fiboŋgo* from this medicine.

in the compound (*nsenzele*). The leaves are cooked in large pots. Fowls are killed, plucked, and cooked in other pots. The vegetables are stirred in the pots with a pestle named *ntovo*.[1]

Meanwhile a crowd of people has collected, men, women, and children. When everything is ready the pots are taken off the fire and the feast begins. The water in which the leaves were cooked has become a vegetable soup, which is eaten with the fowls. The *anyaŋga* begins by eating the liver of the fowls. The food is placed in the hands of the people and they sup ceremonially. The verb which expresses this action is *kukweva*. Women who are expectant mothers must not partake of this meal, but the *anyaŋga* gives them a little of it, mixed with medicine made from charred and pounded roots (*nsita*) and they rub it on their arms and bodies. Women who have babies must feed them at the breast ceremonially.

The chief buries the leaves from which the *kahola* medicine (*muri wakuhola*) was prepared in a hole and they rot away. The *anyaŋga* puts aside in a wooden bowl some medicine made from uncooked leaves and water. This is the water which he afterwards uses for sprinkling huts to keep the evil spirits and sorcerers away. That day all the fires are extinguished in the huts of the people. If they should keep their fires alight, they would lack food at harvest time, the seeds would not grow in the fields. Four assistants are sent out to scour the country far and wide to see that no fires have been left alight. If they find one still burning by inadvertence, they would promptly extinguish it. The *anyaŋga* himself puts out the fire in the chief's hut. The only fire left burning in the district is the large sacred fire kindled by the *anyaŋga* himself, and continually replenished with fuel by the wives of the chief. At sundown, all the fires in the kraals are relighted from this big sacred fire by means of torches carried by the adjutants. The *anyaŋga* himself relights the chief's fire. He then marches solemnly round the chief's kraal accompanied by two servers, one carrying the bowl of sacred water, and the other plucking a fowl and scattering its feathers in all directions. The *anyaŋga* dips a spray of *ŋkuɫu* leaves into the water and sprinkles the huts with it outside. He then stands in the doorway and throws some of the water inside. His helpers afterwards go to the other kraals and bless them by asperging the huts with the water to protect them from the evil influences of sorcerers.

This day is called the day of *muzilo* apparently because cohabitation

---

[1] The Va ka Nya ku Ntovo sib of N. Tʃopiland is said to derive its surname from this implement.

is prohibited during the night of the *kahola* rite, and on the day of *muzilo*. But afterwards, it must be confessed, an amount of sexual licence is permitted which would lead one to think that these are fertility rites.

After a few weeks the seeds that the *anyaŋga* planted at night have grown several inches. It is tabu ever to gather these plants. Any one who gathers them would die.

A variation of the *kahola* rite took place at Masiyeni in 1930. The chief invited the Ndau *anyaŋga* to come to his kraal to doctor the seeds. All the women were ordered to bring their baskets of seeds and their hoes to the chief's kraal. Then the *anyaŋga* sprinkled the seeds with medicine, and anointed the hoes with oil of *Trichilia emetica*.

*The Lumela or Feast of the First-fruits*. On the third month after the *muzilo*, the *lumela* or feast of the first-fruits takes place. No one must reap or gather the produce of the kind of plants of which sample seeds were sown at the *kahola* rite, until the public thanksgiving that the first-fruits have not been destroyed by grubs or worms has been offered. The same *anyaŋga* arrives at the chief's kraal, where a large congregation has assembled. He has a supply of *nsita* medicine with him. He and his helpers provide a plentiful meal of cooked green vegetables of all kinds (*matsavu*), which is served in ten large carved wooden bowls (*tiŋgelo*), borrowed from the chief. He takes some red ochre, and draws a magic ring (*atsala* = he writes), round each bowl with it. Each person takes a tiny pinch of the *matsavu* mixed with *nsita*. The rules for the women are the same as described for the *muzilo*. The *anyaŋga* has offered in his own home sacrifices to the ancestral spirits. In public he gives thanksgiving for the first-fruits. Then the people go home and may gather *matsavu* and mealies (*sifake*). But if any of the people are possessed by Ndau or Ŋgoni spirits they will offer sacrifices to those spirits before they dare to gather the produce of their fields.

These rites seem to be full of symbolism. The *anyaŋga* acts as the priest and representative of the people, but in alliance with the chief. The *kahola* rite seems to represent the birth and death of the spirit of the corn, who possibly appears under another form in the goat slain during one of the most important rites of the women's initiation ceremonies. The *anyaŋga* is usually a near relation of his chief, possibly a cousin, but relationship is not an essential. He may be of Ndau origin. The sacred fire was almost certainly made by friction of sticks in the olden days, but the tendency now is to take a brand from an ordinary fire. It is probable that some potent medicine is mixed with the charred and pounded roots of the sacred plants and trees.

## Ancestral Spirits, Rain Making, and Sacrifice[1]

A rite for rain and the multiplication of fish was described to me as enacted by the Mukavele sib.

Relations of the family were invited. A fowl was caught but not killed. Beer (*vuputso*) was prepared, and maize was pounded. A little hut had been built on a hill near the sea, a small edition of the ordinary dwelling-hut. The family had a ceremonial meal, and some of the mealies and beer were put in a pot (*fiduwana*) and placed in the hut as an offering to the ancestral spirits. The live fowl was dedicated to them and shut up in the house, where it pecked away at the food. Before leaving, the door of the little hut was opened so that the fowl could come out, but it would remain in the neighbourhood of the hut, and return there to roost. It was 'food' for the spirits.

This rite was supposed to bring rain, and also to increase the 'fruits' (fish) of the sea, because 'the sea belongs to the ancestral spirits, the sea is of our forefathers'.

Another rain-making account was given me by one of the Masiye sib.

First when people of old built a kraal in the bush, there where had died their chief, they make a remembrance by building an enclosure. Others build a little house inside the enclosure. They dig a hearth-circle on the ground, they search for clothes. They plant sticks near the hearth, in order that it should be their remembrance. At other times they go there. There gather together there many people, they sacrifice, they kill goats and fowls. The spirits are very pleased indeed, they will send rain and food to help them very much. The people invite each other to go there, they bring out offerings of food to give to the spirits. Also at other times when there was great heat and the rain did not fall, the people invite each other again, they assemble at the place of sacrifice. They sacrifice, they dance, they pray indeed to the spirits that they will make the rain fall again. And also when the rain did not fall, they are very troubled, they return, they seek other *tinyaŋga*, they cast the bones, they ask, saying: 'Why are the spirits angry that there is no rain even for a day?' Another *anyaŋga* tells them that they need to kill an ox, also the person of a young girl, to sacrifice her.

### (B) *Vandau Ṣikwembu and Vaŋgunu Ṣikwembu*

I am about to describe some religious phenomena which are widespread throughout the whole of Gazaland, and which exert an almost unbelievably powerful influence over the heathen people. The cases

[1] For ancestral spirits in connexion with birth, marriage, and death, see Chapters VI, XII, XIII.

of 'possession' (so-called) by Ndau or Ŋgoni spirits are so frequent among the natives that they may be said to be of common occurrence, and to be daily on the increase.[1] The Ŋgoni spirits (of Zulu origin) are connected with the Ndau spirits, because many bands of Ndau having been taken prisoners by the Ŋgoni during the invasions of Gazaland and the Sabi River district (Vusapa), and having settled in this country, have become interpenetrated with the Zulu and Tʃopi elements. There is a saying that the ghost of a Mundau never dies, meaning that if any injury has been done to a Mundau, or if he has been killed by any one in war or otherwise, his ghost will never leave the family of the person who inflicted the injury until full redress has been obtained.

Therefore the world-wide cult of spiritualistic seances (called *Vu-ŋgoma* by the Leŋge) has attained a rank growth in Gazaland, not being restrained by civilized influences. The 'possessing' spirits are maleficent in their origin, that is to say, they owe a grudge of some sort to the person 'possessed' but they may be appeased and propitiated so that in the end, if they do not actually become beneficent, they cease to be troublesome. The psychological motive of the seances is really that of converting hostile forces into friendly ones.

The altar or sacrificial spot for spirits of Ndau or Ŋgoni origin is the *ʃipandzi*, or three-forked branch of a tree inserted into the floor of the hut. I have seen this at the back of the hut opposite the door, or just inside the door on the right. A Tʃopi woman told me that in her sister's hut were two of these three-forked poles, one was for her sister's husband who was possessed by a spirit of Zulu origin, and the other for his wife, who was possessed by a spirit of Ndau origin which would never reveal its identity. But they knew the name of the Zulu spirit.

People who have possessing spirits to propitiate offer the first-fruits of everything to these spirits, especially fermented drinks and oil seeds.

*Description of a Seance*

A description of a seance which took place at Masiyeni recently will illustrate the general procedure.

A Leŋge man named Mabumu Σileŋge had an ancestor (grandfather) named Bembane. The Ŋgoni during the war had given Bembane a girl of Ndau origin named Nyaŋkwavane (whose husband had been killed by a Zulu assegai, and she herself taken captive) to be a sort of

[1] Hysterical religious movements of this kind are usually due to some disturbance or distress in the tribal life.

slave-wife to Bembane, to cultivate his fields. Nyaŋkwavane had been only a few days in Bembane's kraal when she fell very ill. Bembane, not wanting a sick wife of foreign origin, took her into the bush and left her there to die. She, however, being too weak to walk, crawled back to his kraal on her knees. When Bembane's other wives saw her come back they told him. He took a thick cord and made a noose of it, and tied her to a tree. 'She died of starvation and the cord', said my informant, who belongs to the family of Σileŋge. The ghost of Nyaŋkwavane is supposed to haunt all the relations of Bembane in turn. Mabumu's wife is the latest victim; that is to say, that having fallen ill, she attributes her illness to the fact that she 'has'[1]—is 'possessed' by—Nyaŋkwavane's *fikwembu*. The divining bones revealed the fact. Now her whole attention is concentrated on the appeasement of Nyaŋkwavane. She has given Nyaŋkwavane's *fikwembu* a goat, fowls, clothes, and *mahimbe* beer. Nyaŋkwavane expressed through the medium her gratitude for these gifts. What happens to the offerings? The clothes would be put aside for a time, and then worn by Mabumu's wife herself, as the spirit of Nyaŋkwavane was possessing her. The goat would be reserved until it was wanted for food, but if it were killed another must be chosen to take its place. The same would happen to the fowls. The beer would be drunk by Mabumu's wife.

On the night of December 12th and 13th, 1924, I heard the drums in Mabumu's kraal all night long. There was a seance (*ŋgoma*). Mabumu's wife was dancing with the *anyaŋga* of the Ndau spirits, as is usual on these occasions. She was wearing her red-ochred head-dress, and was holding high her ritual axe, the *thema* or *fidzedze*, as she danced. (This axe is curved in form, and has no use beyond a ritual one.) The onlookers were clapping their hands and singing: '*Yo weh! Yo weh! Nyaŋkwavane!*'

Occasionally one sees a little girl with red-ochred hair and heavy brass anklets (*masindza*), who has been offered to one of these spirits. The girl generally lives in a hut, called her 'temple', by herself. I am informed that nothing 'bad' is done to these dedicated children. They are simply 'separated'. If she marries, another girl must take her place —the alternative being that a dedicated girl's husband should come to live in her kraal instead of her going to his home. I once saw a beautifully built little red-earth hut, or temple, of one of these girls, at Σ*ilumbelo*; and in the same district a rather larger one for a woman. The woman's hut was very clean and artistically built. The woman

[1] The Leŋge say 'She *has* the spirit of Nyaŋkwavane'.

herself was covered with red ochre. She was sitting in her hut, or temple, surrounded by interesting looking pots, for she was a potter, like so many of the women in that district.

Some people believe that they can pick up, as it were, these spirits on the road or at the lake, or by seeing a small snake called *fitsetsa*, on the pathway. If a person is ill who has been possessed by a Ndau or Ŋgoni spirit, and the people see a small snake called a *fitsetsa* or a *ndlondlo*, they think it is the spirit which has come out of the sick man, and if it speaks the man will die. If, however, a cloth is offered as a sacrifice the man will live. Some even think that a spirit can haunt the runners of plants. '*Σilavile kumhu, ɡoɡi filavile mina*' = 'It wanted a plant, but now it has wanted me.' At other times a spirit can haunt the walls of a house. If the Leŋge see beads lying in the path, they frequently will not touch them, lest they should be an offering to some *fikwembu*, which might haunt them in consequence of their picking up the beads.

Sometimes if a *fikwembu* is very troublesome, the medium will go to an *anyaŋga* of the divining bones, who will inform her that she must go to a big *anyaŋga* of the Ndau *ɡikwembu*, who advises that the troublesome spirit should have a formal burial in the lake. The person possessed will go with the *anyaŋga* to the lake, carrying her red-ochred garments, which have been put in a *ntundu* basket, with some medicine and the *thema* axe. These are gifts for the *fikwembu*, who will remain in the lake with them. A *fikwembu* which lives in the lake is known as *ndzundzu (tindzundzu)*. (Cf. p. 215).

## The Vanyamusoro and Spiritualistic Seances

*Nyamusoro* is a Ndau word.

A person who is possessed by a spirit may become a servant or *anyaŋga* of that spirit, when, after an elaborate ritual, the spirit has first revealed its identity (*kutwasa*), and afterwards in a dream has intimated that such is its desire. The possessed person can then work on other people (*kufemba*) to make the spirits of which they are possessed reveal their identity also. In order to become an *anyaŋga* of the *ɡikwembu*, the possessed person has to undergo an initiation, and afterwards becomes a regular *anyaŋga*, having patients in the kraal, who are also supposed to be possessed and healing them by bringing to the light the possessing spirits which are causing them harm and making them ill. A secondary important work is to smell out (*kufemba*) criminals and sorcerers and to discover the *ɡigono*, those mysterious thought-entities sent on errands of black magic by their owners. I shall presently describe the *ǵigono*.

## P. Muyanga's Story

The following account was given me by P. Muyanga, a blind Christian woman, of what happened to her in the days of her heathenism, when she was possessed.

She had been ill, had had 'swollen legs for a year or more', and so her father went to the *anyaŋga* of the divination bones. The *anyaŋga* decreed that the father must procure a male goat, which should be all black, with the exception of one white spot above the nose (*ſivhaka*), and after that must consult the omens again. So the father bought a black goat with a white spot for four silver *quinientos*, and then obediently went to the doctor again. Now P. had a sister who was a real *nyamusoro*, and whose work it was to smell out (*kufemba*). The doctor told the father to go home and to tell the womenfolk to stamp grain for making beer, and to advise the *nyamusoro* sister to get the *mandiki* drums beaten, in order to make the spirit (which was causing P. to have 'swollen legs') reveal its identity. P.'s mother also bought two pieces of material from a local Indian store, a white *anjiti* cloth and a black one. Preparations were made for the seance. Crowds of people came, and large quantities of mealie-meal porridge and beer were prepared. The patient was entirely veiled. The white *anjiti* cloth enveloped her head and body as far as the knees, and her feet and legs were covered with the black cloth. The *nyamusoro's* husband and son were to beat the drums. They began the proceedings about five or six o'clock in the evening. The hut was so crowded it was decided to hold the seance outside in the kraal. A huge fire was lighted. The moon arose. The men began to beat the drums, more and more fast and furious. Dukasiyeti, the *nyamusoro*, wearing horse-hair anklets and bracelets, began to dance, her brush for smelling out (*tſovo*) slung on her arms. She continued dancing a solo, while the patient P., her sister, sat in silence with her hands crossed on her knees, and wrapped in grave-clothes, so to speak. Then the *nyamusoro's* own possessing spirit began to reveal its will. She cried: '*Whoo! Whoo! Whoo!*', which was the sign that the spirit wished to communicate the information desired. The *nyamusoro's* husband gave her the ritual assegai and curved axe, and some pieces of material. Dukasiyeti, still continuing the '*whoo*'-ing, danced up to P., and began to brush her with the *tſovo*, tapping her on the head and chest with it, and then smelling the brush.

Then she pretended that she had caught the spirits which were troubling P. on her head, and fell down, clutching her throat. Then her husband and the others, knowing the name of the *nyamusoro's* own possessing spirit, called out in Zulu: 'Greeting! *Waka Njamini waka Ŋgumayo Manukosi!* (name of spirit.) Gently! Gently! Gently!' (i.e. Do not get too excited in revealing your will to us. We are ready to hear and to serve.)

Now in P.'s case she was possessed by two spirits, a man and a woman, and the woman was supposed to be mad, because she had forbidden P. to wash or to do her hair, and had made P. scratch herself all over. P. said her spirits were a Ŋgoni (Zulu) man and a Mundau woman.

The *nyamusoro*, having quieted down a little, sat on a mat, spreading a garment over her knees like a rug. She should have sat on the special stool or *figara*, but her husband had not been able to afford to buy her one. The first remark of Waka Njamini waka Ŋgumayo Manukosi was: 'I want a young girl to give me food.' When the girl attendant came Waka Njamini said: 'I want the husks of maize.' The *nyamusoro* ate, singing, and then she asked for water. The people crowded round, saying: 'Tell us, tell us, what your business is', addressing P.'s own spirits. The drums were beaten more furiously, P. began to shake and quiver. They hastened to take the *fivhaka* goat decreed by the *anyaŋga* of the omens, and raised it by a fore-leg and a hind-leg, cutting its throat, and raising the bleeding neck to the patient, so that she might imbibe a draught of the warm blood. After that P. began to gasp: '*Whaa! Whaa! Whaa!*' The spirit began to speak, saying: 'I will tell you, I will tell you ever so much.' They said: 'Tell us! If you are a Muŋgunu (Zulu), or if you are a Mundau, tell us!' P. said: 'I am *Ŋguŋgunyane* and *Nyabalelane*.' (I asked her when she was giving me this recital, if she remembered what made her think of those names, and she said that her relations must have suggested them to her, telling her that the *ʃikwembu* had revealed them, she being supposed to be still in a trance.) They stretched her limbs and pulled them about, as if she had been stiff in the trance. They said: 'What is the matter?' She replied: 'I was asleep.' 'Asleep!' said they. 'What happened to you?' 'Oh! I don't know!' They said: 'The *ʃikwembu* have come out, now dance.' P. danced all round the kraal. Presently she said: '*ndzi lava nłoko yakubambetela.*' (This was the spirit saying it wanted a red-ochred wig.) It was about ten o'clock at night.

The next morning, very early, they prepared medicine in a potsherd, charcoal and ground monkey-nuts. While it was hot they dipped their fingers into it and licked them. Then the *nyamusoro* drew magic circles round P.'s body with the soot medicine. Next they took a baboon bone and pressed her swollen legs all over with it, and rubbed oil into the pressed parts. The next step was to wash her hair, and dress it in numberless little light twists or curls, covered with red ochre and oil, so that her hair had the appearance of a red-ochred wig (*ſiŋgundu*). In the afternoon, about five o'clock, they put the bladder (*anyoŋgwa*) of the goat in her hair, also two metal rings, one each side of the head. The *anyoŋgwa* was supposed to be a charm for preventing the patient from being ill again.

The remains of the ground-nuts and medicine which had been cooked with charcoal in a potsherd were stirred with a medicine stick and put in a little gourd, from whence it was afterwards transferred to a tiny string bag (*nteve*) to be worn on a shoulder strap.

The same day, later in the afternoon, they gave P. *pupuma* (cf. p. 206) medicine, a decoction prepared from the scraped roots of a plant of that name, put into a little gourd and mixed with a stick. All in the kraal had to take this medicine, dipping the *sisiwana* or poor-finger (i.e. the little finger) into it. This *pupuma* medicine is one which is peculiarly pleasing to the *ſikwembu*. P. had to take *pupuma* medicine every day for three days. Also on the same day a little charm was given her which was supposed to be a powerful charm against sorcerers. It was tied up in a little bit of rag. When the rag in which it was tied was quite worn out, then another must be procured to take its place.

On the fourth day in the morning, before sunrise, P.'s relatives awoke her and escorted her to the cross-paths near the kraal. They took off her clothes and washed her with the *pupuma* medicine, breaking the gourd when the medicine was finished. Then on her return home, she was dosed again with a different kind of medicine called *tsotsoba*, which was mixed with salt, and was also supposed to please the *ſikwembu* very much. This was taken first in the palm of each hand, and raised to the mouth, and then some was placed on the back of each hand, and taken in the same fashion.

There remained still one more charm. Two small tubes of reeds were threaded. Then the *nyamusoro* took a little bit of the nail of each little toe of the patient, and of each little finger, and added to it a short hair from above the temples, and another short hair from the back of the head just above the neck. These were mixed with some medicine, and the medicine put into the little reed tubes, which were stoppered with bees' wax. The fibre thread was covered with black medicine. It was passed over the right shoulder and under the left arm, and the tubes rested just below the waist. This charm was donned after returning from the *pupuma* wash.

The *nyamusoro*, P.'s sister, was rewarded with a fowl and five silver *quinientos*. This was her fee for her share of the performance.

The treatment for the dropsical legs was as follows: On the third day after the *ʃikwembu* had revealed themselves the *nyamusoro's* husband made two little incisions in the legs of the patient, and rubbed in medicine which caused the wounds to smart. In a week's time this operation was repeated. In a fortnight's time P.'s own father went to a *nkanye* tree (*Sclerocarya caffra*) in the bush, and made two holes in the ground against the trunk of the tree, one facing east, the other west, each hole being the size of one of the patient's legs. Then he put some of the medicine which had been used for the incisions in the legs into each hole, and came away. This was a bit of magic to make P. walk properly, so that one leg should not be separated from the other. It was called *matlaŋganisi* medicine.

A week after the coming-out of P.'s *ʃikwembu*, the *nyamusoro* held an 'at home' in her kraal, which all the people in the immediate neighbourhood attended. The patients or *mitenda* were there in force. Some were wearing feathers in their hair. The *nyamusoro* had set up a three-forked *ʃipandzi* of the *ʃitsalala* tree in her hut. This was the sacrificial spot. On this were hung a python's skin and various little gourds containing soot medicines. (The python's skin was a sure sign that the *ʃikwembu* was of Zulu origin.) Fowls tied up were also placed there. A mat outside the hut was placed to receive the *masindza* (brass bangles and anklets) and rings (*ʃiŋgwavelane*). These, being gifts to the *ʃikwembu*, were afterwards taken in and placed at the *ʃipandzi*.

When all the patients and the visitors were gathered together, the *nyamusoro* gave thanks to the spirits on behalf of those who were healed. She washed herself ceremonially after the thanksgiving. Each patient who was healed had to have a *sindza*, brass slave-bangle, hammered on her arm by the husband of the *nyamusoro*. Then food was taken, a little meat was placed in a clean food-bowl, and a little mealie-porridge in another. These two were placed at the *ʃipandzi* as an offering to the *ʃikwembu* of the *nyamusoro*. '*Hi nyika ʃakudla ʃa Wena, Hosi!*' 'We give you your food, Lord!' (in this case of *Waka Njamini*—'Lady'!) Then all the people took a meal. The *vantukulu* of the *nyamusoro's* husband, a boy and a girl, came and ate the food devoted to the *ɡikwembu*. The *nyamusoro's* own children must not touch the food. It is a very great tabu. Next, all the children were served with food and then the grown-up people.

Then there remained one more rite. A fire was lighted in the *nyamusoro's* hut, and medicine was placed on the burning wood. The hut was crowded with people. The door was shut, and the fumes made all the people sneeze most violently. The *nyamusoro* cried out: 'Whetsi! Whetsi! Watʃa! Watʃa! Watʃa!' The children cried: 'We thank you! We thank you!' This sneezing is supposed to be an act of thanksgiving to the spirits, for the 'evil breath' will come out with the sneezing.

When a sufficient round of sneezing had been accomplished, the *nyamusoro* mixed the remains of the medicine with fat, and the patients rubbed themselves all over with it. This was supposed to keep their flesh in good condition. Then all the patients were given two kinds of medicines to go home with in their hand-baskets. Then the *nyamusoro* said peremptorily, 'Go!' and they all went home. They must not say good-bye to her. It is tabu. If they do, their *ɡikwembu* will remain with her.

P. remained about a fortnight with her sister as a patient. Her swollen legs were healed after about a month.

*A Seance at Zandamela*

On August 27th, 1928, returning from a short trip to the Vilaŋkulu sib, with Dr. and Madame Dr. Crinsoz de Cottens and the Rev. H. P. Junod, we passed by the kraal of the chief of Zandamela, in Tʃopiland. A seance was being held. There were crowds of people in the kraal. A tall Ndau woman was the *nyamusoro*. There were five *mandiki* drums being beaten by men. The drums were oval in shape, with single handles. The *nyamusoro* sat on her *ʃigara*, or stool, which was covered with a white *anjiti* cloth. I asked after the seance if I might see the *ʃigara*, and found that it was a beautifully carved one. Her women attendants sat near the *nyamusoro*, and there was one who seemed to be especially her handmaid. Among the crowds of women around her there were many with the insignia of *vanyamusoro*. One had a wig with extraordinary long hair, and an *andoro* ornament on the top. A large pot of some intoxicating drink with a dipper and two wooden goblets (*magombe*), used especially for sacrifices, were standing by. Doubtless the *nyamusoro* had been reinforced by copious draughts.

She presented a striking appearance, being in full dress. Her head-dress (or wig) was of the usual red-ochred curls. She wore the shoulder-straps (*mazaŋgira*) of skin, with charms covered with beads depending from them. She held the *thema* ritual axe in her right hand, and batons or knob-kerries (one in each hand), with red-bead charms attached. The usual ritual brass bangles and anklets (*masindza*) glittered on her shapely limbs, and on her legs were dance-rattles (*mafowane*). She wore a plaited grass (or *minala* palm) short frilly skirt, similar to that worn by women when dancing the *ſitſobe*. A white cloth sash was tied tightly round her chest, the long ends floating behind. A red cloth sash was tied round her waist. Her smelling-out brush (*tſovo*) was hanging on her arm. A shield of some animal skin was slung across her shoulders at the back. (This was probably of ox- or goat-skin.) The possessing spirit sometimes says it wants a shield.

The seance was being held outside the hut allotted to the *nyamusoro*. On the very top of the hut were the sacred white cloths, with a number of sticks piercing them like pins in a pincushion.

I peeped inside the hut and saw great joints of meat (portions of a sacrificed ox) among green branches on the *ſisiku* or fireplace in the centre of the hut.

When the *nyamusoro* sat on the *ſigara* or stool, the *thema* axe was slung over her right shoulder, the smelling-out brush hung from her arm, and the batons were held in the hands.

Then we saw some dances. There were solo dances by the *nyamusoro*, with all her insignia (*thema* axe, brush, and batons). Then when she was tired, one of her *mitenda* (healed women patients) danced. And then, lastly, there was the axe-dance of the *nyamusoro* and her husband. I was told that this dance of the man and woman is a very ancient one, and has come down through the centuries, but in this case the man seemed rather old, and purposely fell down once or twice to show that he was tired and did not want to dance. He occasionally held the woman's *femba* brush while she danced.

### 'Possession' of a Pregnant Woman

There remains to be noted the ritual of possession when the subject is a pregnant woman. Muneŋwasi, the wife of a former wagon-boy of our mission, was unhappy because she had lost one child, and there did not seem to be any prospect of another coming. She therefore went to the *anyaŋga* who cast the omens, and told her that a certain spirit of the Ndau was possessing her and preventing conception. So she must go home to prepare a sacrifice to propitiate the spirit. She did so, and after a time found that she was going to have another baby. She offered another sacrifice as a thanksgiving. But as yet the spirit had not revealed its identity. One day she had pains in her knees and shoulders and sensations of drunkenness. It must be the spirit wishing to reveal itself. A seance was arranged. The doctor of the Ndau *ſikwembu* was summoned. The patient was enveloped in the usual white cloths, and the drums were beaten. Presently M. began to shiver and cry. The spirit was about to come out (*kuhuma*). She continued to weep. Her husband said to the spirit: 'What is your name, *ſikwembu*? You really must tell us your name.' M. uttered the name of the spirit, that of a woman of Ndau origin. The *ſikwembu* ordered her to procure a *ſiŋgundu* or red-ochred head-dress, also the beads and ornaments which are the outward signs of possession. The *anyaŋga* sat by and told her that she must procure these things. Now in her hut was the *mpande* or *ſipandzi*, the three-forked pole on which sacrificial offerings were hung, or under which they were placed. At Muneŋwasi's *ſipandzi*, there were a *ntundu* basket for containing the white garments, and another little basket for containing an important medicine provided by the *anyaŋga*. The *ſikwembu* is said to follow this medicine, so that when the subject is no longer possessed, it must be returned to the *anyaŋga*. Any food offered, such as a fowl or porridge, was first offered to the *ſikwembu* at the *ſipandzi* in the wooden bowl, with a request that it might be pleased with the food, and then bowls were placed in the centre of the hut, and the food divided among the people present.

After the spirit had revealed its identity, Muneŋwasi had to take the usual *pupuma* or *mudlandlopfu* medicine, which is supposed to be very pleasing to the *ſikwembu* and to keep the subject in good health. I believe this plant to be *Tricalysia sonderiana*, which is also used during the eighth month of pregnancy to facilitate the birth. Another plant called *pupuma* is *Helinus ovatus*; and still another, *Securidaca longipedunculata*, which is dangerous, producing gastro-enteritis. M. used to take this medicine at the appearance of the new moon. She procured a little gourd and a stick, with a decoction of the *pupuma*, which was beaten to a froth with the stick. She bent down, lapped the water from the little gourd, rose again, and placed the medicine in her hut. She thought that if she did not take this medicine at the new moon, the *ſikwembu* would make her ill and she would die. She repeated the dose every day till the moon was on the wane, but started again when another new moon appeared. When the medicine began to smell, she threw it away and procured some more from the *anyaŋga*. This practice was continued for two months.

In due time M.'s child was born. There was another seance two or three days after the name-giving of the child (it was given the name of the *ʃikwembu*) when the spirit is supposed to have said that it was very glad because the child had been born. My informants were very emphatic that the spirit had not been born again in the child, but they thought that the spirit had become favourable to the birth of the child and no longer prevented it.

## Some General Remarks on 'Possession'

Σ*ikwembu ʃihumile* = the spirit has come out. The word *kuhuma*, when said with regard to a spirit, has a dual meaning, first of revelation, and secondarily of exorcism. The idea in most seances is to make the possessing spirit reveal its identity and its will, and therefore the revelation is more important than the exorcism. The spirit can be said to be exorcized only when having obtained its desire, and having made the necessary revelations, it ceases to trouble the possessed person. Exorcism in this sense is not a driving-away of the spirit, but the causing it to reveal itself, in order that the necessary sacrifices may be made for propitiation, when it will give power to the medium to perform acts impossible before. These acts are now done in the power of the possessing spirit. They are the healing of others, and the detection of criminal cases, sorcerers, and *ʒigono*. The medium has now become the master or owner of the spirit. The verb which expresses the action of causing the spirit to reveal itself is *ku twasisa* ( = *ku vitana ʒikwembu leʒaku ʒihuma. Amunhu atayendla ahosi ya ʒikwembu loku atwasisiwile*) (to call the spirits to reveal themselves. A man will make himself lord of the spirits when they have been revealed through him).

Spirits never come singly, but there is always a predominating one. Perhaps it is a man, and his wife and child who come. In that case, if a woman bears a child when possessed, she will give it the name of the man spirit if the baby is a boy, and of the woman if it is a girl. If a possessed person wishes to get rid of one spirit, she may pass it on to a child, after performing the necessary sacrifices. If the child is ill after that, the people will think it is due to the *ʃikwembu*.

Sometimes if the spirits are numerous, one after another will 'come out', and the seances are continued indefinitely. Cases of possession among women are much more frequent than among men. The former are increasingly frequent, and the latter are becoming rare.

A woman named Madevane was ill, and her baby too. So she offered sacrifices to the possessing spirit, which is supposed to have remained with her for five years. She certainly looked fat and well when I last saw her. Sometimes a spirit will rest for years, and then return to its former medium. At other times the possessed person is ill for years, and tries to drive away the spirit which refuses to leave. When the medium thinks that the spirit wishes to leave her, she gives the *anyaŋga* the baskets and the medicines, takes off her red wig, washes herself, and becomes a normal member of the community.

This was described to me as follows:

When the spirit wishes to leave the medium, it says: 'Take off your beads and wash. I want to leave you. I want to rest there by the *mpande* (or *ʃipandzi*).' If they see a blackish or a reddish snake there by the *mpande*, they will think it is the *ʃikwembu*. It is a good sign, for if they do not see the snake, perhaps the *ʃikwembu* is angry and has gone to the bush. Some will offer additional sacrifices to ensure that the spirit rests by the *ʃipandzi*.

(C) *The Ŋgoni or Zulu ʃikwembu*

The Ndau and Ŋgoni spirits seem to be so much mixed up in the seances that they can scarcely be described separately. If the possessing spirits are of Zulu origin, Zulu songs are sung by the medium and those taking part in the seance. Some such words as these will be sung: 'Oh! When they come from Zululand, over the mountain-tops!' When the spirits are of Ndau origin, the songs will be in Ndau.

These are some of the questions which are put to the communicating spirits at the time of the seances. After the songs, accompanied by hand-clapping:

After that, they must ask, one after the other, inquires: 'How long shall I be well?' Another says: 'Why in my kraal is there illness every day?' Also the spirits will inform that: 'You will be well if you produce money and give it to the *anyaŋga*. He will put your kraal right for you, by beginning to set up a new gateway, that although some one bad wants to come in and do your kraal an injury, he will fail to enter. If a person comes in with evil intent, he will not be able to return, he will be caught by that medicine.'

The following description of a seance was given me by eyewitnesses:

*An Eyewitness's Story*

A medium was sitting enveloped in the usual white cloth. The *mandiki* drums were being beaten with force by some men relatives. Presently fantastic contortions were seen under the white cloth. The shoulders of the medium were being jerked from side to side—he

PLATE XX

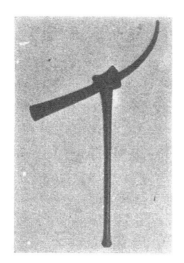

(*a*) *THEMA* AXE (reduced)

(*b*) *ANDORO* ORNAMENT (2½ in. diameter)

PLATE XXI

WOMAN MAKING *ΣIŋGUNDU*

muttered, he muttered, he muttered, he rolled about, he gasped *'Ndzifunuŋgule'* (uncover me). They took away the cloth. He was in a violent perspiration. They bent and stretched his limbs, as if he were coming out of a trance. They gave him a little stool (*ʃigara*, the sacred stool) to sit on. They said, 'Gently, gently! Sir (addressing the possessing spirit), we greet you! We are your children. We await your will.' The medium made indescribable whistling noises like a toy-bird, beginning on a top note, and coming down in a kind of chromatic scale. (My informants made these noises for me to hear.) He then cracked his finger joints. (This also is a very peculiar noise, something like castañets. I have tried to do it myself and failed.) The audience grabbed hold of him, saying: 'Gently! gently!' &c. The medium gasped brokenly: *'He! Ugh! Ha! He! Mayi-wayi!'* 'I see, I see.'

Audience (anxiously): 'Yes, tell us what you see!'

Medium (still more brokenly, and with more violent contortions): 'It is he!' (mentioning a boy at Johannesburg).

*Audience*: 'Yes! Yes! what about him?'

*Medium*: (Gasp!) 'I see the sorcerers . . .' (gasp).

*Audience*: 'Yes! Yes! what next?'

*Medium*: 'He must—(gasp)—get a *ʃisuŋgunu* (charm), (gasp—rolls about in more convulsions).

And so it went on. From which it may be inferred, quite rightly, that a good deal of consummate acting goes on during the seances.

*Ritual Accessories*

Among the ritual accessories and ornaments used at spiritualistic seances the most important are (1) drums; (2) rattles; (3) clothes; (4) the stool (*ʃigara*); (5) the head-dress (*ʃiŋgundu*); (6) ornaments (*mazaŋgira, timbamba, andoro, kota, mbuwa*); (7) baskets; (8) skins and tails; (9) the ritual axe (*thema*); (10) batons.

(1) *The Drums.* When visiting in a hut of some Ndau people at Ŋguzeni in 1928, I saw a collection of drums against the side of the wall. I was told that they were the *mandiki* drums (*mandiki* = spirits, a Ndau word). There were five drums, rather more shallow than Tʃopi drums, carved from a dark red wood and covered with tight skin membranes fastened to the body of the drum with the usual little wooden pegs. One drum was double, each half being a complete drum in itself, but joined to the other by horizontal bars, probably all carved out of the same piece of wood. During two of the nights which I spent at Ŋguzeni I heard the *mandiki* drums all night. I was informed that

when the spirit had 'come out', i.e. revealed its identity through the medium, the seance would end, and the drums be silent. But one seance being finished, another would start, in order to get still another spirit to reveal itself. About sunset every day would be heard quite another set of drums in a different direction. This announced the annual *nzumba* or harvest-dances, which were in full swing.

I noticed five drums being used at the seance at Zandamela on August 27th. They were of varying sizes, but all were oval in shape, and three had single handles.

It is quite possible to hold seances without drums, as sometimes they are not available, but if the spirit decrees that it must have drums, then these will be used. Certainly they have an inciting effect upon the patients.

(2) *Rattles* are made of spotted gourds with a handle; they are shaken with the reiteration of the word *Kotſa! Kotſa! Kotſa!*

(3) *The Clothes*. White, red, and black garments are requisitioned. These are bought at local stores. Sometimes the spirit, if it is a Zulu one, is not satisfied with garments, it must have a python skin, which is worn by the *nyamusoro* in seance, and hung over the *ſipandzi* when not required. The Zulu spirits prefer black garments rather than white. The Ndau prefer white and red. Pieces of red and white print or cloth are put on graves, and become spirit clothes. It is the duty of the medium's husband to provide the clothes and other accessories of the seances, and the ornaments which the spirit desires.

(4) *The Stool or ſigara* is of great value from a ritual point of view. It is usually covered with a cloth when the *nyamusoro* sits on it. It is generally beautifully carved of wood, in an apparently lotiform design. The stool can never be purchased by strangers, although a copy will be made if asked for.

(5) *The Head-dress (ſiŋgundu)*, shown in Plate XXI, is of an *anyaŋga* of great importance. His possessing spirit is supposed to be such a bad one that the sight of the head-dress will frighten a patient into recovery. The *anyaŋga* will wear this only on professional visits when he goes to doctor patients. Sorcerers can have no power at all over the patients when the *anyaŋga* wears this head-dress. He makes it himself with threads of *mintſalu* fibre and ornaments it with white beads.

A woman *nyamusoro* or a medium will make her own wig or head-dress of vegetable fibre, worked over a gourd as a frame. I have watched a woman making hers. She laboriously makes the whole wig with small knots, taking one little fibre at a time, and netting it with a knot to the

PLATE XXII

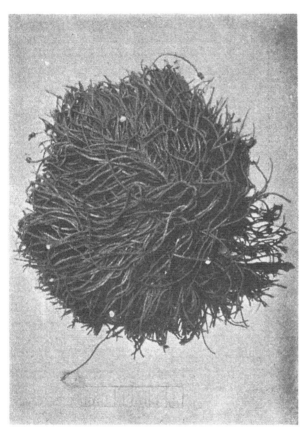

ΣIIJGUNDU OF MAN DOCTOR

PLATE XXIII

ΣIŊGUNDU OF WOMAN DOCTOR

loop above. The wig, when finished, is a mass of tight little curls covered with red ochre and *Trichilia emetica* oil. If the medium's own hair is dressed, she does it in this fashion:

They take *nlelwa* (*Harpagophytum procumbens* DC.), they roll the hair into tiny knots, and make a curly wig of it. Also another way, those who have spirits, seek for red ochre and fat, they anoint the hair, they twist all of it, they cause it to be *kumfi!* very long indeed.

These head-dresses may be decorated with metal rings tied on, or with three little triangles of beads, red, black, and white (the spirit colours); Muneŋwasi wore three such in her hair during her possession; one, red and white; one, black and white; one, red, black, and white. The triangular form of decoration is supposed to please the *ʃikwembu*.

(6) *Ornaments*. A chain of beads is sometimes hung round the neck of the medium in order to please the spirit which is about to reveal itself. This chain or necklace is of tubular black wooden beads, possibly ebony, alternated singly with annular shell beads roughly shaped. Generally a little horn of medicine, the *gonha*, depends from the chain. These chains are sometimes of great antiquity. The wood is known as *nsuta*. In the olden days, death was the penalty for burning this wood.

(*a*) *Mazaŋgira* and *timbamba* are ornaments worn by the *vanyamusoro*. The former consist of bands of vegetable fibre woven with cross-over shoulder-straps, with white, red, and black beads attached. They owe their name to the fact that the ends are sealed with the important *zaŋgira* medicine (of Ndau origin). The *timbamba* consist of a head-band and waist-girdle of cowrie-shells. They can be worn only by those who have undergone the sea-immersion, to be presently described. If, during the immersion, the initiate fails to bring back a shell, preferably a cowrie, the spirit by which she is possessed is supposed to be an idiot or a foolish one, and she can never become a *nyamusoro*.

In cases of Zulu possession, metal rings are sometimes strung together and hung round the neck. If offered to the spirits, they must be placed in a bowl of water. They are worn by men and made by native smiths.

(*b*) *The andoro*.[1] In Theal's *Records of South-Eastern Africa* a ritual ornament, named *andoro*, is mentioned several times. In vol. vii of this work we read: 'Monomotapa and the Mocarangas his vassals wear a

[1] Reproduced by kind permission from *Annals of the Transvaal Museum*, vol. xi, pt. ii, 1925, pp. 125–6. On some ritual objects of the Ndau in S. Chopiland, Gaza, by E. D. Earthy.

white shell on the forehead, hanging from the hair as an ornament, and Monomotapa wears another large shell on his breast. These shells they call andoros, and they are looked upon with hatred by Quiteve, as they are insignia of his enemy Monomotapa, and therefore neither Quiteve nor his vassals wear andoros, although they are all of them Mocarangas.'[1]

In vol. iii of Theal's work are references to a certain Diogo Simões who, in June 1614 or shortly afterwards, presented the Monomotapa with a gold *andoro* set with false stones but very beautiful, which *andoro* was a round medal such as the Mokaranga kaffirs used to wear on their heads.[2] It is an interesting fact that the name *andoro* for this ornament persists to-day in Portuguese East Africa. It is looked upon by the natives as a very sacred votive offering to the spirits. Copies in porcelain have been made by traders which are worn as amulets.

In Smith and Dale's *The Ila-Speaking Peoples of Northern Rhodesia*, vol. i, pp. 26, 35, and 101, this ornament, or something very similar to it, is called the *impande* shell, but the name *andoro* is not used at all in this connexion. The *impande* shell is referred to as 'an emblem of Chief-ship introduced by the Baluba', who came originally from the Congo region. The *impande* appears to be the base of a univalve shell, although trade copies in celluloid and porcelain are also in circulation.

It is interesting to note that the *andoro* was one of the insignia of royalty of the Monomotapa, and that it was a religious or ritual ornament. To-day the *andoro* still has religious significance; according to my informants it is worn only by a person who is a medium for a Ndau spirit of very high rank, one who is 'the lord of all the other spirits'. A great spirit by whom the people swear is that of a Monomotapa named *Mamba Ka Jekwa*.

(c) The *kota* is a large hollow brass bead of cylindrical shape, the circumference of the middle, however, being much larger than that of the tapering ends. It is a religious symbol and an important amulet, for it is supposed to have great healing powers when worn on the neck. The specimen which was brought to me was strung together with ring-shaped dark blue beads, and it was described to me as 'a very

---

[1] Theal is translating here from Friar João dos Santos, 'Eastern Ethiopia, Bk. II, ch. xvi. Concerning other Customs and Insignia of Monomotapa and his Vassals,' *Records of South-Eastern Africa*, vol. vii, p. 289.

[2] See Theal, *Records of South-Eastern Africa*, vol. iii, p. 405. Translated from Antonio Bocarro, *Extracts from the Decade of the Performances of the Portuguese in the East*.

great sacrificial offering of the ancients'. It is of very rare occurrence, and is used by the TſOpi in connexion with their initiation ceremonies, but it was introduced by the Ndau, according to native opinion. Metal beads of this shape have been found in collections from ancient Egypt, and were also used by the Sumerians (cf. British Museum collection).

(d) The *mbuwa* is a large red bead with a white spiral porcelain core. It is worn as an amulet by the *vanyamusoro*, people who have first become mediums of the Ndau *ſikwembu* (spirits) and have then undergone the initiation for becoming witch-doctors for 'smelling out' (*ku femba*) offenders in criminal cases, sorcerers, or the attacking spirit in case of illness. A bead of this kind is worn at the neck, chiefly by women *vanyamusoro*. A portion of the red glass is chipped off in order to show the spiral core underneath. The fragments of glass are ground to a fine powder, mixed with medicine, and the aperture of the bead is filled with the mixture.

It may be noted here that the possessing spirit is supposed to command the medium to procure the various ritual ornaments. The medium takes great pains to obtain the ornaments, especially the *mbuwa*, for if the spirit has really commanded the medium to obtain this bead and the latter fails to do so, then death may result unless the spirit's command had been wrongly interpreted.[1]

Ritual ornaments not being procurable in TſOpiland, a medium has often to make a long journey to Vusapa to procure them. I am informed by a TſOpi mistress of the initiation ceremonies for women that her ancestors long ago paid visits to Vusapa, and to the Ba-Farawu of Nyafokwe (Inhambane), taking sacks of beans with which to feed themselves on the road, for the journey took a long time. From the foreigners, who were called 'Ba-Farawu', after their chief *Farawu*, were bought beads of various kinds, girdles of ebony and ivory cylinders, trumpets made from the very long horns of a sacred animal named *aſtogonono*, large and small metal collars and rings, and small gold (?) ornaments named *mipiri*.

All my informants agree that the Ndau hid their treasures in the ruins of the Sabi district during the Ŋgoni invasions, and that some were recovered afterwards, but that a great many still remain buried. The treasures consisted of ivory, because the Ndau 'ruled with ivory', i.e. had to pay dues of ivory to the chief and used the remainder for *akulobola*. Other treasures were horns of the *tinyau* (which resemble

---

[1] The *mabuwa* beads are probably medieval Venetian.

oxen according to my informant), musical instruments, beads, and other votive offerings to the spirits—'all that they valued very much'.

(7) *The Baskets* (*mitundu* or *kandu*). The rattles and some of the vestments are kept in the *mitundu* (*ntundo*). This kind of basket is very common in Southern Rhodesia, and I have seen them used for all kinds of ordinary purposes, such as for holding vegetables.

A smaller kind known as *kandu* or *nkandu* is used for keeping the medicine or anything else supplied by the *anyaŋga* to the medium, which must be returned to him in the *kandu* when the medium is no longer possessed.

It is a curious fact that, among the Bantu, an object of common use in the country of its origin may become an object of magical or religious value when used in another country. A striking example of this is this *ntundo* basket; and also the bamboo staff which Ndau women carry with them to help them climb the hills in the mountainous part of Southern Rhodesia. This bamboo staff becomes a ritual staff of a *nyamusoro* in Gazaland. It is called a *museŋgele*.

(8) *The Use of Skins and Tails.* When the spirits have come out they want skins to wear. If you lack these skins, they will trouble you very much. Also the *tinyaŋga* want very much the skin of a hyena, in order that they may take the tail and smell out with it, because they say: If a person has died, they take the tail, they go and search with it, they will find where the sorcerers have put the person who has died, they will return with him, they will arouse the body of the person who has died. Others use the brush of the *ntoto*[1] (wild cat?) they take its tail, they make a brush to smell out with it. Therefore others search for the tail of an elephant and return with it, they will arouse a person who has fainted.

(9) *The Axe.* See p. 198. (10) *The Batons.* See p. 205.

*The Initiation of a Nyamusoro*

The *fikwembu* of a woman, who is possessed by it, comes to her at night in a dream, and speaks to her in this fashion: 'You, Machazi (or whatever her name may be), go and dig for such-and-such roots, and return with them. 'You must procure two goats, a male and a female. You must arrange a *fipandzi* and make a circle.' The woman wakes her husband and tells him that the *fikwembu* has appeared to her in a dream, and what it has said. The husband asks if she knows the trees and plants which the *fikwembu* has mentioned. She says 'Yes'. In the early morning the husband and the wife go out with an axe and a hoe, procure the roots and leaves, and return with a little bundle of them.

[1] The skin of a kind of leopard known as *ndlhoti* is also much in requisition.

Then they pay a visit to the divining omens. The omens say: 'Wait! you will be told at night again in a dream what you must do!' The woman waits about a fortnight, and on the same day of the week as before the *fikwembu* comes again in a dream and takes her off to the bush, where beads are hung on the trees. There is a hut there with many people who all wear red-ochred wigs. There is also a smaller hut filled with medicines. The *fikwembu* shows her all the medicines and how to use them. So she wakes her husband, and tells him. Then they get ready the *fipandzi*, and the medicines are placed there on the *fitsalala* pole. (The *fitsalala* tree is a botanical species not yet determined.) A very important *nyamusoro* arrives and conducts the woman to the sea, and she is immersed in it. She must drink quantities of salt water, and return with a shell as a sign of her office. She is now called a *nyamusoro*. Before returning home a feather is put into her mouth to make her vomit. On return she is given by the *anyaŋga* a draught of goat's blood. Then she takes medicine and vomits again. The fourth time she takes medicine and does not vomit.

Then she must be separated from her husband for a time. If he takes another woman during the time of separation, the *nyamusoro* falls ill—her limbs are paralysed. She will recover if he buys clothes for her and comes to thank her.

This initiation of the *nyamusoro* is really a rite of Ndau origin. It can only be studied properly in its native setting. It is difficult to say how much the Leŋge have borrowed of the original rite, and how much they have omitted.

(D) *The Tindzundzu Spirits*

Sometimes if the possessing Zulu or Ndau spirits are very troublesome, the *anyaŋga* will tell the possessed person to bury the troublesome spirits in a lake. He will accompany the patient to the lake, and will place in some secluded spot the *ntundo* containing the spirit garments and some medicine, and the curved axe or *thema*. The spirit remains with its paraphernalia, but one day will choose a person in whom to enter among the many people who come to the lake. The kind of spirit caught at the lake is *ndzundzu* (plural *tindzundzu*).

Another informant described the *tindzundzu* spirits to me as follows:

There are some people who are taken by the *tindzundzu* (spirits living in the lake). They capture perhaps a grown-up person, perhaps a child. They will remain with him in the lake. One remains in the lake for six months. When he comes out of the lake, when the spirits are tired of living with him, they have taught him everything he ought to do outside to save people. Also he will become a very great *anyaŋga* indeed. If it happens there is a person who has stolen something they call him (the *anyaŋga*) saying: 'Tell us the person who has taken our things.' Indeed he-of-the-*ndzundzu* will begin to call the name of the person who has taken things. He tells him: 'You must produce that which you have taken.' Indeed he who has taken something brings it out, because he-of-the-*ndzundzu*, they believe that he has spoken truly, because he had been taken to be taught by the spirits—therefore everybody knows him.

Another woman gave me the following information about the *tindzundzu*:

People think sometimes when they have become possessed by a spirit that they have got the spirit sometimes at a spring of water, or a river or a lake. They will dip themselves in the sea, but they do not think the spirits are in the sea. But Ndau or Ŋgoni spirits dwell in the lake or spring or river. *Ndzundzu* is the kind of spirit they get at the lake or river. It dwells below the water. Sometimes the person captured and the *ndzundzu* will dwell in the lake, and when the master (or owner) returns from the lake, he will have great snakes coiled round him, sometimes one, sometimes two. These snakes are called *tiłaru* (pythons). The person may be either man or woman.

### (E) *The Mifukwa or Mademona Spirits*

The *mifukwa* are demons. If one makes people ill, and the person dies, it will go off to seek another place, it seeks another person. *Mifukwa*, they say, want people to die. If they cannot find a way of going to heaven, they return, they make *mifukwa*. *Mifukwa* begin by persecuting the souls of people who are well because they have lacked a place to dwell in. It is like the pigs which were driven away, they beg a place, they go to the sea in the depths of the water.

(This last piece of information was given me by a Christian man.)

### (F) *The Ṣitukutwane or Ṣiruŋwa*

The *ṣitukutwane* is a kind of spirit which lives in the sky. If it falls from heaven and speaks with a person, that person will die.[1]

I knew of two cases of girls who had said they had met and spoken with a *ṣitukutwane*, which had made a revelation to them.

This idea approximates somewhat to our idea of an angel, but it seems that the people believed in *ṣitukutwane* before they had ever heard of angels—for this reason we use the word *tiŋgelozi* now when speaking of angels, in order that there may be no confusion between them and the *ṣitukutwane* or *ṣiruŋwa* (messengers). Some few years

---

[1] Cf. 'The *ṣitukutwane* fell from the *ŋkułu* tree' (see p. 43).

ago, just before the epidemic of Spanish influenza broke out, Machazi, a heathen Leŋge girl, said that she had met a *ſitukutwane* in the road who had told her that she would die. Curiously enough, she did die of this epidemic. Some time afterwards I asked a Leŋge the native name for Spanish influenza, and he said it was called Machazi. I said, 'Why, that is a woman's name.' 'Yes,' said he, 'there was a girl named Machazi, who died last year. She said she had seen a *ſitukutwane* in the fields, which told her that she would die, and that all the people 'would mourn her with grass'. 'Have you not noticed', he continued, 'that many of the girls about here have been wearing plaited grass shoulder-straps? (worn over one shoulder, and under the other arm)'. I had noticed it. 'They wear it as a charm to protect them from the influenza,' said he.

## II. SORCERY

A man gave me this account of sorcery as it is practised here in Gazaland:

The people of this country have many ways because when they die people think that it is the sorcerers who bewitch them, therefore they begin by going to the divining dice. They divine at the *anyaŋga*, and the *anyaŋga* tells them that a man who is ill is killed by a person who is a sorcerer. It is he who has a grudge against him. You must call him in order that he may make an offering that he may be well. Indeed they go, they call him, he comes saying: 'Very well, if it is I who am killing him, let him live!' Indeed sometimes he is well. But sometimes he is not well. Also this way the people of this country of ours, they are very afraid of sorcerers, therefore they believe that the spirits have power to drive away sorcerers, because if a person is ill, they will call the *anyaŋga* of the *ſikwembu*, whose spirits will come, saying: 'Oh! that man was killed by such-and-such a person.' They say: 'We have found his *ſigono*, which told us by whom he was sent.' It says the name of the person from whom it came. Therefore, all the people of this country are very afraid, they do not agree that when a man has died, he died of himself—they don't say that. They believe that he was bewitched by other people. Therefore they do not say that those who die go to heaven. They think that we all when we have died we change, we make *ſikwembu*, that we may trouble other people. Also all the people of this country, when one man tells another man, saying: 'You are a sorcerer', it is a very big matter. They must go to the chiefs, also the chiefs will make them go to the *anyaŋga*. Also when they have arrived at the *anyaŋga* the *anyaŋga* will divine, and when he finds one who says that: 'You, you bewitch', he [the accused person] must return and produce money, perhaps £10, because the way of the sorcerers is not good to people, because they know that the sorcerers it is they that bewitch people. Therefore the way of people of this country when they say, 'You, you are a sorcerer', you make a great matter, because he, he will be very upset, he will want you to go with him to the *anyaŋga*, they will divine for you. This is like when you say: 'You, you have stolen my wife, or my money.' It will trouble people very much. All this they bring before the *anyaŋga*.

## The Ṣigono

Sometimes the *vanyamusoro*, when practising the 'smelling out', find that the cause of a person's illness is not a spirit but a mysterious entity called a *ṣigono*. These *ṣigono* figure very much in folk-stories. They are spiritual in that they do not seem to have a material existence at first, although they can assume human or animal shape according to the will of their masters and owners, the sorcerers. They may therefore be considered thought-creations, and are used only in black magic by the sorcerers. For instance, a woman may create several *ṣigono* by her thoughts, and put them in a pot or an *aŋgula* (bin for monkey-nuts); so that if any one goes to that pot or *aŋgula*, the *ṣigono* may bewitch and perhaps kill that person. If a woman has several *ṣigono*, they are known as her *ṣivanana*, little children.

Sometimes the *ṣigono* are made to assume the shape of animals, and to join other animals in a herd (perhaps of goats) and bewitch or kill the other goats or the shepherd. Sometimes their owner or creator will put them in a hollow of an old tree trunk, where rain-water can collect. This is a very favourite spot in which to place them. Now when a person is bewitched or made ill by a *ṣigono*, it is one of the functions of the *nyamusoro* to smell out the *ṣigono*. The following account of such a proceeding was given me:

The bewitched person Seneta sits in moody silence, with head bent. The *nyamusoro* arrives on the scene with her divining-brush, and an *induna* or helper. She sets to work, the people present calling out: '*Ye-hayi! Ye-hayi! hayi! Nyamusoro!*' Her attendant takes a long white cloth, and ties it round her waist, leaving a long end free. These two resemble children playing at horses with toy-reins, for the *nyamusoro* crawls about on all fours, her helper following her about holding up the long end of the white cloth like reins. The *nyamusoro* holds her divining-brush in her hand, sweeping the floor and the various articles in the hut with it, and holding it up to smell continually. At last she smells a *ṣigono* on the chest of the person who is ill. The helper calls out: 'You are hot! You are hot! Mamma!' (just like children playing at hide-and-seek). The *nyamusoro* having smelt the *ṣigono* is so overcome that she falls down on the top of the sick person, and they both roll over together. The *nyamusoro* gasps and carries on a little conversation *sotto voce* with the *ſigono*, who says, using the *nyamusoro* as a mouthpiece, 'tſelanjekanje! tſelanjekanje'. (This word or combination of words occurs often in folk-story songs when the *ſigono* are the subject of the story. When you ask what it means, the answer is, 'We don't know'.)

The attendant then drags the *nyamusoro* outside the hut, still holding her firmly by the white cloth, while she rolls about in convulsions. It is to be noted that the *nyamusoro* has now possession of the *ſigono*, which speaks through her.

The helper says (addressing the *ſigono* in the *nyamusoro*):
*Helper*: 'Tell me, who sent you?'
Ʃ*igono* (in *nyamusoro*) 'Oh! no! I couldn't! I die of fear!'
H. 'Oh! but just whisper! I shan't tell anybody! You were sent by whom?'
N. 'Oh! no! no! no! I should die!'
H. 'Oh! but I shouldn't tell a single soul! Not one!'
N. 'Oh! no! no! I can't! I can't!'
The *nyamusoro* shrugs her shoulders peevishly and pettishly, and turns her back on H., saying: 'I can't! I can't! I can't!'
H. 'But Mamane—I will give you . . .'
N. 'What will you give me?'
H. 'A cloth from Johannesburg.'
N. (*whispers*) 'A cloth from Johannesburg . . .'
H. 'Yes, a beautiful one! Listen, just tell me!'
N. 'You won't tell a single person, You promise?'
H. 'No! No! No! I promise!'
N. 'Well then, it was . . . Hush! sh! sh! sh! sh!'
H. 'Yes, Yes, who was it?'
N. 'Oh! I die of fear! It was . . . Machazi!'
H. '(In extreme astonishment). Machazi!!!'
N. Yes! yes! yes! (brokenly) she put me . . . among the monkey-nuts in the *aŋgula*, so that when Seneta came to take them out (she was jealous of Seneta because she had so many nice clothes), she sent me to kill her—she said . . .'
H. 'Yes! Yes! What did she say?'
N. 'Oh! You will promise not to tell a single person?' And so it goes on.

Seneta is then told that the *ſigono* has come out, and that she must procure a charm or amulet to prevent bewitchment in future. These charms are generally mysterious little packages of medicine tied up in a bit of rag, ornamented with white beads, and hung round the patient's neck.

From all of which it may be inferred that the *vanyamusoro* are fine actresses.

A Leŋge woman gave me this information about the *ɟigono*. If Mevasi wishes to kill Machazi, she will make a *ʃigono* and put it in Machazi's neighbourhood. Machazi becomes very ill, her relatives summon an *anyaŋga*, who finds the *ʃigono*. Old *ɟigono* are very sophisticated and are not easily caught.

They run away quickly because they are wise but a new one can't run very fast, and so the *anyaŋga* finds it. He or she arouses the patient, who is near death, with medicine (*zaŋgira*). This medicine is believed to be made from an assegai (*tlhari*), it is reddish. The patient inhales it and begins to revive. The *anyaŋga* says to her: 'Rise, I have snatched you from the hands of your enemies.' The patient sneezes.

The *anyaŋga* calls the patient by name. She assents, showing that she has heard him. He asks her where she has been. She tells him: 'Oh, my enemy placed me in the kraal of the *ɟigono*.' The *anyaŋga* says: 'What did you see there?' She said: 'Oh! I saw many people—some were my own relations. I saw my own husband, who was killed before me.' The *anyaŋga* gives her some soot medicine which is very healing. When she is quite well, then he will give her a charm to wear to protect her from future attacks of the sorcerers.

When they make a *ʃigono* they make an image, like this: perhaps they make a monkey, perhaps they make a buck, it becomes their child; perhaps birds, that they may be their children. When a sorcerer has drunk the *mondzo* he says that it was my child who did it. He makes an animal of Machazi, and kills her in the bush inside the animal.

My informant added these remarks about a similar case.

The sorcerer will hire a man to go after a herdsman and his flock. The man pretends to go hunting. He follows the herdsman and says: 'I want one of your flock.' The herdsman says: 'I suppose you want to get money from me.' 'No, I want to kill one of your flock.' The herdsman is obliged to give way, because he is afraid the man will kill him if he does not. And he is afraid to tell tales afterwards. So the man kills the animal, saying: '*Ndzi kukumile*' ('I have caught you')—thereby killing the bewitched person as well, so he thinks—and buries it in the bush.

They take an animal which lives in the bush to be the child of the sorcerer. Perhaps he takes a crocodile to be his child, he commands it to kill people. When it has killed a person, he converts the soul of the person into a *ʃigono* of his. When he wants to kill a person again, he sends these *ɟigono* to kill another.

Also when an *anyaŋga* has smelt out a *ɟigono*, he can return home with it, and make it a real person to be his servant.

These creatures are described as misshapen, ill-formed, hunch-backed, with all kinds of abnormalities, and they speak in a pettish and petulant voice, like spoilt children.

My informant declared roundly that there were *tinyaŋga* in the old days who could do that, and although I scolded her for believing such rubbish, she said most firmly, 'Oh! but they could! There really were such *tinyaŋga*', and nothing I could say would convince her. She told me that when people were walking in the bush at night and stepped on hot ground, it was a fire of the *ɟigono*. That person must get out of the way quickly. Also they must take a little bit of hair from the temple and another little bit of hair from the back of the head, near the nape of the neck, and chew it, keeping it in the mouth as a charm against the *ɟigono*, till they had reached the journey's end safely.

The following remarks on sorcerers were given me by a Leŋge man of the Masiye sib:

The people of our country say they are constantly troubled by sorcerers; also some when a living relation is very much troubled say, 'My relation is being killed by sorcerers. I must seek for an *anyaŋga* to give the *mondzo*.' Also when they have drunk it, many people fall. One says: 'It is I who have killed that person. I have taken his leg and given it to another, I have taken his arm and given it to another. Also his bowels I have eaten with my children. Also his head, I will invite the big sorcerers that I may eat it with them.' But this makes very angry the heart of the person who is being bereaved of his relation because he hears it is they who killed him. Also others of this country often take assegais and kill those who are intoxicated with the *mondzo*, who—because they do not know what they are saying—say, 'It is I who killed your relation.' Also now there have arrived white people, foreigners. They forbid indeed these laws, because they see people deceive themselves by the lies of the *tinyaŋga*. Also they kill indeed, because of old the Ŋgoni said, when people fell by the *mondzo*, even if it were five hundred, they must all be killed, because they did not want that there should be some people who killed others by witchcraft. Also now if the magistrates hear of a person who makes people drink the *mondzo*, they send to capture him, they will shut him up in prison because they do not want people to bear bad laws. Also those who are said to be sorcerers, it is they who go by night, they fly with fire in order to hunt and kill people; and also the sorcerers—we do not see them with our eyes; we hear that there are sorcerers, we are told by the *tinyaŋga*. On other days when we go by night, it is their fires[1] which flare up there in the fields. Very much

[1] These mysterious lights are seen at night above the tops of the trees. The natives say that they are not fire-flies nor will-of-the-wisps.

indeed in the time of the young shoots of mealies, one is accustomed to see indeed their fires in the fields, therefore the heathen know that the sorcerers want to plot to take the food. Also when people die at this time, the heathen believe that they are killed by sorcerers, that they may dig up their food. Also when the sorcerers kill a person they take his shade to remain with them, to be their servant. But they cannot take the souls of people because they have no power to take their souls. (This last sentence shows Christian influence.)

*The Blessing of the Kraals*

The blessing of a new kraal or hut (*kupuŋga muti*) is an important ceremony to ward off malign influences of sorcerers. It is evident that with a population of such mixed origin, different *tinyaŋga* may use a ritual varying in order and detail, and four different ways of doing this have been described to me.

The oldest way, which seems more or less to have died out now, is thus: The *anyaŋga* arrives bringing with him small branches and leaves of *nsaŋgula* (a species of *Euclea*, generally *Euclea natalensis*). This is considered a very important medicine. All sorts of leaf medicines are in the *anyaŋga's* little skin bag. The *Euclea* medicine he cooks with a fowl and a *fisimbu* (little fibre-bag containing root medicines) in water in a pot on a fire which he has lighted himself. All the fires in the kraal must be extinguished first. Kaffir-corn (*fikombe*) and maize have been pounded previously by one of the women in the kraal. The *anyaŋga* takes the fowl and the *nsaŋgula* and the *fisimbu* from the pot, and proceeds to asperge the new hut. He sprinkles it with the soup in the pot, twice inside the hut and three times outside. Then the pounded maize and Kaffir-corn are cooked in the remaining soup.

Meanwhile the people in the kraal are all lined up, the men with bows and arrows, and the women with their field-baskets and hand-baskets. The *anyaŋga* gives them balls of the cooked porridge. The owner of the kraal and his wife, and the other members of the kraal with their wives, will run in turn in pairs to the entrance to the kraal, tossing the balls of food from one to another as they go. Each couple will have ritual intercourse in the bush, and then return. The sorcerers cannot bewitch, and the people do not die if they fall ill, if this rite is performed. The bows and arrows are taken because they kill game and bring food, and the hoes will help people to dig, and the field-baskets will bring home food.

Then the *anyaŋga* tells the chief wife of the owner of the kraal to take a lighted brand and place it in the new hut. All the others will follow suit and place new fire in their huts. The remaining charcoal of the fire will be placed in a potsherd or broken gourd (*ſikambatso*) and put at cross-paths near the house, together with the brush which swept up the ashes.[1]

Then the *anyaŋga* (if the kraal is a new one) places two poles at the entrance, drawing a red and black ring round each.

A more modern rite, one performed in July 1925, was as follows: On passing along a path in the Marameni district, I saw on the left-hand side some ashes and charcoal, a tattered old winnowing-tray, and a brush made of *minala* palm. On the other side of the path, a little farther on, were a broken gourd and more charcoal of the *nzole* and *ſiɫaŋgwa* bushes. I was told afterwards that a new hut had been blessed. An *anyaŋga* had arrived with *nsaŋgula* leaves (*Euclea* sp.) and other leaf medicines in a skin bag. He had apparently taken a pot, and drawn a circle round the edge with red ochre, and had then 'written inside the pot' with red ochre (this time mixed with water, not fat). The 'writing' inside the pot was apparently drawing a diametrical line from north to south and from east to west (of the pot).

The leaves were cooked in this pot at the entrance to the kraal. Then two fowls were killed and cooked in another pot. He then took a fibre-bag, containing root medicines (*ſisimbu*), and dipped it into the pot containing the fowls, having taken out the fowls and placed them in one of the wooden food-bowls. Then in silence he sprinkled himself and the owner of the kraal with fowl soup. The decoction made from *Euclea* in the red-ochred pot was poured into another wooden bowl. The branch of *nsaŋgula* was used to spray the new hut with the decoction. He held the bowl of *Euclea* decoction in his left hand and sprinkled with his right hand. He added salt to the fowls, and all who were there ate a little bit of one fowl. The headman had a breast and a leg, his wife a leg also. He went home with the other fowl to give it to his wife and child, reserving the liver and the entrails for himself. He then took the *nsaŋgula* branch and hung it up on one of the poles at the entrance to the kraal. (I have often seen branches of *nsaŋgula* hung up at the entrance of a kraal.)

He then told the women to take the ashes of the old fires, each woman sweeping up her own ashes, and place them with the brush and dust-pan (an old winnowing-tray or bit of a gourd) at the cross-paths near the house, and never to look behind while they did it.

---

[1] This process of spraying the new hut is called *kutotoviya yindlu*. It is curious to note that stripes on old black beads *matotoviya*, and the magical sprinkling of a hut are called by the same name. (Cf. p. 60.)

Everything that was used for sweeping up the ashes of the old fires was placed at the cross-paths. It was a sign to all that the kraal had been blessed.

The new fires were lighted by the brands or logs or sticks taken from the *anyaŋga's* own fire, 'which was cleansing, because it took away the *khombo*'.

The poles at the entrance to the kraal had to have two magic circles drawn round them by the *anyaŋga*, one of black charcoal and the other of red ochre. These anointed poles are a very frequent sight at the entrance to a kraal.

Another way of blessing the kraal was described to me in this way:

The *anyaŋga* is invited, he will come bringing his medicines in order that he may asperge the kraal with them. He prepares the medicine in one bowl, and encircles the kraal sprinkling the huts with it. Then he takes a live fowl by the feathers and the neck and dips its tail into the medicine, and sprinkles the kraal with it. Then he opens the mouth of the fowl and puts medicine in it. After that he kills the fowl, and scatters its feathers all round the kraal. The poles are then set up.

A Tʃopi woman told me that in this rite as practised in the district of Nyantsumbu there is no procession of couples to the gate of the kraal, but the *anyaŋga* tells all the people to go into their huts. No one must be in sight or see anything. He then walks round the kraal naked. She did not know what rite he performed, probably the sprinkling of the kraal with the leaf medicine, as no one must see him. But the substitution of the *anyaŋga's* new fire for the old one was a marked feature of the proceedings. If this sib is of *Vetʃa* origin, probably this rite has the same source.

These remarks by a Leŋge man on the blessing of the kraals are rather illuminating:

When a person has built a kraal, they invite *tinyaŋga*. When one has arrived first he tells them that: 'You must collect fowls, that I may work well.' Also if the kraal is a big one, get ready a pound, if it is a small one, prepare half-a-sovereign. When he has finished working, they bring out the money and give him. Also he tells them that: 'This kraal is blessed; sorcerers cannot enter, because I have used my medicines—because I have driven away evil spirits, also there will remain good (ancestral) spirits.' Also when he gets up and goes, and they remain overwhelmed with many misfortunes, they say, 'that *anyaŋga* did not work well,' they will call another *anyaŋga* who will set up another gateway and leave the old one.

On May 10th, 1928, as we passed through a kraal, we saw a group of people gathered under the roof of a cooking-hut. There were an *anyaŋga* and another man, and the head of the kraal and a boy. Some women were gathered together in a hut. The boy was holding the goat, which was about to be killed. It was a black and white one. In a winnowing-basket was some Kaffir-corn. One of the native women with me said she had seen the Kaffir-corn smeared over the breast of the goat. The remaining corn in the winnowing-tray was afterwards to be made into porridge, and some medicine of the *anyaŋga's małuŋgu* or soot medicine in a little gourd (*noŋgovane*) to be added to it. The *anyaŋga* would kill the goat saying as he did so, 'Help me, my Father, that I may work well for the people in this kraal.'

The object of the rite was to protect the kraal from evil influences and the enemies which surrounded it.

## XVI
## FOLK-LORE AND PROVERBS

FOLK-STORIES are told in the evening round the fire, for amusement, by the women and girls and boys. The men, especially those who have been to Johannesburg, already look upon this form of amusement as childish. In spite of that there is a very rich folk-lore originating from many sources. There are stories of Leŋge, Tʃopi, Ndau, Arab, Indian, and Portuguese origin.

Always when beginning a story, a Leŋge woman will say, '*Kariŋgani wa kariŋgani!*' (Story of stories!) The audience chimes in '*Kariŋgani!*' (Story!) The relater goes on: 'There went out a young man to capture a bride, &c.' The audience chimes in '*Kariŋgani!*' and as the story proceeds, a woman here, or a girl there, will softly repeat '*Kariŋgani!*' By this they mean to impress upon themselves that the story is only fiction after all.

Only a small selection can be given here. The stories will speak for themselves. To me, the distinguishing note is the recital of all the little details of the daily life and work of the women. A literal translation of the text is given. Owing to expenses of publication, it is impossible to give the native text.

*Dipumbane. Told by Marian Nsevele and Peresina Muyaŋga*

A woman starts off, she seeks for pot clay. She returns, she models the clay, she makes an image. She places it on the hanging shelf (*tsala*), then she kindles a fire. It dries. When it is dried it says, '*Whetsi!* (*sneezes*). Take me off, Mamma!' Then there arrive young girls, saying, 'Let us go to the dancing contests.' She refuses, saying, 'I may dissolve.' Then they say, 'We will protect you with our clothes.' She refuses, saying, 'You may leave me, I shall be drowned with the rain.' They say, 'Oh, no, no! Let us go. We will cover you up.' So they start off; they go to the dances. They seek the dancing. So then clouds begin (to gather) above. Then there falls a great rain. Then they protect her with their clothes. Then when they are tired with the cold of the rain, they begin to take their clothes. They cover themselves with their clothes. Then Dipumbane remains without anything. Then the rain falls on her. Then she begins to be wet. Then she returns home. She arrives in the path. Then she (sings), 'Mamma,

*Wawulele*,[1] I am dissolving. They have deceived me, saying, "Let us go to the dances." I am the bearer of the divining-bag. I am dissolving.' And then another leg comes off. Then she goes on one leg only. Then there comes off another leg, she is finished. Then her mother goes and takes her there at the gateway, and pounds her, and adds more clay and makes an image. She places her again on the hanging shelf. Then she dries. Then when she is dry, she says, '*Whetsi!* Take me off, Mamma!' So her mamma takes her down. Her mamma says, 'Don't go again to the dances.' She says, 'No! no! I will not yet go to the dances.' But when her mother has gone to the fields they remain again, they deceive her saying, 'Let us go to the dances.' She says, 'She may scold me, my mamma, because she said, "Don't consent to go again to the dances".' 'The girls say, 'We will give you an umbrella.' She says, 'You may deceive me again because you began by deceiving me, saying, "We will give you clothes" while you take them away again.' They answer, 'Oh, no! no! We are certain to-day that we will give you an umbrella.' She starts by going into the house, she takes her clothes, she puts them on, and goes to the dances. Then they arrive at the dances. Then when they have arrived at the dances, and begin to see the contest, there come clouds black indeed, those which bring great rain. So then it rains indeed, and then they give her her umbrella, saying, 'Protect yourself with it.' When the owners of the umbrella feel the rain, they say to Dipumbane, 'Give us our umbrella.' They take their umbrella. So then Dipumbane begins to cry, she says, 'You deceived me, saying, "Let us go to the dances." When I refuse, you say, "We will give you an umbrella."' They say, 'Oh! We feel the rain.' So they take their umbrella, they run, they leave Dipumbane. She is drowned with rain. Then she (sings), '*Mamane, Wawulele, Wawulele!* I am dissolving. They deceived me saying, "Let us go to the dances," there at the dances, I am dissolving. I am the bearer of the bag, of the bag, I am dissolving. There at Mamma's, there at Mamma's, I am dissolving.' So then one leg comes off. She goes on one leg. Then she tries to reach home. Another leg comes off. And then when she has arrived at the doorway, both her arms come off, there remains her head. Then she (sings), '*Mamane, Wawulele, Wawulele,* I am dissolving! They have deceived me saying: "Let us go to the dances," there at the dances, I am dissolving. I am the bearer of the bag, of the bag, I am dissolving, There at Mamma's, at Mamma's, I am dissolving!' Her mother begins to scold her, saying, 'To-day I shall leave you, I shall not

[1] *Wulele* = in this case, grass placed between pots to prevent their breaking.

mould you. You will crumble there in the bush.' So then she leaves her, and does not mould her again. So then the rain muddies the clay and makes it dust, it dissolves.

*Dzinyaŋga. Told by Marian Nsevele, Mbalweni*

A woman starts off to seek mealies. She gives them to her daughter-in-law, saying, 'Pound (them)!' While there are two grains only. Then that woman sets out to go to the fields, there remains the young girl, saying, 'You! You gave me two grains only, I shall be filled with that!' (Ironical!) She enters the house to find maize, she climbs up on the hanging shelf (*tsala*). She seeks maize there on the *tsala*, but cannot find it. She finds a water-pot without a mouth, and brings it down. Then she lets it go, it breaks below. Then there come out little creatures[1] (children) of that woman, she had put them there in the pot. So then these children (five of them) go into the fields to their mamma. So then while they stood in the path they said, 'Mamma! Mamma! your daughter-in-law has killed the pot, saying, "Mealies!" while it was we. *Dzinyaŋga! Dzinyaŋga! Dzinyaŋga!* Make haste! Mamma! We are finished with the cold. *Dzinyaŋga! Dzinyaŋga! Dzinyaŋga!*' So then there dies one in the way. There remain four. While they are on the way, they stop again, they sing again, saying, 'Your daughter-in-law has killed the pot, saying, "Mealies!" while it was we. *Dzinyaŋga! Dzinyaŋga! Dzinyaŋga!* Make haste, Mamma! We die with cold! *Dzinyaŋga! Dzinyaŋga! Dzinyaŋga!*' Then there die three on the way without reaching the fields. So then there remains one. It arrives in the fields. It sees its mamma! Then it cries, saying, 'Mamma, Mamma! Your daughter-in-law has killed the pot saying, "Mealies!" while it was we. *Dzinyaŋga! Dzinyaŋga! Dzinyaŋga!*' So it also dies in the fields. Then its mother cries and goes home. Then she arrives and drives away her daughter-in-law saying, 'You have killed my children.'

This is a story of the *ʃigono* which a sorceress calls her children. The belief about *ʃigono* is that the sorceress kills people, and then makes the 'spooks' of the people she has killed, her servants or children, to do her will. The *ʃigono* may be of all sizes and forms (some are in the form of animals) and they are generally protected by a mortar or a pot, or perhaps placed in the hollow of a tree.

*The Python Husband. Told by Amy Nyantsumbu*

A python starts off saying, 'You, Mamma, seek for me a girl who is

[1] See p. 218.

very pretty.' His mamma starts off to seek a girl. She found one who was pretty, she asks, (tells) her that, 'I want you, you are wanted by my son, he has gone to Johannesburg. He said, "Mamma, seek for me a girl who is very pretty indeed." Now I have found you, you are very pretty indeed.' That girl says, 'All right, I want him, your son.' That woman starts off, she goes to her home, she takes the money to lobola. That girl starts off, she goes to her husband's home, with her younger sister. They arrive at the husband's home, they show them their hut. The mother of the python sleeps, she has shown them their hut, they sleep. There arrives the python saying (sings), 'Mamma don't you open, open for me then?' The mother of the python says (sings), 'She was opening for you, my child. Makhowana[1] is with me now.' She opens, he enters, saying, 'Mamma, where is then my water?' His mother says (sings), 'It is there by the side of the hut, my child. And now I have Makhowana.' He takes water, he washes himself saying, when he has finished washing, 'Mamma, Mamma, where is then my food?' Mamma says, 'It is there at the side, my child, my child! And now I have Makhowana.' He takes his food, he eats. When he has finished eating he says, 'Mamma, Mamma, where is then my wife?' His mamma says, 'Don't you see her, my child? don't swallow her. It is she of the *fikava*.[2] And now I have Makhowana.' He starts off, he sleeps with his wife. He gets up, he goes to the bush, there remains the younger sister, she says to her sister, 'Your husband is a snake.' Her elder sister denies it saying, 'It is lies, my husband has gone to Johannesburg.' Her younger sister says, 'It is lies, he came into the house, he is a snake.' The elder sister denies it, the younger sister saying, 'To-day cease to eat their food here at home. Eat my little cucumbers (*nkaka* fruits) only.' The elder ceases to eat the food there in the kraal, she sleeps, she does not eat anything. Her husband arrives saying, 'Mamma, Mamma? Why did you not open for me then?' His Mamma says, 'She was opening for you, my child, my child! And now I have Makhowana.' She opens. His wife begins to fear, she clings to her sister. Her younger sister says, 'Let me go. I told you. I said your husband is a snake. You annoy me saying, "My husband has gone to Johannesburg." Now don't fear! it is he, your husband.' She says, 'All right, cover me with a garment, that he may not see me.' She covers her up. The python says to his mother, 'Mamma, Mamma, my wife, where is she then?' His Mamma says, 'Don't you see her, my

---

[1] *Makhowana* = pots and pans, the bride's own name.

[2] *fikava* = enlarged umbilicus.

child, my child! It is she of the *ſikava*. Don't swallow her. Now I have Makhowana!' His wife is afraid. Her younger sister catches her that she does not run away, she sleeps. At dawn in the morning they say good-bye, saying that they are going home. The Mamma says, 'All right, Farewell.' They go. When they have reached home the elder says to her father and her mother, 'That husband, I do not want him. Take his money and give him, because I can never go back to my husband's home.' They take the money and give him, he goes to his home.

### Ɖwamukoki (*The Little Hunchback*). Told by Amy Nyantsumbu

Many young girls start off saying, 'Let us go to the teeth-filing.' Ɖwamukoki follows them. They send her back, she refuses, they run, they leave her, because she cannot run because she is a hunchback. They arrive, they go to have their teeth filed. Ɖwamukoki arrives afterwards: she asks, 'There where they file teeth, where is it?' They show her, saying, 'Go.' She goes, she arrives, saying, 'I want to have my teeth filed, doctor!' The *anyaŋga* consents, saying, 'Come, I will file them for you.' He files them, he finishes. She says, 'Show me there where our people are having their teeth filed.' The *anyaŋga* shows her, saying, 'Let us go.' He shows her her companions, they are surprised, saying, 'But we left you at home, yet you follow us.' They put them all in a hut: they say, 'Smile, we see the teeth! How pretty they are!' Those girls, many of them smile, their teeth are black, because he has powdered charcoal, their *anyaŋga*, he powders charcoal to polish the teeth. He says, 'Smile!' They smile; black are their teeth! They say, 'You smile too, Ɖwamukoki.' The hunchback smiles, it lights up the house with the teeth of the hunchback. Those many girls say, 'Let us go home.' They get up and go. Ɖwamukoki goes, they kill her in the way. They put her in the hollow stump of a tree—they put her there. They start off home, they arrive. Ɖwamukoki's mother asks, saying, 'Where is Ɖwamukoki?' They say, 'We do not know, because we turned her back. We do not know where she is.' She weeps, the mother of Ɖwamukoki, she starts off, she takes an axe, she says she is going to seek wood. She arrives at the tree where they put her child. She cuts wood. Ɖwamukoki says (there in the tree stump), '*Ve vetso vetso!*' (pants for breath). Her mother looks, she does not see that which is breathing. She begins to cut again. She begins to sing. Ɖwamukoki (sings): 'Who is that saying *ghe! ghe!!* (noise of cutting wood). Call me, Mamma, you cutting wood. Ɖwamukoki has perished, You, she has perished.

*ghe! ghe!* She perished at the teeth-filing! you! *ghe! ghe!* Is it you? *ghe! ghe!*' Her mother takes her out there from the hollow tree, she carries her home. She cooks beer, she invites the chief of the country, she will show him her child, saying, 'Smile, my child'. She smiles, in her mouth there is light. She invites the very many girls who killed Ɖwamukoki. The chief says, 'You smile also.' They smile, their teeth are black. They say, 'You have all failed, Ɖwamukoki's teeth are pretty.'

*The Woman and the Bird. Told by Rindawu Nyamavili, Nteteni*

A woman starts off with her child, she reaches the fields, she puts the child to sleep in the shade of the *muhimbe* tree. She digs, she gets tired, she rises and pulls up manioc, she lights a fire, she roasts (the manioc), and wakes the child. She takes the manioc, she eats and gives it to her child also, and puts it to sleep again. She gets up and goes to dig. The bird comes and kills the child, it takes the head, it makes a drum. It takes the stomach, and makes a skin membrane, it takes the arms, and makes strikers (drumsticks). It takes the legs, it makes a Tʃopi-piano (*timbila*). It ascends aloft in the *muhimbe* tree. It begins to beat the drum, saying, 'Mrs. Digger, I am you! You dig very much! The child you have—sing bird, resound! khe vhe! khe vhe! khe vhe! khe vhe! khe vhe! khe vhe!' The woman leaves her digging, she goes home, she tells her husband that there is a dancing contest in the fields. The husband says to his wife, 'Go back there, if there are people seeing the dances, you will return and tell me.' The woman returns and searches there where she has put the child to sleep. She misses the child, she gets up and stands far off. The bird sings again, the woman returns, she goes home, she tells her husband saying, 'My child has been killed by a bird.' That man invites his companions who are married men. The woman also calls her companions who are married women, they take a pestle. The men take a gun and bow, they go, they say they are going to kill the bird. The bird sees them and says, 'Mrs. Digger! I am you, you dig very much! Sing bird, resound! He takes a head, he makes a drum. He takes the arms, he makes drumsticks. He takes the legs, he makes a Tʃopi-piano. Sing bird! resound! khe vhe! khe vhe! khe vhe! khe vhe!' The men put down the guns. The women put down the pestle. They dance. They tire themselves out with dancing. They return, they go home. And it also, the bird it goes away.

This story is interesting as showing that the idea of a skull being used as a drum, and arm-bones as drumsticks, is not an unfamiliar one with the Leŋge, and indirectly affords further proof of the truth of P.'s account of her initiation. It will be remembered that she declared that the drum used on that occasion was the head of a man, and one of the drumsticks, his arm-bone (cf. p. 127).

*The Doll. Told by Silivia, a schoolgirl of Masiyeni, whose mother belongs to the Nyantsumbu sib*

Nsatimune sets out to seek a *sala* (*strychnos* shell). She makes a baby with the *sala*. Elidina says, 'Nsatimune has beaten (surpassed) me.' Then she gives notice to her child companions to search for *masala* to make babies with the *masala*. Then they decorate their children with beads and fringes. Then they bring out their babies to show, that people may see which is the prettier. They choose that of Nsatimune, saying, 'This is pretty.' They (the girls) go into the districts to show the babies again. The districts say, 'This of Nsatimune is pretty.' They return home again. They say, 'Let us go far again indeed.' They produce their children again. The people say, 'Nsatimune's is the prettier.' They return home. They are angry with Nsatimune, saying, 'Let us go to the lake to wash the children.' So when they have arrived at the lake they begin to wash their children. Nsatimune is overcome with weakness. They say to her, 'Why do you not wash your child?' Then she enters the lake while overcome with weakness. She dips the child, she then loses it there in the lake. She looks and fails to find. Then her sisters say, 'Let us go home. You will look for another *sala*.' She says at once, Oh! no! no! I want this one. I will dip under the water, and go with my *sala*.' She dips, she goes, there in the water. Then she meets a hippopotamus, and inquires of it. She passes on and meets a crocodile, saying, 'Have you seen my children?' The crocodile says, 'Pass, go on farther, and ask there.' So she passes, she finds a house. That house is a house of Mystery.[1] She asks it, it says, 'Pass on, go farther.' She passes on and finds an old woman, and asks her, while the old one was standing on her head, 'Have you seen my child?' (The old woman) says, 'Come to me,' so she goes. (The old woman) says, 'Wash my back with water.' She washes her back, and remains with her. The (old woman) gives Nsatimune an earth-pea, saying, 'Stamp! there in the mortar.' She stamps. The mortar is filled with one earth-pea. She cooks, they eat, they go to the lake. When they

---

[1] The word *Sikuŋgumari* is used here. See initiation ceremonies, p. 131.

have arrived at the lake the old woman says to Nsatimune, 'What is this?' She says, 'It is a water-dipper,' while it was an arm. The (old one) says, 'And this?' she says, 'It is a water pot,' while it was a head. (The old one) says, 'And this?' She says, 'It is a head-ring,' while it was a snake. (The old one) says, 'And this?' She says, 'It is leaves for a pot covering,' while it was bowels. Then she says, 'I have finished questioning you. Lift up my pot on my head! We are going home.' Nsatimune says, 'Lift up mine for me.' She raises it. They return home. She helps her to put the pot down, (the old one) seeks one grain of maize and gives it to her saying, 'Pound.' When she has pounded it the mortar is full. (The old one) says, 'Cook!' When she has cooked (the food) and it is done, she serves it. The old woman says to Nsatimune, 'Husks or maize, which shall we give to my young men?' Nsatimune says, 'We will give them husks.' So she gives them husks. They themselves eat samp. The old woman says to Nsatimune, 'Go and sleep with the boys.' She refuses saying, 'I will sleep with you.' Then they slept. At dawn the old one says, 'Home or here, which do you want?' Nsatimune says, 'I want home.' (The old woman) calls her inside the house, taking a garment (ŋguvo), and gives it to her with a box and pounds, saying to Nsatimune, 'Go to your home. When you have gone and you find a kraal, when the sun has set, and you ask saying, "I want a place to sleep"—if they agree do not take their mat if they give it you—you will say to them, "I will sleep on my garment".' Indeed Nsatimune does this. She goes, she finds a kraal, she asks saying, 'I want somewhere to sleep.' When they agree, they want to give her their mat, but she says to them, 'I will sleep on my garment.' Then she spreads out her garment and sleeps on it, with her *sala*. Then in the middle of the night when she lies awake, she hears that the *sala* is restless, it makes itself a baby. When it dawns the owners of the kraal are surprised to see the *sala* changed into a baby. She says good-bye and goes and reaches home, does Nsatimune. They are pleased, her mothers and sisters. Then her sister says, 'I will go also to the lake, I will lose my *sala*, because Nsatimune lost her *sala* and followed it, and we wept because we missed her, saying she was lost, while she returns with a baby—and I, I will do as Nsatimune (did), who returns with a baby.' So she goes also, the sister of Nsatimune, she plunges into the water. The *sala* refuses to sink. She refuses (to give in) and does it with force. So the *sala* is lost. Then she says also, 'I will go with my *sala*.' Where she has gone there is a hippopotamus, she asks it, it says, 'Pass on farther, and ask there.' She passes, she finds a crocodile and passes and finds the house of Mystery. She inquires there. It says, 'Pass.' She abuses the house. She finds the old woman standing on her head. She makes inquiries. The old one says, 'Come to me.' She goes, the old woman says, 'Wash my back.' She refuses saying, 'There is dirt. My hands to touch filth! I cannot!' The old one gives her an earth-pea. She says, 'Oh! no! I cannot take one and return many.' They give her (earth-peas) angrily, because she has broken many laws. When she stamped the earth-peas and they were spilt, she takes and throws them into the bush. Others were pecked up by the fowls. She cooks them. When they are done, the people eat. At dawn they go to the lake. The old one says to the sister of Nsatimune, 'What is this?' She says, 'It is an arm by which you draw water.' The old woman says, 'And this?' She says, 'It is the head of a person.' The old one says, 'And this?' She says, 'It is the bowels of a person.' The old one says, 'Lift my pot on my head.' They return home, she helps to put down the pot. The old woman takes a single mealie grain saying, 'Stamp.' She stamps, she winnows, she cooks, it is not done well. (The old one) says, 'Serve!' She serves the old woman, (who) says, 'Husks or mealies, which shall we give to the boys?' The sister of Nsatimune says, 'We will give them mealies, we will eat the husks.' The old woman angrily takes the mealies to the young men, while they ate the husks. The old one says, 'There or here, where do you want to sleep?' She says, 'I want to sleep at the boys, because it is horrid with you. Also it is smelly. I do not want you.' (The old one) takes a mat and gives her, she goes to the young men's hut and sleeps there. She wakes saying, 'Why do they not return? They will return at what time?' She waits, and when at another time she wakes and does not see (them), there begin to arrive young male rats. When they reached her, they begin to bite because they are many. They finish her body eating it, because she broke the laws of that old woman.

## TIDEKADEKA (DOUBLE ENIGMAS)

The *tidekadeka*, which are in the nature of proverbs or riddles, are taught by mothers to their children. Young people remember more of these riddles than older ones. M. Junod calls these riddles 'enigmas of two statements or propositions'. The second statement or proposition explains the first, but the topical allusion or esoteric meaning is not stated, but understood.

M. Junod tells us that these double enigmas are known as *psitekatekwane* among the Roŋga, who begin by saying, '*teka, teka, teka*' ('take!

take! take!'), whereas the Leŋge always begin by saying, '*dhe! dhe! dhe! dhe! dhe!*' Several examples of *titekateka* are given in a spelling book published by the American Mission at Inhambane in 1922, in Landina (*Tswa*).

Bishop Smythe, in his grammar of the Leŋge language, gives, '*ku dekadeka* = to shake, not to be firmly fixed.' *Dekadeka* = a story, fib, tale which is not true.

The study of *tidekadeka* among the Leŋge confirms the following statements made by the Rev. H. L. Bishop (*South African Journal of Science*, vol. xix, 1922, pp. 401–15):

'It is difficult at the best of times to define a proverb. It is perhaps still more difficult to decide just which sayings should be grouped under that name. It is often difficult to decide between the riddle and the proverb. . . . One might have thought that, the great facts of life being the same everywhere, there would be frequent close parallels between [African] proverbs and those of European peoples. I have, however, found it very difficult to find such equivalents, for more than a very few of the proverbs. The same subjects crop up constantly, but the angle of vision is so different, that often one can only link our proverbs to theirs by a loose paraphrase.

'From the linguistic standpoint, a large collection should be very useful. The language is, as was to be expected, highly idiomatic and frequently archaic. In the present state of the language, when old words are dying out rapidly, and when hard sounds are being softened, contact with forms that have a relatively high antiquity may help us to clear up doubtful points of more than one kind.'

I am very grateful to the Rev. H. L. Bishop for so concisely summing up the true facts of the case of African enigmas and proverbs. I have also noticed the same grammatical phenomena in the Leŋge enigmas as those which Mr. Bishop mentions as occurring in the Roŋga ones, i.e. the use of shortened forms, suppression of the copula; irregular constructions; omission of conjunctions; irregular pronominal concords, irregular noun-formations, and suppression of the nominal prefix.

*A few Leŋge tidekadeka.*
    *Dhe! Dhe! Dhe! Dhe! Dhe!*
    *Dekela wadekela* = Totterer of totterers.
    *Koku waku wakhale* = Your old grandparent.
    *Litaŋga liheta nti hikunava.*
    *Σikosa ſaheta nti kunzunza.*

The gourd creeps all over the kraal, the old woman moves herself about all over the kraal (finishes the kraal) sitting down (she is too old to walk).

*Magoŋgolo mambidi yatsanzeketana.*
*Şikosana şimbidi şisela nambu.*
Two old logs cross each other, two old people drink together at the river.

This possibly means that people choose companions of their own age.

*Ɽidwamana tʃalatʃala, tʃalatʃala.*
*Tsumela, ŋwanaŋga, niyakule.*
The young hare scuttles, scuttles. Go back, my child, I am going far.

This refers to a woman who is fond of gadding about, and does not want her child to follow her.

*Ɽisalana koyo.*
*Ɽikhunzwana namu.*
= Sala heavy with fruit, initiation candidate back of neck.

As the young *Strychnos* tree bends with the weight of the oranges, so do initiation candidates sit with bent head.

*Gubata! Gubata! Mitaŋgu yimbidi ʃiseloni.*
To flip with the finger, two little loaves of mealie-porridge in the winnowing-tray.

If there are two children in the family, and one dies, the other will die also.

*Kusu baleka ni manemba, muhorana lowola nititiho.*
The *ukułu* tree (*Trichilia emetica*) bends beneath its weight.
The young girl is lobola-ed with fingers (pounds which are counted on the fingers).

*Ku alakanya lembe landlala, koŋgolo koʃa marambu yaʃena.*
To remember the year of famine, roll over the baboon's bones.

*Tʃomo didimwa, rola ahahane.*
Let an orange fall, Aunt picks it up.

The brother's child has let something fall, the aunt picks it up. There are tabus about picking up things.

*Ɽipalana thoko thoko, atu vatu, higumelamu.*
The grave is deep, we people end there.

*Tinyeleti rhee, kugya vuswa wena.*
Glittering like stars—to eat porridge you.
(This refers to white ants.)

## FOLK-LORE AND PROVERBS

*Tihuku ta Nyapondzweni tiŋgena hiſisuka, mahuŋgu ya
Nyapondzweni yakukambiwa hi ɡiłangi.*
The fowls of Nyapondzweni enter the coop backwards.
The matters of Nyapondzweni are examined by children.

Here are two riddles:

*Leſowa vaŋgaroli iſiyini? I mati!*
What is that which cannot be picked up? It is water.

*Leſoka vaŋgakanzihi iſiyini? I tinzulu.*
What is that which cannot be climbed? It is sedge [*Cyperus natalensis*].

## CONCLUSION

IF I tried to sum up very shortly the characteristics of the Leŋge, I should say: They are religious and punctilious in observing even the small details of their ritual. They have a decided scientific bias. This is shown in the way they have one name, or more, for every tiny blade of grass, every little bird which sings, and in their minute observation of all natural phenomena; by their very careful preparation of food, and the numerous stages in its preparation (ill-cooked or ill-prepared food is not known among them); by the native industries of pottery and basket making and the extremely careful preparation of the materials, and the good work resulting; by their liking for medicines; the careful dosage in a mussel-shell, and the counting the drops (*ku-minyeta*) of the right dose. When the Leŋge are interested then they will take infinite pains.

They are musical and artistic: who that has ever heard it will forget the galloping rhythm and blazing sounds of a full orchestra of Tʃopi pianos, drums, and dancers, in a native kraal (not the imitation performance which is staged in a Johannesburg compound) in the height of the dancing contests? Or what can surpass those quaint little tunes which are sung as refrains during the recital of folk-stories in the evening, and which take one back to the olden days when animals walked the earth as men, and vice versa; when mischievous elves hid in basket-bins; when little clay dolls in the rafters woke to life with a sneeze; and rabbit skins jumped down from the wall and danced and sang—these little tunes in their right setting belong to the morning of life, when the earth was young.

The real artistic sense of the Leŋge is shown in their beautifully constructed huts, some of which resemble a Brobdignagian basket inverted, and superimposed on a clay pot decorated with white, red, and black designs. The wood-carving and bead-work also show the artistic sense in many ways.

And what about their faults? The Leŋge are lazy, yes, but only if not vitally interested in their work. They are immoral (or rather un-moral?), yes, but there are those among them who have made of their sex 'a spiritual achievement'. They are covetous of money and clothes, yes, but this is not altogether their fault, for rapidly advancing civilization is not finding the African able to make new adjustments to changing circumstances at a moment's notice. But there are occasions when the

# CONCLUSION

coin of Leŋge culture in its spinning is so nearly falling, with the reverse side uppermost, that a glimpse of it can clearly be seen. A sympathetic Government with Christianity and education can engrave that reverse side as it should be, and also provide the elixir to infuse new life into the people.

And so I close this sketch of the old testament of the Leŋge women. To others more worthy than I will be given the task of writing the new testament of this little people, tucked away in a corner, between the great grey-green, greasy Limpopo River, and the violet Indian Ocean.

# APPENDIX
## THE SIBS OF GAZALAND

### I. List of Independent Chiefs and their Districts, *as given by Johane Makamu.*

VaBila. Bila. Σikonele. Małalele. Nhuvuŋga. Σisano. Mandlati. (There are also Suto-Pedi and Ndau elements in Bilene.)

VaNhlave. Makamu. Novela. Mavundza. Ɖkwinika. Nhloŋgo.

VaNtlava. Matavele. Tsakalu. Pelembe. Dzimba. Nyambaŋga. Masiye.

VaKosa. Kosa. Sambo. Ndzukula. Likotso. Σivuri. Nyambendze.

VaƉwaluŋgu. Ɖkuna. Valoyi. Masaŋganye. Maluleke.

VaHleŋgwe. Mazive. Tʃauke. Makondzo. Muhuŋgu.

VaDzivi. Hlavaŋgwani. Zuŋguza. Yiŋgwani.

VaMhandla. Matʃanise. Σikatsa. Mbinyavukari. Σirundzu. Ɖguluve. Vilaŋkulu. Mawelele.

MaKambana. Mondlwana (Makwakwa by origin).

VaƉwanati. Makwakwa. Matsinye.

VaPuwa. Mhula. Nyabaŋgo. Novele.

VaManyisa. Manyisa. Σirindza.

VaLeŋge. Ɖwamusi. Ɖkavele. Ɖkumi. Nyoko (Kosa Lipaŋga). Mpumule. Marame. Masiye. Mahumani.

Vatʃopi or VaTsoŋga. Ɖkandze. Maŋgundze. Muŋgwambi. Nyantsumbu. Zandamela. Bahule. Zavala. Σilundu. Nyaŋkale.

Each of these sibs had its own chief, and self-government.[1]

(Some of them are really of Thoŋga origin, but are considered Tʃopi now.)

Ndau sibs which settled in Gazaland under Manukuse were the Ɖkomo or Sitoyi, Nqibi, Simaŋgu, Nyamukume, Mwoyana, Muhlaŋga. Mandlazi. Małalele or Ɖgwami.

### II

In *Bantu Studies*, vol. iii, 1927, pp. 57–71, M. Junod gives a list of Leŋge chiefs and of the headmen of the districts which they govern. I have visited most of these districts, and spent a short time in each, and can amplify the list as follows:

Regulo 1. Σihału Ɖwamusi

Ɖwamusi governs the following *ʒigava*:

| Σigava. | District. | Present Surname of Chief (1930). | Origin. |
|---|---|---|---|
| 1. Nyampfumo | Nyampfunwini | Σihału Ɖwamusi | Thoŋgo |
| 2. Ɖkumayo or Ɖkumi | Ɖkumini | Ɖkumayo | Partly Thoŋga, partly Ntama |

[1] In olden times the system of self-government was called *Makomana*. Each sib had to settle its own affairs without reference to any big chief.

# APPENDIX

| Σigava. | District. | Present Surname of Chief (1930). | Origin. |
|---|---|---|---|
| 3. Marame | Marameni | Marame | Thoŋga |
| 4. Masiye | Masiyeni | Masiye | Thoŋga |
| 5. Ŋgaŋgale | Ŋgaŋgaleni | Ŋwamusi | Thoŋga |
| 6. Venye | Venyeni | Venye | Thoŋga |
| 7. Nyahule | Nyahuleni | Nyahule | Ntama |
| 8. Ŋkumbe | Ŋkumbeni | Ŋkumbe | Ntama |
| 9. Nyatsembe | Nyatsembeni | Muthemba | Chief is of Ŋgunu (Ŋgoni) stock |
| 10. Nyampheke | Nyamphekeni | Matʃayı | Chief is of Ŋgunu stock |
| 11. Ntete | Nteteni | Ntete | Thoŋga |
| 12. Nyamavila | Nyamavileni | Ndava | Zulu (probably Ntama) |
| 13. Seleve | Seleveni | Seleve | Zulu (probably Ntama) |
| 14. Σisano | Σisaŋwini | Matavele | Ntama ? |
| 15. Ŋkavele | Ŋkaveleni | Ŋkavele | Thoŋga |
| 16. Ŋkunzule | Ŋkunzuleni | Ŋkunzule | Partly Thoŋga, partly Ntama |
| 17. Ŋgoŋwani | Ŋgoŋwanini | Ŋgoŋwani | Thoŋga |
| 18. Σavane | Σavaneni | Σavane | Partly Thoŋga, partly Ntama |
| 19. Σavi | Σavini | Nyampʃumo | Partly Thoŋga, partly Ntama |
| 20. Makamu | Makaŋwini | Makamu | Partly Thoŋga, partly Ntama |
| 21. Σiluvane Nyapondzo | Nyapondzweni | Nyapondzo | Thoŋga (Vilaŋkulu) |

All Σihaɫu's territory is under the Administration (Portuguese) of Vila de João Belo, and immediately under the Chefe do Posto, native sub-commissioner at Choŋgoene ( = at the lake Ntʃoŋgo).

Masiye is greeted by the title of Mayazi Kosa. Ŋgoŋwani is greeted as Madleyapandle, Duvane. Seleve is greeted as Muthimba; and Ndava as Zibiya.

The old surnames or titles by which chiefs are greeted at ceremonies are interesting and important as showing their origin.

REGULO 2. *Nyafoko.*

There are seven *ṣigava*.

| Ṣigava. | District. | Surname of Chief. | Origin. |
| --- | --- | --- | --- |
| 1. Mukodwani | Mukodwanini | Muyaŋga | Tʃopi-Zulu |
| 2. Ʃagwala | Ʃagwaleni | ,, | ,, |
| 3. Nyafoko | Nyafokweni | ,, | ,, |
| 4. Maŋgundze | Maŋgundzeni | ,, | ,, |
| 5. Mafaŋge | Mafaŋgeni | ,, | ,, |
| 6. Tʃithembe | Nyatʃithembeni | ,, | ,, |
| 7. Mbole | Mboleni | ,, | ,, |

All the chiefs of this regulo, as well as those of Mahumane, belong to the Muyaŋga sib. There are, however, BaVetʃa settlers among the people.

REGULO 3. *Mahumani.*[1]

The premier chief is Mugoŋgonola of Mahumane of Konjweni.[2] He is the 'Chief of the Stone' of Nyokweni also, but this district has been separated from that of Mahumane for administrative reasons.

[1] Mahumane borders on Nyaŋkutse, or Banyini, which is in the Khambana district. The dividing-line is really a geological one. The red sand, *jihu*, of the Mahumane district becomes the whitish argillaceous sand, *banyi*, of Banyini. This ground provides pot-clay. My informant brought me two little lumps of sand, one red, one white, to show the difference, adding, however, that the boundary-line was not strictly adhered to.

[2] Reference has been made (p. 38) to the Stone of Chieftainship which VaLeŋge chiefs swallow at their accession. The *anyaŋga* of the chief usually places the stone or stones in porridge mixed with medicine, and gives the mixture to his master to swallow. A chief is called 'the chief of the stone', meaning that he is the real chief. Mugoŋgonola of Konjweni is called 'the chief of the stone' of Nyokweni, although at present he is not actually ruling Nyokweni in addition to his own district (cf. p. 244).

A crocodile is said to swallow the stone when it has killed a man, in order to aid digestion; but a stone found in the crocodile is more likely to be a natural concretion or oolith. If three ooliths are found, it is said that at different times the crocodile must have swallowed three men. The natives calculate that on an average a crocodile swallows one man a year. When a crocodile is killed, the chief of the district is at once informed, and he comes and takes possession of any stones found.

One woman told me that when a crocodile was killed in the lake near our house, she and some others went to see it, but they were not allowed to see the stone.

If a chief has two or three stones in his possession, he may sell one to a neighbouring chief.

Every new chief on succession not only swallows a new stone for himself, but that of his predecessor as well. He is said to retain the latter stone in his body and to be buried with it, but his own stone is ejected before his death. When he sees it, he considers that it is a sure sign that he is going to die, because his stone has no more virtue in it. (Cf. Junod, *The Life of a S. African Tribe*, i, 393, ii, 339.)

The oolith resembles a pearl. I have seen discoloured ones only. I once heard a Leŋge say that he thought chiefs sometimes swallowed diamonds in olden days, and that a diamond would *lobola* a chief's daughter.

# APPENDIX

| Σigava. | District. | Surname of Chief. | Origin. |
|---|---|---|---|
| Mahumane | Mahumaneni | Mahumani (Muyaŋga) | Tʃopi-Zulu |
| Makamu[1] | Makaŋwini | ,, | |
| Mafumisane | Mafumisaneni | ,, | |
| Ntsamba | Ntsambeni | ,, | |
| Σibiyelo | Σibiyeleni | ,, | |
| Mpumule | Mpumuleni | ,, | |
| Ŋgumula | Ŋgumuleni | ,, | |
| Mbalo | Mbalweni | ,, | |
| Botsamu | Botsaŋwini | ,, | |
| Nyoko | Nyokweni | Kosa Lipaŋga Mahumani Muyaŋga | |

The chief and petty chiefs of this regulo are all saluted by the title of *Mahumani, Zari*, or *Zayi*, and they all belong to the Muyaŋga sib. The people whom they govern are of very mixed origin.

The Mahumani, Zari, they are all Muyaŋga beginning at the regulo Σizavani and the regulo Makupulani, and the regulo Maŋgundze, and the regulo Mugoŋgonolo Mahumani, all those are of one kin, all are Muyaŋga. All are descendants of Ŋkandze Muyaŋga, and the Nyoko Lipaŋga Kosa. It is they who are Mahumani Muyaŋga. They left their old name of Nyoko because the Vaŋgunu had forbidden them to use it, they said it was insulting the Vaŋgunu. Then they say they are Lipaŋga Kosa, but their chief is Mugoŋgonolo Mahumani. Also all the kindred of the Mahumani, their chief is Muyaŋga. The third regulo, they are ruled by Muyaŋga Σizavane, therefore the rulers of the Mahumani Zari, are those of Maŋgundze and Makupulani. Their old chief is he, Σizavane Muyaŋga.

The story goes that the Muyaŋga came north in search of ivory. They are all very vague as to the time when they came. They say it was so long ago that they have forgotten. According to the information given me by Mudoŋgole, who is the present *ŋganakana* (petty chief) of Mbalweni, one of the lineages of Mahumani, they found on arrival a people who were 'poor and miserable' of the *ʃiboŋgo* of Nyakule. (Not to be confused with Nyahule.) These people lacked 'iron' weapons to kill the elephants, and so they begged the invaders to remain and be their rulers, and to provide them with iron weapons (*matlhari*). The invitation was accepted, and the new-comers speedily absorbed the old Nyakule stock by intermarriage. There are, however, just a few people left in this district who still have the surname of Nyakule. The first-comers of the Muyaŋga appear to have been Mahumani and Ŋkandze. Mahumani was the founder of the sib which now bears his name. Ŋkandze went to rule Ŋkandze, also called after him. With regard to Nyokweni, a woman of the lineage Lipaŋga Kosa told me this story which explains the insult to the Ŋgoni by using the surname Nyoko. It appears that a woman of Mabuyindlela origin

[1] Another district of this name is in Σihalu's country.

was taken in marriage by a man of the Lipaŋga Kosa sib while these people were still living in Ŋkoseni, and had not yet migrated to the other side of the Limpopo. The woman was accused of witchcraft by her husband's relations, given the *mondzo* ordeal, and driven away. Her little son remained for a time, and then they drove him away, too, saying, '*Hamba ka nyoko*' ('Go to your mother', the term *nyoko* being an impolite one). The poor boy trudged for many weary miles trying to follow his mother. He met a party of people on the road. They asked him his name and where he came from. He was too young to know his real origin, but he knew that his father's people, in driving him away, had said, 'Go to Nyoko' and so he answered, 'I am of the Nyoko'. This boy is said to have been the founder of the Nyoko sib of Nyokweni. But the Ŋgoni Zulus, objecting to the name Nyoko, made the people of Nyokweni use their old true surname of Kosa Lipaŋga.

REGULO 4. *Makupulane*.

The present chief, George Makupulana, has the following districts under his rule. He belongs to the 'Laŋga' sib of Zulu extraction. Laŋga and Muyaŋga are now used interchangeably. Some prefer one form and some the other, of this surname, but all agree that it is the same name. Although the rulers are of Zulu origin, many of the people whom they govern are of Tʃopi origin, and the Tʃopi language is the prevailing one. The rulers have identified themselves with the people. Large numbers of Ndau have settled in the district, especially at Ŋguzeni, and carry on the work of pot-making.

The *ǵigava* are: Ŋguzeni (the Chief's seat), Σilumbelo, Malembe, Nyakoko, Kuku, Nyambendze, Nyaŋkale, Ruku, Kadi, Makanyule.

REGULO 5. *Ŋkandze*.

(Regulo Ŋkandze and his *chefes* (*Port.*) on the border of the sea. He has to be differentiated from the Ŋkandze, who are to be found in true Tʃopiland, but both are Laŋga people.)[1]

The *ǵigava* are: Bahaneni (Head-Chief Ŋguŋguya Muyaŋga), Σizavanini, Moŋgonyeleni, Nyatʃitseneni, Σikwaŋgeni, Nyamboŋgweni, Kwambeni, Masaŋgweni, Madimini. The rulers of these *ǵigava* all belong to the Muyaŋga sib.

Regulos 4 and 5 should now be comprised in Tʃopiland, and not in modern Leŋgeland.

*The Khambana Sib*.

This extremely interesting and important sib belongs to the Bilene group. The Khambana country presents some ethnographic, botanical, and geological features which are distinct from the regions surrounding it.

The folk-lore of this district is very rich, and the language preserves an ancient dialect incorporated into the modern Thoŋga. The Mondlana sib

[1] Rev. H. P. Junod, loc. cit.

# APPENDIX 245

appears to be of Thoŋga origin (Makwakwa). I was told that at the time of the Ŋgoni invasions, the invaders found the Makhambana and the VaTʃopi living as one people, and they made fortified kraals by barricades of tree trunks, to keep out the invaders.

The beautiful tree *Brachystegia venosa* grows in the Khambana district in lovely profusion. The Government botanist at Pretoria tells me this is the most southerly record for this tree. The spring foliage in the Khambana is marvellous in its colouring, and the ground is carpeted with leaves of the *Brachystegia*. I am informed by Maria Mondlana, a Khambana woman, that the people of the Khambana had no initiation ceremonies for girls originally, but if any girl of that district were taken in marriage by a Leŋge man, he would insist that she should go to the initiation ceremonies of Leŋge girls. This was up to 1929.

The following sibs of Bilene are not governed by Leŋge chiefs, but are mostly of Mambu or Ntama origin: Nyatʃekeni, Mbalaneni, Nyaŋkumeni, Mbunzuleni, Nyambaŋgeni, Ŋkonzweni, Mahiyeleni, Σiluŋgwini, Mpinini, Nɬoteni.

# INDEX

Abortion, 63, 64, 82.
Adultery, 107, 147.
Aggregation, 81, 125.
Agriculture, 22, 24, ch. IV; rites, 192–5.
*Akulobola*, 12, 21, 137–40, 143–5, 147, 150; and 'avoidance', 12; *hahane* and, 16; of widows, 169–70; tally of, 108, 138.
Altar, sacrificial, the, 189, 197.
Ancestral spirits, *see* Religion, *sikwembu*.
*Andoro* ornament, 204, 211–12.
Animals, domestic, 24–5; sacrificial, 190 ff.
Anyaŋga, *see* Tinyaŋga.
*Aŋgalaŋga* dance, 177.
Art, designs in beadwork, 60; on walls of huts, 132; food-bowls, 50–1; gourds, 52; lizard pattern, 105–6, 119; pottery, 54, 56; tatu patterns, 59, 107–8.
Asperging, 39, 60, 159, 194, 223.
Avoidance, 12, 64 n.
Axes, 50; ritual, 198, 205, 209, 214; axe-dance, 205.

Bark cloth, 43, 60, 112, 123–4, 125, 137.
Barra, pottery district, 53.
Baskets, 23, 30, 57–9; in spiritualistic seances, 209, 214.
Beads, 59–60; *akulobola*, 137; and spirits, 199, 211; bead girdles, 59, 167; buried, 156; in initiation rites, 124, 125; *kota*, 50, 212–13; *mbuwa*, 213.
Beans, 28, 32, 53.
Betrothal, 16, 122.
Bila, the, a Thoŋga group, 9, 10, 240.
Bilene, district of Bila, 4, 240.
Birth, and the *hahane*, 15, 16; rites, ch. VI; suckling, 84; weaning, 84; death of women in childbirth, 171.
Bishop, Rev. H. L., Roŋga Proverbs, 235.
Blessing the kraals, 222–5.
Bones, divining (*tinlolo*), 16, 61, 62, 76, 80, 113, 138, 164, 190, 200; baskets for, 58; methods of divination, 185–7; string figure, 97; see also Tinyaŋga.
Brides, duties of, 141.
Brown, A. R. Radcliffe, 14.
Buŋgana, pottery district, 53, 54.
Burials, ch. XIII; abnormal, 170–1; of adults, 155–7; of a chief, 163; of infants, 153–5; of women, 56; the *hahane* and, 16.

Cattle, *akulobola*, 137, 138; in Ŋgoni death ceremonies, 163; sacrifice of, 196, 205.
Chai Chai, *see* Vila de João Belo.
Character, 23.
Charms: against falls, 85; against influenza, 217; against sorcery, 41, 46, 80, 202, 220; for procuring a husband or wife, 138; teething, 83.
Chefe do Posto, Portuguese Commissioner, 241.
Chiefs, 4, 5, 11, 41, 88, Appendix.
Children, 61, 151; education, ch. VII; games, ch. VIII; meals, 37; occupations, 23; punishment, 88.
Choŋgoene, Portuguese administration, 241.
Christian influence, 21, 37, 152, 169, 182, 222.
Clothing, 20, 21, 155–6; borrowed, 65.
Cooking, 22, 23, 24, 26, 27; *see also* Pottery.
Cosmetics, 52, 89.
Creation, theory of the, 182.
Crocodile, 24; and the stone of accession, 38, 242 n.; in medicine, 63.

Dances: 23, ch. XIV; bridegroom's, 138; contests, 172; initiation, 115–17, 124, 132 ff.; *masessa*, 174–5, 177, 181; mourning, 180–1; *fiŋgombelo*, 178–9; *timbila*, 177–8.
Death, ch. XIII; in infancy, 153–5; of a chief, 163–5; of adults, 155–7; rites, 157–68, 171.
Depilation, 89, 105.
Divination, *see* Bones, divining.
Djoŋga, the, a Thoŋga group, 4, 9. 10.
Dolls, children's, 87; in folk tales, 42–3, 232; *mayika*, in initiation ceremonies, 114, 119, 124, 129.
Drink, cashew-nut (*Anacardium occidentale*) beer, 28, 31, 44; gin, 44; malt, 48; *mahimbe* (*Garcinia Livingstonei*) beer, 31, 44, 164; *makanye* (*Sclerocarya caffra*) beer, 46–8; manioc gin, 45–6; palm-wine, 30, 43; *pepeta* beer, 49; pine-apple beer, 43; *vuputso*, 29, 48–9, 140, 141, 192.
Drums, dancing, 174, 176, 180 n.; in initiation ceremonies, ch. XI, *passim*; in ritual, 209, 210.
Dzivi, Gaza sib, 240.

# INDEX

Ear-piercing, 104, 105.
Education, of children, 23, ch. VII.
Elephant, 5, 8, 243.

Fires, ceremonial, 164, 165, 166, 194, 222–4; fire-place, 26.
First fruits, rites of, 42, 44, 195, 197.
Fish, 30, 124, 196.
Flora, 24, ch. IV; *see also* Trees.
Folk-lore, 42, 88, ch. XVI.
Food, 22, ch. V; and the rite of kraal-blessing, 222; distribution, 37–8; nutritive values, 32; prohibitions, 38, 49, 52, 65, 79; storage, 26.
Food-bowls, 37, 39, 50, 112; sharing of, 15, 37; washing of, 77.
Fowls: 25; and ancestral spirits, 191, 196; and fish, 196; in agricultural rites, 194; in birth rites, 81–2; in death rites, 166; in initiation rites, 115; in marriage ceremonies, 139, 142, 143, 146; in religious rites, ch. XV; in seclusion rites, 122; rain-making sacrifice, 196; to procure a husband or wife, 138.
Funeral feasts, groups at, 160.

Games, 23, ch. VIII; counting, 90–2; string figures, ch. IX.
Gazaland, 3; agriculture, ch. IV; chiefs and sibs, Appendix; climate, 24; ethnology, 7; flora and fauna, 24.
Genealogy, 7 ff., 17, 19.
Girdles, 20, 59, 82, 108, 124, 167.
Goat, 22, 24; *akulobola*, 137; in initiation rites, 114, 119, 120; in death ceremonies, ch. XIII, 181; sacrificial, 146, 147, 190–2, 196, 200, 201, 214, 225.
Gourds, 29–30; beaded, 60.
Granaries, 24, 52–3.
Greetings, 12, 13, 23; of chiefs, 5 *n.*, 241 *n.*, 243.
Ground-nuts, 28, 29, 30–1, 32, 36.

*Hahane* (father's sister), role of, 14 ff.
Hairdressing, 43, 50–1, 77, 89, 118, 125, 166.
Hall, R. N., *Prehistoric Rhodesia*, 4.
Head-hunting, 51.
Head-rests, carved, 52.
Hlaŋganu, the, a Thoŋga group, 9.
Hleŋgwe, the, a Thoŋga group, 4, 9, 10, 240.
Hoes, 50; for *akulobola*, 137; handles, 39, 50; in birth rites, 79; string figure, 101.
Horn, in initiation rites, 113, 116, 119.
Houses, 3, 24; construction, 25; contents, 26–7.
Hunting, 29, 37–8.

Implements, axes, 50; domestic, 49 ff.; food-bowls, 50–2; gourds, 52; hoes, 50; mortar and pestle, 49–50; spoons, 52.
Initiation, 110–36; badge, 112; dances, 115–17, 124, 132 ff.; ornaments, 59, 124; preparation, 111–14; sacred symbols, 113, 117–19, 129; school, 114–17; seclusion, 120; secret language, 125–7.
Iron work, 50, 103.

Jealousy, 23; remedy for, 148.
Johannesburg, 1, 26, 153, 219.
Johnston, Sir H., *Comparative Study of Bantu Languages*, 9.
Junod, Rev. H. A., *Life of a S. African Tribe*, 4, 9, 14, 25, 30, 77, 78, 123, 185.
Junod, Rev. H. P., *Tſopi Origins*, 7, 9, 11.

Khambana, district of Gaza, 4, 240, 242 *n.*, 244–5.
*Khambanyane*, Leŋge chief; *see* table, 8.
Kinship, ch. II *passim*.
Kinship system, 12 ff.
Konjweni (Kondȝweni), Leŋge sib, 173, 242.
Kosa, Gaza sib, 240.
Kovelane Nyapondzo, Leŋge chief; *see* table, 8, 241.
Kwakwi, Leŋge sib, 4, 5, 6.

Language, 4; bad, 68; secret, 125–7, 130.
Leŋge, agriculture, ch. IV; character, 23, 238–9; clothing, 20, 21; cooking, 27; daily work, 22, 24; dances, ch. XIV; death ceremonies, ch. XIII; folk lore, ch. XVI; food, 22; greetings, 23; houses, 24–7; language, 4, 9, 10; meals, 37; origin and history, 3 ff.; physical features, 20; religion, ch. XV; tatu marks, ch. X.
Leper, burial of, 171.
Levirate, 14, 151, 167–8, 169.
Limpopo R., Bar, 1; *see also* Barra, map.
Lizard, in art, 52, 105–6; in initiation rites, 119; in medicine, 77.
*Lobolo*, *see Akulobola*.
Log, in marriage rites, 143, 146.

Magic, 32.
Mahumane (or Mahumani), Leŋge chief, 5, 240, 242–3.
Maize, 28, 31, 32; first fruits, 28–9; *pepeta*, 49; preparation, 34–5.

## INDEX

Makamu, Johane, 3, 7, 240; Leŋge sib, 240, 241.
Makloŋgwe, Leŋge chief, 6.
Makupulane, Tʃopi chief, 5, 243, 244.
Malahisi, pottery district, 53.
Malinowski, Dr. B., 149.
Mamba Ka Mhula, the, 5, 6, 7; old Leŋge sib, 240, 245.
Mambu, see Mamba.
Mamitele, Leŋge chief; see table, 8.
Manioc, 30, 31, 32, 33-4; gin, 33, 45; grater, 33.
Manukosi, Zulu chief, 3.
Manuse, Leŋge sib, 4 n.
Manyisa, Gaza sib, 240.
Maphamu, Leŋge chief, see table, 8; Maphamu Ntete, 8, 241.
Marame, Leŋge sib, 239, 241.
Marriage, ch. XII, akulobola, 137-40, 143-5, 150, 169; bridesmaids, 140-1; ceremonies, 146; Christian, 152; illegitimate children, 150, 169; levirate, 151, 169; polygyny, 151; sex relations, 122, 149; songs, 148-9; tatu and, 102; the hahane and, 16.
Masiye, Leŋge chief and sib, 4, 10, 240, 241.
Matsemane, ancestor of Vilaŋkulu, 6.
Mayika, see Dolls.
Mbaŋgu, pottery district, 53.
Meals, 37.
Medicine, crocodile, 63-4; for abortion, 64; for children, 85, 86; for forgetfulness, 84; in birth rites, 66-8, 77-82; in death rites, ch. XIII; in initiation ceremonies, 114, 116, 117, 120; in religious rites, ch. XV; jealousy, 148; lizard, 106; mondzo ordeal, 183-4; mourning, 106; oil-making, 41; potsherds and, 56; prevention of twins, 79; puberty, 110, 111; soot, 47-8, 68, 193; sorcery, 107, 153.
Mhandla, the, Gaza sib, 7, 240.
Mhula (Va Ka), Gaza sib, 54, 240; see also Mamba Ka Mhula.
Mifukwa mademona spirits, 188, 216.
Miners, return home, 2.
Miscarriage, rite after, 154.
Monkey, 24, 38; belief about, 66; bones, 138.
Monomotapa, insignia of, 211-12; kingdom of, 4.
Moon, and birth rites, 74, 77; and planting, 34.
Mortar, and birth rites, 80; and pestle, 49-50; child's, 86-7; string figure, 100.
Mpalaneni, pottery district, 53.

Mukumbe, ancestor of Vilaŋkulu, 6.
Musical instruments, ráttles, 176, 178, 205, 209, 210; Shangaan harps, 174; figoriha, 173, 177; trumpets, 173; Tʃopi pianos, 96, 174, 176, 177, 178, 231; whistles, 174; see also Drums.
Musika, ancestor of Vilaŋkulu, 6.
Muyaŋga, Leŋge and Tʃopi sib, 242, 243, 244.

Names, 76, 79; of dolls, 87-8.
Ndau, the, history, 3, 4; nyamusoro, 214-15; pottery, 53, 54; sibs, 240, 244; ʂikwembu, 42, 49, 196 ff., 205, 208, 215-16.
Nhlave, Gaza sib, 240.
Ntakula drum, ch. XI passim.
Ntama tribe, the, 5, 6, 240, 241.
Ntete, Leŋge chief and sib, 8, 241.
Ntlava, Gaza sib, 240.
Nyafoko, Leŋge chief and sib, 5, 242.
Nyahule, Leŋge (Ntama) sib, 5, 6, 193 n., 241.
Nyakule, Hleŋgwe sib, 4.
Nyakwadi, belief in, 62-3.
Nyamavila, Leŋge sib, 241.
Nyambutsi, mistress of initiation rites, ch. XI.
Nyampfumo, the, Leŋge sib, 6, 7, 8, 240.
Nyampfuŋwini, Leŋge district of Σihaɬu, 5, 240.
Nyampheke, Leŋge sib, 241.
Nyamusoro (priestess), 182, 199, 210, 213, 214, 218; and love charms, 138; and sorcery, 218-20; initiation, 214-15; methods, 200-5, 218-20.
Nyane, the, old Leŋge (Ntama) sib, 5, 6.
Nyaŋkuŋgwane, ancestor of Vilaŋkulu, 6.
Nyapondzo, Leŋge chief, see table, 8, 241.
Nyatsembe, Leŋge sib, 241.
Nyaviri, the, old Leŋge sib, 5.
Nyoko (Kosa Lipaŋga), Leŋge sib, 240, 243.
Nyokweni, pottery district, 54.
Nzuŋwe, ancestor of Vilaŋkulu, 6.

Ŋgaŋgale, Leŋge chief and sib, see table, 8, 241.
Ŋgoni (Vaŋgoni, Vaŋgunu), akulobola rings, 137-8; beadwork, 60; death of chief, 163; history, 3, 4, 10; ʂikwembu, 42, 49, 61, 182, 188, 195, 196 ff., 201, 203, 208, 215-16.
Ŋgoŋwani, Leŋge sib, 6, 241.
Ŋguzeni, pottery district, 53.
Ŋkandze, Leŋge chief (now Tʃopi) and sib, 5, 240, 244.

Ŋkavele, Leŋge sib, see table, 8, 240, 241.
Ŋkiriŋgwane drum, ch. XI passim.
Ŋkumayo (Ŋkumi), Leŋge sib, 240.
Ŋkumbe, Leŋge sib, 4, 7 n., 8, 241.
Ŋkunzule, Leŋge sib, 241.
Ŋwaluŋgu, the, a Thoŋga group, 9, 240.
Ŋwamusi, Leŋge chief and sib, 4, 5, 7, 8, 240.
Ŋwanati, Gaza sib, 240.
Ŋwavumbulane, Leŋge chief, see table, 8.

Ochre, red (*tsumane*): and birth rites, 76, 81; and initiation rites, 112–14, 118, 123, 124, 129, 131; as depilatory, 89; in mourning, 166–7; in pottery, 55; preparation of, 123.
Oils, 22, 28, 29, 30, 31, 38–43, 103.
Orange trees, 32.
Ordeal, trial by (*mondzo*), 183–4, 220, 221.
Ornaments, *andoro*, 204, 211–12, anklets, 20; rings, 20, 50, 156, 203, 205; *akulobola* rings, 112, 137, 138; mourning, 167; ritual, 204, 206, 209, 211–14; see also Beads.

Palm trees, 24; wine (*vutfema*), 30, 43.
Pereira Cabral, A. A., *Moçambique natives, tribes and customs*, 9, 128.
Phonetics, see note, xii.
Pigs, 25; ceremonial gifts, 140, 143, 146; food-bowls, 50.
Pineapples, 28, 32, 43.
Polygyny, 151.
Possession by spirits, 42, 44, 47, 61, 196–205, 207, 208–9, 213–17; and beer-drinking, 31, 44, 48, and first fruits, 42; of a pregnant woman, 205–7.
Pottery, 53–7; method of making, 54–6.
Prayers, 42, 61, 67, 72, 76, 113, 117, 146, 158, 192, 225.
Pregnancy, 63 ff.; 'possession' of pregnant woman, 205.
Proverbs, 234 ff.
Puberty, ch. XI; prohibitions, 109–10.
Punishment, of children, 88.
Puwa, Gaza sib, 240.
Python skin, and spirits, 210; in sacrifice, 66–7, 203; in sorcery, 153.

Quintinha, D. J., see Toscano and Quintinha.

Rain, 24, 31; protection from, 56; rain-making rite, 196.

Rattles, 210.
Rattray, Capt. R. S, anthropology and missionary work, vii–viii.
Reed, supposed origin of Leŋge from, 181.
Religion, ch. XV; agricultural rites, 192–5; blessing the kraals, 222–5; rain-making, 196; sacrifices, 189–93, 195, 196, 197; spiritual seances, 198–205, 208–9; *ẓikwembu*, 188–207; *tinaŋga*, 16 n., 158–9, 164–5, 182–5, 190–6, 199–201, 205–8, 215–16, 220–5.
Rings, *akulobola*, 112, 137, 138, 156.
Rites, aggregation, 81; agricultural, 192–5; after a miscarriage, 154; birth, ch. VI; blessing the kraals, 222–5; burial, ch. XIII; fertility, 151, ch. XV; initiation, ch. XI; *Kahola*, 193; marriage, ch. XII; mourning, 157; puberty, 110; purification after death, 151, 164; rain-making, 196.
Roŋga, the, a Thoŋga group, 9.

Sacrifices, 112–13, ch. XV; agricultural, 192 ff.; by *hahane*, 15; family, 24; for children, 61; in birth rites, 66–7; in initiation rites, 112, 113, 114, 118; in marriage ceremonies, 145; in death ceremonies, ch. XIII.; to spirits, 188 ff.
Salt, 33, 36, 37, 104.
Sand, 32, 85; *banyi, jihu*, 242 n.
Scarification, see Tatu.
Seasons, 28.
Seclusion, after initiation, 120.
Seleve, Leŋge sib, 241.
Sex relations, 149; ritual intercourse, 122, 162, 165, 168.
Shangaan, 4 n., 9.
Shells, cowrie, 211; see also *Andoro*.
Sibs (Ṣigava), 4, 7, 8, 10, 11, Appendix.
Simaŋgu (Va Ka), Ndau sib, 38, 240.
Skins, sacrificial, 214.
Sleeping mats, 26 n., 65.
'Smelling out', 199, 200, 205, 214, 218.
Smith, Rev. E. W. and Dale, A. M., *Ila-speaking Peoples*, game of initiate, 129.
Smythe, Bishop, *Xilenge (Σileŋge) Grammar*, 235.
Snakes, in Gazaland, 24; omens, 208; see also Python.
Sneezing, 204.
Social organization, 11 ff.
Songs, 21–2; at marriages, 148, 149; at seances, 208; for dances, 179–80; for games, 93.

# INDEX

Sorcerers (*valoyi*), 41, 46, 153, 217–25.
Sorghum, 29, 31, 35, 48; *vuputso*, 48–9.
Sororate, 14, 151.
Spider, in medicine, 120, 148.
Spirits, ch. XIV.
Spitting and sacrifice, 190, 192.
Stick, bridegroom's, 139, 142, 144, 145.
Stone of accession, 38, 242 *n*.
Stool, ritual, 210.
Suckling, *see* Birth.
Suicide, and burial, 170.
Sumerians, metal beads used by, 213.
Surnames (*şiboŋgo*), 10, 241.
Σavane, Leŋge sib, 241.
Σavi, Leŋge sib, 241.
Σigono, 218.
Σihału, Ɖwamusi, Leŋge chief, 5, 7, 240.
Σikavele lineage, 5; *see also* Ɖkavele.
Σikonele, Leŋge sib, 29, 240.
Σiluwane Vilaŋkulu, chieftainship, 6, 7, 8; Leŋge sib, 241.
Σiŋgundu, 178, 206, 210.
Σisano, Leŋge sib, 239, 241.
Σitsumbuli, Leŋge chief, *see* table, 8.
Şikwembu (spirits) and agricultural rites, 192–5; and initiation, 116; and rain, 196; beliefs about, 207; propitiation of, 188–92; Ndau and Ɖgoni, 196–208.
Şitukutwane, messenger spirits, 188, 216, 217.

Tabu: concerning baskets, 58; birth, ch. VI; death, 162, 163, 171; fire, 166; food, 38, 49, 52, 65, 79, 88; hairdressing, 125; head-dresses, 125; initiation, 112, 121–2, 125, 136; mortar and pestle, 50, 70, 80; oil making, 41; pottery, 56; pregnancy, 38, 64 ff.; puberty, 109–10; tatu, 103, 104; teeth, 82–3.
Tatu, 42, ch. X; decorative, 59, 107; designs on pottery, 56; implements, 103; incisions, 107–8; keloid scars, 108; ritual, 106; totemistic, 105; tribal marks, 104.

Teeth, cutting, 82–3; filing, 105, 230.
Thoŋga, the, history, 3, 9.
*Tindzundu* spirits, 188, 215–16.
*Tinyaŋga* (priests), 16 *n*., 46; and agriculture, 193–5; and birth rites, ch. VI; and death, 158–9; and distilling, 46; and first fruits, 46; and puberty, 110; and religion, ch. XV; and sorcery, 217; and tatuing, 103; *see also* Bones.
Titles, chiefs', 5, 241, 243.
Toscano, D. F., and Quintinha, D. J., *A Derrocada do Imperio Va Tua*, 3.
Totemism, 10, 105.
Trees, 25, ch. IV, 243 (Brachystegia venosa); sacred, 25, 39, 46, 65, 189; *see also* Oils.
Trilling, 173 ff.
Troughs, 45, 47, 53.
Tʃopi, the, history and origin, 3, 7 *n*., 9, 10, 240, 242, 243, 244; tatu marks, ch. X.
Turtle, and food prohibition, 38.
Twins, 79, 86; burial of, 154, 155.

Utensils, 39, 49 ff.

VaLeŋge, VaNdau, VaƉgoni (Vaŋgunu), VaTʃopi, &c., *see* Leŋge, Ndau, Ɖgoni, Tʃopi, &c.
Venye, Leŋge sib, 6, *see* table, 8, 241.
Vetʃa tribe, 10, 242.
Vila de João Belo (Chai Chai), 1, 2.
Vilaŋkulu, the, Tʃopi (old Leŋge) chief and sib, 4, 6 ff., 240.
Vu Tsoŋga, district, 3, 9.

Weaning, *see* Birth.
Widows, and widowers, 166–70.
Wig, red-ochred, in rites, 198, 201, 202, 204, 205, 208, 209, 210–11, 215.
Witwatersrand Native Labour Association depot, 1.
Women, position of, 11, 88; work done by, 22, 31.

Zandamela, Tʃopi sib and district, 9 *n*., 240.
Zulu in Gazaland, 3, 4, 241, 242, 243, 244; *see also* Ɖgoni.

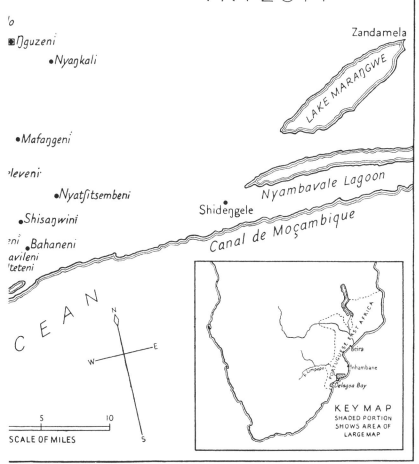